SOCIAL WORK WITH YOUNG PEOPLE IN CARE

This introduction to social work with children and young people who are looked after (in care or accommodated) by statutory or voluntary agencies is the only textbook on the subject which addresses this area of work across all four nations of the UK.

Providing a clear theoretical and ethical basis, it introduces and develops a set of core themes, reflective of contemporary developments including:

- the influence of, and tensions between, dominant discourses that shape the social work service (relationship-based practice, early intervention and prevention, social innovation, evidence-based practice and outcomes)
- the use and abuse of concepts of 'children's needs' and 'best interests';
- ideas of parenting and parental responsibility, and the relationships between children, families, communities and the state;
- the importance of recognising that children and young people have rights and considering their views;
- trauma, trauma-informed practice, transitions and resilience.

With chapters addressing a sequence of topics – assessment and planning, residential and foster care, leaving care, and permanence – there is a specific focus on working with disabled children, children from minority ethnic communities, and marginalised groups of children and young people, including refugees and asylum seekers, LGBTQIA+ children and those who have been trafficked.

Packed full of useful pedagogical features, including material on the legal and policy context, summaries of research evidence, notes for good practice, group teaching exercises, references to legislation and guidance, and guides to further reading, it will be core reading on any child and family care modules, general preparation for practice courses, Frontline, Step Up, as well as for all social work practitioners.

Nigel Patrick Thomas is Professor Emeritus of Childhood and Youth at the University of Central Lancashire. He was a social worker and team leader for 20 years before becoming an academic. He led the establishment of the first all-Wales Postqualifying Child Care Award.

Karen Winter is Professor of Children's Social Care at Queen's University Belfast. Prior to her academic career, Karen worked for 16 years as a social worker and team manager with children and families, and latterly as a guardian, representing children in court proceedings.

Student Social Work

https://www.routledge.com/Student-Social-Work/book-series/SSW

This exciting new textbook series is ideal for all students studying to be qualified social workers, whether at undergraduate or masters level. Covering key elements of the social work curriculum, the books are accessible, interactive and thought-provoking.

New titles

Becoming a Social Worker, 3rd ed.
Viviene E. Cree

Mental Health Social Work in Context, 3rd ed.
Nick Gould

Social Work Practice with People with Dementia
Peter Scourfield

Social Work, 2nd ed.
A Reader
Edited by Viviene E. Cree and Trish McCulloch

Social Work with Young People in Care, 2nd ed.
Looking After Children in Theory and Practice
Nigel Patrick Thomas and Karen Winter

SOCIAL WORK WITH YOUNG PEOPLE IN CARE

Looking After Children in Theory and Practice

Second Edition

Nigel Patrick Thomas and Karen Winter

Routledge
Taylor & Francis Group
LONDON AND NEW YORK

Designed cover image: © Getty Image

Second edition published 2025
by Routledge
4 Park Square, Milton Park, Abingdon, Oxon, OX14 4RN

and by Routledge
605 Third Avenue, New York, NY 10158

Routledge is an imprint of the Taylor & Francis Group, an informa business

First edition published by Palgrave 2005

British Library Cataloguing-in-Publication Data
A catalogue record for this book is available from the British Library

ISBN: 978-1-032-82149-8 (hbk)
ISBN: 978-1-032-82151-1 (pbk)
ISBN: 978-1-003-50319-4 (ebk)

DOI: 10.4324/9781003503194

Typeset in Sabon
by codeMantra

CONTENTS

BOXES, EXERCISES, FIGURES AND TABLES

Boxes

Exercises

Figures

Tables

ACKNOWLEDGEMENTS

Acknowledgements are due to the following for permission to include extracts from published material: British Association for Adoption and Fostering for permission to reproduce Chart D, 'People's Needs' from Bryer, *Planning in Child Care: A Guide for Team Leaders and Their Teams* (1988) (reproduced as Figure 2.1, page 19); for extracts, Barn, *Working with Black Children and Adolescents in Need* (1999), Fahlberg, *A Child's Journey Through Placement* (1994) and Ince, *Making It Alone* (1998); Charles C. Thomas Inc. for permission to reproduce Figure 6 on page 199 of Plumer, *When You Place a Child* (1992) (reproduced as Figure 7.1, page 146); and HMSO for permission to reproduce Figure 20.1 on page 251 of Biehal, Clayden, Stein and Wade, *Moving On: Young People and Leaving Care Schemes* (1995) (reproduced as Figure 10.1, page 233). Unfortunately, it was not possible to contact the copyright holder for permission to use the extract from Hitchman (1966) *The King of the Barbareens*, although Penguin Books Ltd. indicated that as the publishers they have no objection to the use of the material in question.

PREFACE TO THE 2ND EDITION

In preparing this new edition of a book originally written nearly 20 years ago, we have been struck by how much, but also how little, has changed.

There has been plenty of new legislation in that time, in the United Kingdom and doubtless in many other states too. As demands and expectations of services change, so the legal framework comes to be adjusted, along with agency policies and professional standards. In the UK, there is the additional impetus of devolution, which over time is producing greater divergence in policy, with a consequently greater number of different legal provisions applying variably to the 'four nations'. A primary aim for us in producing this new edition has been to take full account of the impact of devolution, and ensure that the book is relevant and useful for practitioners and students working in Wales, Scotland and Northern Ireland, just as much as in England. We have in general aimed to be up to date with current legal provision in all four jurisdictions. However, as with the first edition, our main focus has been to produce a text that will still be relevant when those particular laws and policy frameworks are no longer current.

Readers may notice that the list of references has undergone extensive and thorough updating. Only about 50 of the original 300-odd references remain, and something like 400 new ones have been added, reflecting changes in legislation, new publications on practice and a considerable volume of new research. Research in this field has continued to grow nationally and internationally, not only in volume but also in its theoretical and methodological approaches. However, it is still often difficult to secure funding, and with that comes a concern that some areas remain relatively invisible.

There have of course also been wider social and political changes in the two decades since the book first appeared, which have had in some cases quite major implications for the care system and for social work practice with children and young people. Obvious examples include the increasingly fraught issue of how to respond to refugees and asylum-seekers, especially unaccompanied children, a growing concern and awareness of child sexual exploitation, and a significant rise in the numbers of children and young people who are questioning their gender, seeking to transition or identifying as non-binary. All these are issues which pose challenges for practice, and which we have tried to address in the new text.

Arguably an even greater challenge to established ways of working comes from the fast-growing 'digitalisation' of society, with all its ramifications, including vastly greater availability of information for those who have access, and growing exclusion for those who do not. In particular, children's lives have in some ways been transformed by the use of smartphones and social media, as have the ways in which practitioners relate to them. We cannot forecast what further impacts of technological innovation are on the way, but we have done our best to take account of those that have emerged so far. There have also been some trends in practice that we have tried to reflect in the new edition – some new thinking on assessment and planning, and perhaps (we hope) a revitalised emphasis on the importance of relationships in professional practice with children and families.

The first edition appeared at a time when the political climate in the UK was in many respects hopeful, from the perspective of social work and children's services more generally. A government committed to reform of services, and willing to invest public money in health, welfare and education, had introduced the Every Child Matters strategy, the Sure Start programme for the early years and a host of other projects aimed at improving life chances for children in England. A similar atmosphere prevailed across the UK; for example, all four nations established an independent Children's Commissioner during that period. Since then we have had the financial crash followed by 14 years of savage cuts in public services under the guise of 'austerity', delivered by a government which often seems unconcerned for the wellbeing of all but the richest members of society. As a result, the demand for social work services to children and families, including the provision of care and protection, has steadily increased, while the human and financial resources available to meet that need have steadily reduced.

In view of that sustained lack of investment, it is perhaps not surprising that our overall impression in looking back to the first edition is of how much has *not* changed. The same issues about quality of services, about children being moved from placement to placement, about care leavers being cut adrift without proper support, about the slow progress in enabling children and families to participate fully in decision-making – all those issues are as salient now as they were in 2004.

That does sound rather bleak. By way of contrast, we would point to the many social workers, managers, local authorities and other agencies who are genuinely trying to do things better, despite all the difficulties that stand in their way. If you are reading this as a practitioner or a student, we hope that you will join them, and that this book will be of some help to you. Notwithstanding all the research and changes in law, policy and practice, children in care tend to want the same things as they did 20 years ago – to have safe, secure, loving relationships, to be respected and treated with dignity, to have choice and to be heard. And children in care tell us that we still have a way to go to succeed in these things.

Our sincere thanks to Professors John Devaney, Sally Holland and Michelle Lefevre for reviewing the entire manuscript in draft and making some very helpful suggestions for improvements. (Thanks also to John for persuading us to produce this new edition in the first place.) Finally, Patrick thanks Karen for doing most of the hard work of updating the text and references.

A NOTE ON TERMINOLOGY

The title of this book refers both to 'young people in care' and to 'children looked after'. These terms do not refer to two distinct groups; rather, they are different ways of describing the same group.

Whilst legal provisions in the UK refer to anyone under the age of 18 as a 'child' – as does the United Nations Convention on the Rights of the Child – people in their teenage years do not generally refer to themselves as children, nor do they necessarily like others to refer to them in this way. The phrase 'children and young people' is commonly used to include anyone aged up to 18, and often to 21 and beyond. In this book, we sometimes use the word 'children' alone when it seems more relevant or simply easier. We also use the phrase 'children and young people', and we sometimes speak simply of 'young people'. After all, even the smallest child is a person (and a unique individual, regardless of the labels we use for different groups).

The Children Act 1989 made a distinction between children *in care* by order of a court, and those who are 'accommodated' under a less formal arrangement, with 'looked after child' as an all-embracing category. This has not really penetrated into popular discourse, and in this book, we generally use the terms 'care' and 'in care'. Many of these technical or legal terms can be alienating to children and young people, as social work 'jargon', and they are hardly ever used by children and families. Nor might they be meaningful to a non-British professional readership; in other countries, terms such as 'children and young people in out-of-home care' or 'cared for away from home' are more commonly used. For all these reasons, we generally use the word 'care'.

Otherwise, with regard to the many of the terms used in this book, whether technical terms in law and policy or words used to refer to particular social groups, the ones used are those current and accepted at the time of writing. We recognise that later readers may find that these terms have dated with changes in language, policy and practice.

1

INTRODUCTION

Themes and key principles

CONTENTS OF CHAPTER

- Introduction
- Children's needs and 'best interests'
- Listening to children and children's rights
- Working with difference and oppression
- Parenting and the state
- Conclusion – working together
- Guide to further reading

Introduction

Working with children and their families can be one of the most stressful, and most controversial, areas of social work practice. It can also be one of the most rewarding.

The work is stressful and controversial for several reasons. First, the current social, economic, political context in which social work to children and families is delivered is challenging. Collins (2022) highlights the impact of COVID-19, the current cost of living crisis and economic challenges on the wellbeing of service users and social workers alike. Second, the legal mandate and nature of the responsibilities that social workers carry is a contested area (Featherstone et al., 2018), and decision making about the wellbeing, protection and development of children and young people is often complex and challenging (Munro, 2019). The families involved often experience multiple issues representing the coalescence of difficulties such as abuse, addictions, violence, mental and physical health issues, compounded and exacerbated

DOI: 10.4324/9781003503194-1

by the impact of social structural issues such as poverty, unemployment, homelessness and discrimination. Often there are no obvious answers or easy solutions. And yet, as highlighted in the media, there are often serious consequences of making the wrong decision (Munro, 2019). Third, there is research (Orsi-Hunt et al., 2023; Henson et al., 2023) that suggests the stresses and hazards are greatest in child protection work.

Having said this, the work can also be rewarding because of the satisfaction when things do work out: when a child's life that was insecure and disrupted is placed on a sound foundation, when parents receive help and move forward in their lives in positive ways, or when in your work with children you build meaningful, positive relationships and enjoy spending time together (Cree, 2022; Ruch et al., 2018).

Social work in child protection and with children in care are two areas of practice that overlap considerably – more than half the children in the care system at any one time are there because of child protection concerns. Other children come into the care system and quickly return home, often from families which require continuing family support. This means that work with children in care (or 'looked after') also involves a good deal of work to support families.

In a sense then, it is artificial to separate work with children in care, or 'looked after', from work with children and families in general. Books that introduce or explain work with children and families in general can be very useful, and this book is not intended to be a substitute for them. However, there is enough that is distinctive about working with children and young people coming into care, living in care and leaving care to justify giving it separate attention; and that is why we hope this book will be useful too.

The aim of this book is to enable the reader to develop a sound understanding of the field of social work with children and young people who are in care and their families, in order to provide a foundation for ethical and effective practice. This will involve looking at the political and legal context that shapes and informs services for children in care, and at the social and ethical context. It will also involve exploring the range of service provision for children and their families, and the research evidence for what kinds of services produce the most desirable outcomes. Finally, it will involve studying what happens in working relationships between social work practitioners and children and their families, what are the skills needed for this work and how they can be developed.

The purpose of all this is to lay the groundwork for developing practice skills and knowledge in work with children and young people who are looked after, and with their families. This is a process which does not begin, or end, with this book. Our aim is to enable the reader to use and build on whatever existing knowledge they may bring to the subject, to introduce readers to new key texts and research, and most importantly to provide a basis for further study and professional development in practice.

This book has, we hope, a clear theoretical and ethical foundation. In this chapter, a set of core themes is introduced, which will be developed in the rest of the book as we look together at different aspects of social work with children and young people in care. The first is concerned with ideas of children's needs and 'best interests', and the ways in which they are used. The second is about the importance of listening to children and young people, and of recognising that they have rights as well as needs. The third is about working with difference and oppression. The last is to do with concepts of parenting and parental responsibility, and the relationships between children, families, communities and the State.

Children's needs and 'best interests'

These two concepts were both used for the first time in relation to children during the twentieth century. Psychologists in the 1920s began using 'needs' in the sense of human drives or wants, and developmental psychologists applied the concept in a particular way to children; while lawyers developed the concept of 'best interests' in order to promote the idea that the law, in dealing with matters concerning children, should consider what was best for them. More recently, from the 1980s onwards, these concepts are embedded in child care law and the United Nations Convention on the Rights of the Child (UNCRC) (United Nations, 1989). Both concepts are useful, but both need to be handled with care, as we shall see.

Children's needs

Much discussion of services relating to children is now expressed in terms of 'children's needs'. The term is central to child and family social work practice; so much so that professionals' understanding of the term is usually taken for granted and often there is a lack of exploration as to what it actually means. Related terms can include 'basic needs', 'additional needs', 'complex needs' and 'children's developmental needs'. Sometimes specific needs are also mentioned, for example 'special educational needs', 'identity needs' and 'spiritual and religious needs'.

The concept of 'children's needs' is used both to suggest that all children have needs which must be met if they are to develop into healthy adults, and to point practitioners to identifying the particular needs of individual children (Cleaver and Unell, 2011). In some respects, the concept is clearly a progressive one. Putting 'what children need' at the centre of concern is arguably an advance on earlier preoccupations with moral decline, or with the costs of dealing with troublesome and destitute children. However, there have also been criticisms of the concept and the way it is used. Martin Woodhead (2005, p. 72) has pointed out that the term 'children's needs' is complicated and carries with it different meanings; he also notes how statements about 'needs' mix up fact and value. When we make a statement in the form of 'a child needs A' what we really mean is 'a child needs A in order to achieve B, and B is something desirable and important'. However, these steps in the argument are left unsaid, and so cannot be questioned. The result is that the 'need' is constituted as an inherent part of children's nature, rather than as a means to a particular end, which may be promoted by some groups and accorded less priority by others.

According to Woodhead (1997), 'need' may refer to children's psychological nature, as evidenced by drives such as those for sustenance or attachment (or by the known pathological consequences of childhood experiences such as institutionalisation). On the other hand, 'need' may also represent 'a judgment about which childhood experiences are most culturally adaptive', or 'a prescription about which childhood experiences are most highly valued', as illustrated in Table 1.1.

Because it is not always clear in which sense the word is being used, it can be easy to overlook the extent to which statements about 'children's needs' contain assumptions that are culturally specific or based on particular sets of values. At the most basic level, contemporary Western culture seems to set a high value on having an enquiring and independent mind, while other cultures may set much greater store by being compliant and obedient.

TABLE 1.1 Definitions of 'need'

Description of need	*Meaning*
Children's physical and psychological nature	'Need' refers to the essential basic requirements for healthy, human survival and development – their physical, social/relational, emotional/psychological and educational needs.
An experience/condition to replace/restore impact of loss/harm	'Need' refers to what is known about the potential negative consequences of particular childhood experiences and their impact on children's developmental needs. This meaning is evidenced in statements such as 'this child needs stability and security' (the inference being that the lack of it impacts on developmental outcomes).
An expression of societal preference linked to views of children/childhood	'Need' is an expression of what childhood experiences are most valued in society. This meaning is evidenced in statements such as 'children need to play' or 'children need to be children' both of which reflect specific cultural norms and expectations regarding children and childhood. These 'needs' might hold true in some cultures and not others where other cultural and structural norms mean that children 'need to look after their siblings', for example.

Woodhead (2006) even suggests that the concept of 'children's needs' is so muddled that it might be better to do away with it. In this book, we will use the concept, but we will try to do so in a critical spirit and be aware of the pitfalls. In particular, we will try to remember two things:

1 that many assumptions about children's needs are dependent on a cultural context, and there is often room for more than one view of them;
2 that although children's needs are usually discussed in developmental terms, children are people living in the present, not simply pre-adults in the process of development.

When we look more closely at children's developmental needs in Chapter 2, we will be bearing these points clearly in mind.

'Best interests'

The same caution applies to the notion of children's 'best interests'. It is now common for laws and conventions to refer to children's 'best interests' and to suggest that they should be given priority over other considerations. Examples include the Children Act 1989 in England and Wales, UNCRC (United Nations, 1989) and the supporting UN General Comment No. 14 (Committee on the Rights of the Child, 2013) which gives detailed advice on the implementation on the right of a child to have their best interests taken as a primary consideration. Section 1 of the Children Act makes the child's welfare the 'paramount consideration' in all court proceedings about the care or upbringing of children. Article 3 of the United Nations Convention says that 'in all actions concerning children ... the child's best interests shall be the primary consideration'. General Comment No. 14 reminds us that 'best interests' is a substantive right, a fundamental interpretative legal principle, and a rule of procedure (Eriken and Backe-Hansen, 2018).

The concept of 'the best interests of the child' represents progress compared with the past in that children are now seen as individual people rather than the property of their parents. Applying the concept means that each child and their interests has to be considered in their own right, even if there are sibling groups. However, a challenge lies in the assumption that it is possible to know objectively what is in a child's 'best interests'. Application of 'the best interests' principle to individual cases can be tricky. The work of Sutherland and MacFarlane (2016) provides in-depth analysis and commentary on these issues; here we note four main reasons. First, as noted, there is not always an obvious answer as to what is in the best interests of a child, but rather there are competing options, each with benefits and limitations. Second, there may be conflict between the short- and long-term interests of children, and deciding which comes first may be a matter of values rather than objective fact. In the short term, for example, it might be in the best interests of a child to place them with alternative carers, but the long-term consequences of this decision might be less clearly in the best interests of the child, because of the potential for further instability or loss of identity. Third, different cultures have different assumptions about what is in the best interests of children. Finally, there is the question of *who decides* what is in a child's best interests – experts, family members, adults or children themselves? It has been argued that it is vain for the state to try to calculate objectively what is in the interests of an individual child, and that it is better to follow some simple general principles such as the value of continuity – and to give children themselves a role in determining what happens. Importantly, on the last point, the Convention on the Rights of the Child and the accompanying General Comments suggest that it is not possible for others to determine what is in the best interests of a child (Article 3) without first seeking the views of the child where possible and taking these into account (Article 12). In seeking the views of children and young people, we should also be mindful of related Articles that include the right to non-discrimination (Article 2), the evolving capacities of the child (Article 5), the right to life, health and development (Article 6), and the right to express views in any medium of the child's choice (Article 13).

The issue of what weight should be placed on children's interests as against other factors can also be a difficult one and can cause misunderstanding (O'Halloran, 2022). For instance, it is a common misconception that child care legislation in the UK makes the child's welfare the *paramount* consideration in all matters governed by the legislation, including local authority services to children and families. In fact, it only does so in relation to court proceedings about the care of children. A little reflection shows why it would create difficulties if the paramountcy principle applied to other matters. As noted above, 'paramount' means 'supreme over all other considerations'. If, for example, a local authority providing services for thousands of people was required to treat each child's interest as paramount, it could be very difficult to set aside resources for all its other responsibilities such as maintaining highways or collecting rubbish, and impossible for it to take decisions over conflicts of interest between different children and their families. That is why, as we shall see, the duty to children in the care of public authorities (local authorities, health and social care trusts) is *to safeguard and promote their welfare* – but not to put an individual child's interests over all others. 'Best interests', then, is another concept which will be used with care in this book. It is a powerful tool, and so can be dangerous when misused.

Listening to children and children's rights

As illustrated above, listening to children and young people is a central theme of this book. As a phrase, it may sound trite or obvious, but it has real content, and if understood properly presents one of the greatest challenges to social work practice with children and families. The theoretical basis for it is twofold.

One is that above all else *a child is a person*, as noted in Lord Justice Butler Sloss's famous words in the Report of the Inquiry into Child Abuse in Cleveland (1987), where she states, 'a child is a person, not an object of concern'. That is a moral statement that emphasises respect for the child as an individual person who is entitled to be considered in their own right. It also connects with themes in the study of childhood by sociologists and psychologists, who have emphasised the need to see children as individual human beings and active participants in social life and in their own development, not just as passive recipients of 'socialisation'. Psychologists, building on the tradition of Piaget and Vygotsky, have emphasised the extent to which children contribute to their own development in their social interactions (see for instance Trevarthen, 1995; Woodhead, 2006). Sociologists and anthropologists have moved on from studying socialisation and 'upbringing', and now study children as social actors in their own right, even having their own cultures which children have invented, contribute to and sustain by themselves rather than being designed by adults for children. Good examples of children's own cultures include 'street play' in which children create the rules and the social norms. Sociologists and anthropologists also analyse the ways in which childhood is 'socially constructed' (understood differently in different societies), rather than being simply a natural, biological phenomenon (see James and Prout, 1997; James et al., 1998). If we accept that this perspective is right, then in practical terms it means that we must respond to children as persons, not just as the objects of our caring, and involve them actively in making choices about their own care.

The other part of the theoretical basis for listening to children is that they have *rights*, both individually and collectively. There has been a great deal of debate among lawyers and philosophers about whether children have rights, and also about whether they have the same rights as adults or whether there are distinctive children's rights (as summarised in Chapter 3). However, since the adoption by the UK of the UNCRC (United Nations, 1989) on 16 December 1991, there has developed a widespread agreement that children have rights to certain kinds of provision and protection such as a family life, identity, education and health care, and freedom from abuse and exploitation. The rights as defined in the UNCRC are interrelated, interdependent and indivisible. For example, although the extent to which children have the right to determine their own lives is still a matter of debate, there is also general agreement that children have a right to be heard and consulted in relation to all decisions regarding them in child protection, child care proceedings and when in care (Diaz, 2020; Križ and Petersen, 2023). This principle is outlined in Article 12 of the UNCRC but is also related to Articles 2, 3, 5, 6, 13 for example. Further detailed guidance about a child's right to be heard can also be found in the UN General Comment No. 12 'The Right of the Child to be Heard' (Committee on the Rights of the Child, 2009), and in other General Comments such as No. 7 'Implementing Child Rights in Early Childhood' (Committee on the Rights of the Child, 2005). The right of each child to express a view and have their views taken into account has become part of the accepted ideology of child welfare. It is not always easy to follow through in practice, and sometimes it receives more lip service than actual implementation in practice. However, it is certainly one of the core principles on which this book is based, and in the chapters that follow we will look at some of the ways in which it can be made effective.

The practical implications of seeing children and young people as individual people each with individual rights to certain kinds of provision and protection, and also having rights to be heard and consulted, is that their views about what happens to them, about where they live, and about the plans that are made for them, should be actively sought by those providing care – whether they are parents, foster carers, social workers, or others. 'Listening' is a shorthand for this – sometimes children and young people don't say very much, at least not in words – but this does not mean that their wishes and feelings are any less important. It is not just a matter of individual children, either. Children as a group have collective rights, and the views of children and young people in general about the services provided (or not provided) for them should also be sought actively – and notice taken of them. In Chapter 3, we will look at some of the ways in which we can listen to children, both individually and also in groups.

Working with difference and oppression

The third theme that deserves a chapter to itself, and which we will therefore deal with only briefly here, is that of working with difference and oppression (Tedam, 2020; Dominelli, 2017). The diversity of background and context of children and young people who come into care is one obvious reason for this to be a major concern for practitioners. Whatever our own background, much of the time we will be working with children, young people and their families who are from different backgrounds from ourselves, be this as a result of social class, religion, ethnicity, family type, language, culture, lifestyle or life experience. This is the first challenge – to understand these differences, the unique meanings they have for people, and the effects they may have on their lives.

Another reason for this to be a concern is that any child who comes into care is by definition at a disadvantage, and in most cases their life chances and those of their families have already been limited by individual and social structural factors outside their control – whether that be the impact of social class, poverty, discrimination, trauma caused by war and conflict, mental illness, substance addiction and so on. This is the second challenge – to understand these different patterns of disadvantage and the specific ways in which people may be discriminated against or oppressed (including ways in which they may be discriminated against or oppressed by professionals, often without intending to). These issues provide the focus of Chapter 4 and will be explored in some depth there. They will inevitably recur in the second part of the book.

Parenting and the state

Children in care have experienced parenting in a variety of family types, including one-carer and two carer families, intergenerational/reconstituted households, carers with varied, differing sexualities and/or gender identities, multiple partner households and multi-lingual, multi-culture families (Kiima, 2021). For the children and young people we are considering, style and quality of parenting are likely to be important issues. Most of them still have birth parents, even if they have not lived with them for years. Many have parents who are separated, and many have step-parents. Most children in care are placed at one time or another with foster carers or 'foster parents', and some acquire new parents through legal adoption. For many, a key issue in planning their future is that of whether the parenting provided to them is 'good enough' parenting.

It is important, as noted above, to remember that any child who comes into care is by definition at a disadvantage, and that in most cases their life chances and those of their families have already been limited by individual and social structural factors that are outside their control (Featherstone et al., 2018; Parents, Families and Allies Network, 2022). It is important to understand these different patterns of disadvantage and the specific ways in which people may be discriminated against or oppressed and respond appropriately. By being sufficiently informed, self-reflective and aware, we can help mitigate against the impacts of stigma, discrimination and social exclusion faced by young people and children in care.

For all children and young people who are looked after by the state – or by voluntary or private organisations, – 'corporate parenting' is an important part of their lives. In England, the principles of corporate parenting were set out in Section 1 of the Children and Social Work Act 2017, followed by statutory guidance (Department of Education, 2018). According to the guidance the critical question for a local authority should be 'would this be good enough for my child?' (2018, p. 6).

It is essential to be clear about what we mean by parenting, who can be a parent, how far and in what ways it may be shared, and what counts as good enough parenting. There seem to be two distinct meanings of 'parent': someone from whom one has one's biological origin; and/or someone who takes responsibility for upbringing – who takes care, hence 'parenting' as the activity of caring for a child. We suggest that 'parenting' incorporates these key elements:

- caring and responding to needs;
- offering intimacy and connectedness;
- providing advice, guidance, opportunities;
- taking responsibility for outcomes.

Theorists such as Goldstein et al. (1973) have argued that only one or two people can provide what they call 'psychological parenting'. Their theory was based on a psychoanalytic theory of human development which emphasises the importance of a single, primary attachment between child and parent and the long-term negative consequences of disrupting this bond. However, in a contemporary context where we know far more about diverse caregiving practices across cultures, and where children are cared for in large family and community networks, it is now generally accepted that children can have significant attachments with more people than this, especially if those people have good relationships with each other (see Richards, 1986; Fahlberg, 1994). At the same time, it does also appear from attachment research that the emotional aspects of parenting (positive attachments) are of crucial importance for the development of a healthy personality.

What does this mean for the state as the 'corporate parent'? Clearly, the state, or a local authority cannot, as a corporate body, directly provide the elements of intimacy and connectedness that seem crucial to a concept of 'psychological parenting'. But what it can do is ensure that each child or young person has someone with whom they can establish that kind of relationship by providing high-quality caring arrangements. However, the state does have a direct role both in providing caring and in assuming responsibility for outcomes, as indicated in the most recent children's legislation in the UK and its accompanying guidance (Carr and Goosey, 2019). These are therefore major issues for anyone involved in planning children's care, or in making decisions about who should look after children and young people, and they do raise wider questions about the relationship between the state, parents and children and when the state should intervene.

Fox Harding (1997) identifies four competing value positions in relation to the state's interventions in parenting. These she describes as *laissez-faire*, state paternalism, parents' rights and children's rights, as depicted in Figure 1.1.

Laissez-faire	**State paternalism**
Minimal state intervention and only in cases of serious abuse, neglect and harm. Below this, state intervention is described as 'interference' into the private life of the family, undermining autonomy.	The state has a legitimate role in scrutinising the care of children within the family and in intervening because of the vulnerability of children. The role of the state is broad combining protection and support.
Modern defence of the birth family and parents' rights	**Children's rights and child liberation**
State intervention to support families to stay together and maintain their relationships with each other even when separated because of the underpinning emphasis on parents' rights and the enduring nature of biological relationships or 'blood ties'.	Children are understood to be a group lacking voice, power and control and discriminated against. There is an emphasis on children's voices and participation.

FIGURE 1.1 Fox Harding's value positions.

Although Harding's work is nearly 30 years old, her conceptualisation is still of relevance today. Applied to contemporary society, the four positions appear to contradict each other, but they are often found to co-exist, in that the same legal or policy system may contain elements that represent more than one of these value positions. Linked with these longstanding conflicts over values is a debate about what standard of upbringing children in the care of the state should receive. Recent policy developments highlight the expectation that not only will alternative care be of the highest quality to meet the complex needs of children in care, but that all carers (whether foster carers or residential social workers) should aim to support children to achieve their full potential and improve their outcomes. 'Being in care' is seen therefore as more than being cared for; rather it is seen as aspirational, as a means of connecting children to new opportunities, experiences and events to enhance their wellbeing and outcomes.

When thinking more broadly about parenting, there are no easy answers to questions about what constitutes 'good enough parenting', about who can or should parent a child, or about what should be the precise role of the state in relation to parents and children. Indeed, this is reflected in court decision making as seen in these comments by a judge:

> Society must be willing to tolerate very diverse standards of parenting, including the eccentric, the barely adequate and the inconsistent. It follows too that children will inevitably have both very different experiences of parenting and very unequal consequences flowing from it. It means that some children will experience disadvantage and harm, whilst others flourish in atmospheres of loving security and emotional stability. These are the consequences of our fallible humanity and it is not the provenance of the State to spare children all the consequences of defective parenting. In any event, it simply could not be done.
>
> *Mr Justice Hedley in Re L (Care: Threshold Criteria) (Family Division 26 October 2006)*

Still, these questions cannot be ducked in practice, even if we have not resolved them in theory. In Chapter 5, we look a little more closely at how parenting and the relationship between parents and the state are handled in particular legal systems. Issues about the quality of parenting and who provides it will recur in the second half of the book.

Conclusion – working together

The first half of this book is about the theories and principles that should underpin social work practice with children and young people. In the second half, starting with Chapter 6, we look at how these theories and principles work in different aspects of practice. There are some common threads that run through all this, of which one is the idea of *partnership* or working together.

As noted in the introduction to this chapter, working with children and their families can be one of the most stressful and controversial areas of social work practice, because of the importance of the responsibilities involved and the difficulty in making the right decision. Fortunately, these responsibilities are not usually carried alone. As we see in Chapter 5, and in all recent policy developments, partnership is emphasised as a key principle in work with children and young people in care. For social workers, that means partnership in teams with one's own immediate colleagues, with other workers such as foster carers and volunteers, and with professionals from other agencies and disciplines. Sharing difficult decisions with managers and within teams is crucially important, given the nature of some of the decisions we have to take. Inter-agency working is increasingly acknowledged as important in all areas of social work practice, and this is no exception. There is increasing recognition too of the multi-disciplinary and corporate nature of responsibility for the welfare of children and young people, especially if we really start to see their needs for care, health, education, and community in a holistic way. Finally, of course, partnership means working together with parents and other family members, and with children and young people themselves.

GUIDE TO FURTHER READING

Introductory texts to social work with children and families in general include: O'Loughlin and O'Loughlin (2016); Douglas and Fourie (2021); and for Scotland, Hothersall (2013).

For further exploration of children's needs, best interests, resilience, and attachment, see Horwath and Platt (2018).

Parenting and its cultural aspects are considered by Kiima (2021). Tedam (2020) provides an up-to-date text on anti-oppressive social work practice. Perspectives on child participation are further explored in Diaz (2020).

Guidance on further reading regarding other key themes covered here can be found in the next four chapters.

References

Carr, H. and Goosey, D. (2019) *Law for social workers*. Oxford: Oxford University Press.

Cleaver, H. and Unell, I. (2011) *Children's needs-parenting capacity: Child abuse, parental mental illness, learning disability, substance misuse, and domestic violence*. London: The Stationery Office.

Collins, S. (2022) *Social workers and compassion*. London: Routledge.

Committee on the Rights of the Child. (2005) *General comment No. 7: Implementing child rights in early childhood*, 20 September 2006, CRC/C/GC/7/Rev.1. Geneva, United Nations. Available here https://www.refworld.org/docid/460bc5a62.html (accessed 23.01.24).

Committee on the Rights of the Child. (2009) *General comment No. 12: The right of the child to be heard*, 25 May – 12 June 2009, CRC/C/GC/12. Geneva, United Nations. Available here https://www.refworld.org/docid/4ae562c52.html (accessed 23.01.24).

Committee on the Rights of the Child. (2013) *General comment No. 14: The right of the child to have his or her best interests taken as a primary consideration*, 29 May 2013, CRC/C/GC/14. Geneva, United Nations. Available here https://www.refworld.org/docid/51a84b5e4.html (accessed 23.01.24).

Cree, V. (ed.) (2022) *Becoming a social worker*. London: Routledge.

Department for Education. (2018) *Working together to safeguard children*. Available here https://assets.publishing.service.gov.uk/government/uploads/system/uploads/attachment_data/file/942454/Working_together_to_safeguard_children_inter_agency_guidance.pdf

Diaz, C. (2020) *Decision making in child and family social work. Perspectives on children's participation*. Bristol: Bristol University Press.

Dominelli, L. (2017) *Anti-racist social work*. London: Bloomsbury Publishing.

Douglas, V. and Fourie, J. (2021) *Safeguarding children, young people, and families (post-qualifying social work practice series)*. Exeter: Learning Matters, Sage.

Eriken, A.F. and Backe-Hansen, E. (eds.) (2018) *Human rights in child protection. Implications for professional practice and policy*. Basingstoke: Palgrave Macmillan.

Fahlberg, V. (1994) *A child's journey through placement*, London: British Agencies for Adoption and Fostering.

Featherstone, B., Gupta, A., Morris, K. and White, S. (2018) *Protecting children: A social model*. Bristol: Policy Press.

Fox Harding, L. (1997) *Perspectives in child care policy*. Abingdon, Oxfordshire: Routledge.

Goldstein, J., Freud, A. and Solnit, A.J. (1973) *Beyond the best interests of the child*. New York: The Free Press.

Henson, M., Cain, M.D., Wilke, D.J. and Radey, M. (2023) 'What makes a case difficult: Definitions from child welfare workers and implications for workload and caseload management', *Journal of Public Child Welfare*, 1–22. https://doi.org/10.1080/15548732.2023.2219649

Horwath, J. and Platt, D. (2018) *The child's world: The essential guide to assessing vulnerable children, young people and their families* (3rd edition). London: Jessica Kingsley Publishers.

Hothersall, S. (2013) *Social work with children, young people, and their families in Scotland*. Exeter: Learning Matters, Sage.

James, A., Jenks, C. and Prout, A. (1998) *Theorizing childhood*. Cambridge: Polity Press.

James, A. and Prout, A. (eds.) (1997) *Constructing and reconstructing childhood: Contemporary issues in the sociological study of childhood*. Abingdon, Oxfordshire: Routledge.

Kiima, D. (2021) *Assessing culturally informed parenting in social work*. Abingdon, Oxfordshire: Routledge.

Križ, K. and Petersen, M. (2023) *Children and young people's participation in child protection: International research and practical applications*. Oxford: Oxford University Press.

Munro, E. (2019) *Effective child protection*. London: Sage Publications Ltd.

O'Halloran, K. (2022) *Children & the law. Shaping the modern welfare principle in the British Isles*. Abingdon, Oxfordshire: Routledge.

O'Loughlin, M. and O'Loughlin, S. (2016) *Social work with children and families*. Exeter: Learning Matters, Sage.

Orsi-Hunt, R., Harrison, C.L., Rockwell, K.E. and Barbee, A.P. (2023) 'Addressing secondary traumatic stress, burnout, resilience and turnover in the child welfare workforce: Results from a 6-month, cluster-randomized control trial of Resilience Alliance', *Children and Youth Services Review*, *151*, 107044. https://doi.org/10.1016/j.childyouth.2023.107044

Parents, Families and Allies Network. (2022) https://www.pfan.uk

Richards, M. (1986) 'Behind the best interests of the child: an examination of the arguments of Goldstein, Freud and Solnit concerning custody and access at divorce', *Journal of Social Welfare and Family Law*, March, 77–95.

Ruch, G., Turney, D. and Ward, A. (2018) *Relationship-based social work. Getting to the heart of practice*. London: Jessica Kingsley Publishers.

Sutherland, E. and Macfarlane, L. (eds) (2016) *Implementing Article 3 of the United Nations Convention on the Rights of the Child: Best Interests, Welfare and Well-being*. Cambridge: Cambridge University Press.

Tedam, P. (2020) *Anti-oppressive social work practice*. Exeter: Learning Matters, Sage.

Trevarthen, C. (1995) 'The child's need to learn a culture', *Children and Society*, *9*(1), 5–19. https://doi.org/10.1111/j.1099-0860.1995.tb00438.x

United Nations. (1989) *Convention on the rights of the child.* New York and Geneva: United Nations.

Woodhead, M. (1997) Psychology and the cultural construction of children's needs. In James, A. and Prout, A. (eds.) *Constructing and reconstructing childhood. Contemporary issues in the sociological study of childhood* (pp. 54–73). Abingdon, Oxfordshire: Routledge.

Woodhead, M. (2005) 'Early childhood development: A question of rights', *International Journal of Early Childhood*, *37*, 79–98. https://doi.org/10.1007/BF03168347

Woodhead, M. (2006) 'Changing perspectives on early childhood: Theory, research and policy', *International Journal of Equity and Innovation in Early Childhood*, *4*(2), 1–43. Available here http://www.edfac.unimelb.edu.au/ceiec/resources/journal.html

2

THE NEEDS OF CHILDREN AND YOUNG PEOPLE WHO COME INTO CARE

CONTENTS OF CHAPTER

- Introduction
- Knowledge of child development
- The 'ecological' model
- Developmental pathways
- What children need in order to develop
- Attachment
- Relationships
- Resilience
- Family and social circumstances of children coming into care
- Abuse, neglect, harm and exploitation
- Needs of disabled children
- Education and health
- Summary and conclusion
- Guide to further reading

Introduction

Let's start with some personal reflection. Find a relaxed setting and try Exercise 2.1 in your own time.

Exercise 2.1 Making it personal

Imagine that a child known to you personally is in a situation in which they need to be cared for away from home. You may choose to think about your own

DOI: 10.4324/9781003503194-2

child, in the present or in the past, or a child belonging to a relative or friend; but you should think about an *actual* child. You can imagine that they need to be cared for either on a temporary or on a more permanent basis, for whatever reason.

Whatever the circumstances, the task for this exercise is the same. Think about what you would want for the child you have chosen, in terms of the care arrangements to be made. What sort of placement would you want the child to have? What services would you want to see provided? What sort of processes would be necessary to plan and make decisions? Above all, what sort of experience would you want the child to have, and what would be necessary to provide this?

Take ten minutes to reflect on these questions; and write down your thoughts. Afterwards, if you wish, discuss your thoughts with a colleague or fellow student.

The above exercise is likely to have raised a lot of issues about how children and young people are cared for, many of which we will return to in later chapters of this book. One of the first issues it should raise is to do with what we think children and young people *need* – both in general and as individuals.

An influential use of the concept of 'children's needs' was in the book *The Needs of Children* (Kellmer Pringle, 1974, 1986), commissioned by the UK Department of Health and Social Security with the following terms of reference:

> To prepare a comprehensive document about the developmental needs of all children about the ways in which these needs are normally met, and about the consequences for the emotional, intellectual, social and physical growth and development of children when, for one reason or another, these needs are not adequately met.
>
> *Kellmer Pringle (1974, p. 8)*

Her focus was on 'western societies', younger children and their psycho-social development. She defined children's developmental needs as:

a 'the need for love and security' – the child needs to experience loving relationships, consistency and familiarity;
b 'the need for new experiences' – the child must have opportunities to explore and to master a succession of tasks;
c 'the need for praise and recognition' – encouragement is of crucial importance;
d 'the need for responsibility' – children should have increasing independence within a secure framework.

You may have noticed that this is a highly selective list. For instance, it is noteworthy that she does not include physical needs for warmth and sustenance – indeed, she deliberately leaves them out. 'Since physical ones are not only more clearly understood but also more easily and now more generally met, the emphasis will be on psycho-social needs' (Kellmer Pringle, 1986, p. 34). Written as advice for parents, teachers and social workers, Kellmer Pringle's approach to children's needs is very focused. Indeed, several of the core messages still have relevance to policy and practice today including the importance of:

- the early years – emphasising the principles of early intervention and prevention;
- establishing strong family support systems – because parenting is a demanding and complex task;
- the environment in which the child lives – including family functioning and access to financial, practical, emotional, social support and family connectedness to community;
- children's rights and parents' responsibilities.

A broader approach is adopted by Margaret Bryer in 'Planning in Child Care' (Bryer, 1988), another book that was commissioned for a specific purpose (as advice to social work team leaders and their teams). Bryer's comprehensive list of 'people's needs' is organised under five headings – physical, social, emotional, educational or intellectual, and ethical. Within these are a total of 87 different categories of need (see Figure 2.1). Again, although written a long time ago, the detailed sub categories of need, under each of the five headings are still very useful. For example, under 'emotional' needs, Bryer has an extensive list including the need for: responsibility; fair treatment; sense of belonging; fun and laughter; acceptance; attention; love; confidence; praise; stability; security; and honesty.

Bryer's argument – like Kellmer Pringle's – is that these needs have to be met both in childhood and throughout life. Bryer also draws a helpful distinction between the general needs that all children have, and the 'priority needs' or 'unmet needs' of individual children in difficulties. In another helpful insight, she also says that when children come into care, it is hoped that some of the unmet needs will now be met or met more effectively. But there is a danger of new needs being created as the child leaves his or her familiar environment. Bonds of affection and friendship can be loosened or broken and precious continuities in the child's life are lost (Bryer, 1988, p. 30). The principles and approach outlined by Bryer will continue to be referred to throughout this book, recognising their currency and applicability in a contemporary context. There are, of course, other descriptions of children's

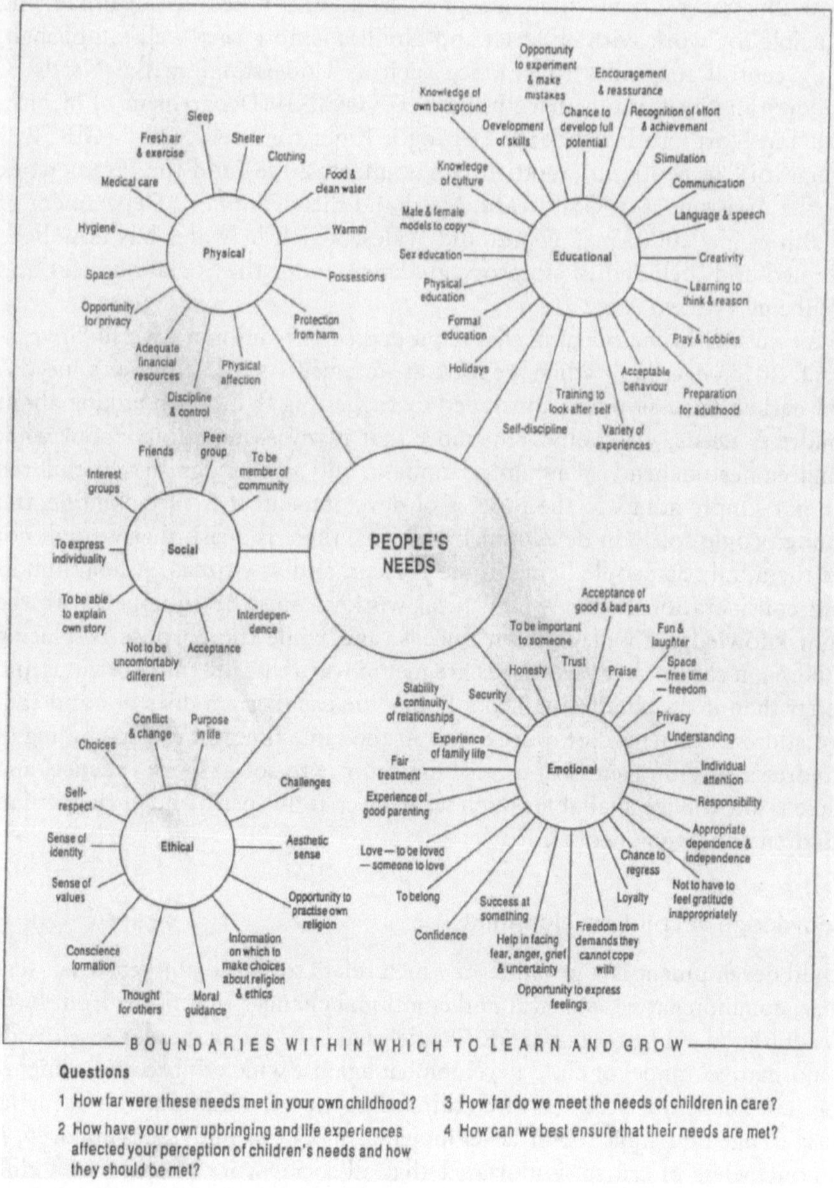

FIGURE 2.1 People's needs.

Source: Bryer (1988, p. 32).

needs which can be found in basic texts on child development, some of which are referred to in the Guide to Further Reading at the end of this chapter.

As illustrated above, the concept of 'children's needs' as an organising principle for work with children and families is now very well established, being central to guides to practice such as Understanding the Needs of Children in Need in Northern Ireland (UNOCINI) (Department of Health, 2011) in Northern Ireland, the Getting it Right for Every Child (GIRFEC) framework in Scotland (Scottish Government, 2008) and the 'Framework for the Assessment of Children in Need and their Families' (Department of Health et al., 2000) in England and Wales, which in Wales has now been adapted and included in statutory guidance under the Social Services and Wellbeing (Wales) Act 2014.

As we saw in the opening chapter, a degree of caution is (Welsh Government, 2015) necessary when we look at statements about children's 'needs'. The earlier discussion was concluded by suggesting that, when talking about children's needs, we should remember that many assumptions about what children need depend on a cultural context, and also recognise that children are not simply adults in the process of development. If we see children and young people solely in developmental terms, there is a risk that we will not see them fully as people living in the present, and as citizens. A final important consideration is that while social workers must be equipped with the right knowledge about children's needs, and while the purpose of placing children in care is that their needs are met in ways that are more obvious and better than if the child remained a home, the care system does not and cannot address every need of every child. At the same time, an understanding of children's development is of central importance to social work practice, and there is knowledge available which we neglect at our peril, and at the peril of children and young people.

Knowledge of child development

Child development is a broad term which refers to the cognitive, social, sensory, communicative, physical and emotional changes that occur from birth to adulthood (Aldgate et al., 2006; Daniel et al., 2011). These changes provide a 'normative' model of child development against which to broadly compare the developmental progress of children. Despite the limitations of applying a rigid 'age and stage' child developmental model to individual children, it is nonetheless of critical importance that all social work practice with children and young people in care is informed by a good understanding of child development. There are several reasons for this. First, it enables us to have a better understanding of children's lives at different ages and stages – what skills and capacities they may have, what particular needs they may have, what conflicts they may be dealing with, and so on. Second, it enables us to identify children and young people whose developmental progress is concerning when compared with the developmental norms that are expected, and to enquire into possible reasons for that. Third, a good knowledge of child development enables us to plan to meet children's needs, and to advise parents and carers. Finally, it puts us in a position where we can engage in constructive dialogue with other professionals, including psychologists and doctors, and advise courts making decisions about children's welfare and 'best interests'.

What do we mean by 'a sound knowledge of child development' in this context? As indicated above, it is not simply an account of the rigid 'ages and stages' approach, of prescribed weights and heights, standard indicators of language development, and so on. There have been enough critiques of 'developmentalism' (James and James, 2012; Shute and Slee, 2015) to make us see that this is not by any means the whole story. First, each child is different. Children do not all follow the same fixed developmental pattern, because of the unique combination of their own intrinsic qualities and characteristics and the influences of the social contexts in which they live. As a result, children learn to walk and talk at different ages, and some very young children can possess highly developed social competencies compared with others. Second, it is now acknowledged that children and young people are not to be defined in purely developmental terms – the adult competencies they have yet to acquire or what they will become – but rather there is an appreciation that their lives *now* are of central importance. Finally, because childhood is itself a socially constructed phenomenon, many aspects of children's lives are not determined by fixed biological processes but are produced in social interaction. As a result, there is a huge diversity within the child population with regard to developmental progress.

That said, it is imperative that we do not reject broad child development frameworks because they do provide a solid foundation from which to appreciate developmental progression over time. For example, there are biological processes at work, subtle and complex ones, and we cannot ignore them. The physical growth of children and young people tends to follow certain patterns. Although these patterns are affected by individual genetic variation as well as by environmental factors such as nutrition, they are nonetheless patterns that can be observed. The development of muscular control in infancy tends to follow a similar sequence for all children. The physical structure of the brain appears to develop in predictable ways (and this structural development of the brain continues into adulthood). Environmental factors can impede or facilitate this growth, but they cannot apparently change the basic pattern. These biological patterns have obvious practical consequences. For example, the normal age of onset of behaviour such as walking or talking tends to be similar in different societies, despite wide cultural variation in child care practice and in other aspects of infant behaviour. The implications for professionals are that, if we are equipped with good knowledge about child development, when a child does not fit expected developmental patterns, we will be in a position to enquire whether there may be a problem.

In Chapter 1, we noted Woodhead's observation that statements about 'children's needs' may refer to basic drives such as those for sustenance or closeness to people, or to the pathological consequences of particular childhood experiences, or they may refer to judgments about which childhood experiences are most culturally adaptive or which childhood experiences are most highly valued in society. As well as knowing about basic biological patterns of development, Robinson (2020) reminds us of the importance of understanding cultural patterns of development. This knowledge can help understand differing cultural expectations in different communities or social contexts and assist in avoiding stereotypes and meeting the particular needs of different children in appropriate ways. There are some highly relevant resources regarding understanding child development from a cultural approach mentioned in 'Guide to Further Reading' at the end of this chapter.

Furthermore, because it is not the purpose of this book to provide a detailed guide as to what is known about child development, or the different theoretical models proposed, we have instead included additional resources in the Guide to Further Reading. We suggest consulting several rather than depending on a single source. It is also important to read critically – some authors are better than others at using the concept of 'development' in a sceptical way and at stepping outside their own culture. In this chapter, we do focus on particular aspects of developmental theory, and on the relevance of these for social work with young people in care. The first is an understanding of children and their development in a wider social context, as explored further below.

The 'ecological' model

One of the most useful insights in developmental theory, particularly for social workers, is the idea that development is not simply a matter of studying what happens in the individual child, or the child in their family, but that an analysis of the influence of various factors within the wider social context also contributes to an understanding of how children develop. The 'ecological model' proposed by Bronfenbrenner (1979), which focuses on the psycho-social determinants of optimal child development, underpins core social work policies and guidelines for work with children and families. For example, the approach underpins the child assessment frameworks in all four nations of the UK. It focuses on the person, the social processes and the context, as illustrated below, providing a systemic approach to understanding child development.

Bronfenbrenner's model (1979) (Figure 2.2) distinguishes between: 'microsystem' – the immediate settings such as the family, a school or peer group

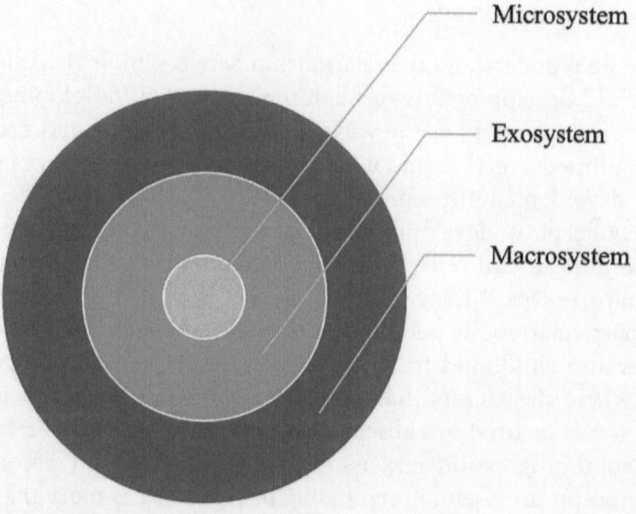

FIGURE 2.2 An adaptation of Bronfenbrenner's ecological model.

within which individuals live and develop; 'mesosystem' – the interaction between these settings; 'exosystem' – wider social institutions such as neighbourhood, government and media; and 'macrosystem' – the broader context of social and economic systems, law, ideology and culture.

Although diagrammatically the model appears static, with clear divisions between the various layers and factors, factors overlap and layers are interconnected with influences that change over time and vary across cultures. Using this model too rigidly can lead to a picture of an individual child as simply a product of external systems, rather than contributing to and being an active participant in their own development. Used flexibly, however, it reminds us that there are many different factors that have a bearing on the lives of children and young people, that they are not all in the child's immediate social environment (see Exercise 2.2), and that it is important to extend the usual focus on the child and family with a wider community perspective.

Exercise 2.2 Mapping children's needs

Think again about the child you chose for Exercise 2.1. Using the chart in Figure 2.1, and the model in Figure 2.2, try to identify some of the key influences on that child's situation in the microsystem, the mesosystem, the exosystem and the macrosystem.

Developmental pathways

One way to help understand the relationship between biological and cultural factors in child development is through the concept of 'developmental pathways'. The concept refers to the ways in which developmental progress can be tracked, plotted overtime and where any positive and negative factors that impact on developmental progress can be identified (and addressed if possible). The concept of 'developmental pathway' is used slightly differently by different authors. It can refer to the opportunities provided for children by different cultures (see Weisner, 2005), and it can refer to the pathways followed by particular young people which are disrupted by adverse childhood experiences and childhood trauma and which can lead to poor outcomes, especially where the factors that mitigate against the impact of harm (personal and social factors) are absent. Another way that this is referred to is 'developmental progression' and associated continuities and discontinuities.

These concepts are useful in reminding us that there is more than one way to grow up, and more than one way of understanding positive outcomes for each child. It also reminds us that a child's future as an adult is not wholly predetermined for good or ill by what happens in early childhood, and that it is important to be aware of the potential impacts of childhood trauma and adverse childhood experiences on the developing child, as well as those factors that help mitigate those impacts. We explore further below what children need to develop, what might interfere with developmental pathways and what might help children navigate their way through to achieve their full potential. These complex processes were helpfully illustrated by Daniel et al. (2011) when they used the image of a sailing yacht to show how a child's progress through life may be affected by a succession of factors, some of which may blow the child's development 'off course' while others help to put it back on track.

What children need in order to develop

It is clear that in order to develop fulfilled and healthy lives, children and young people need certain resources to be available, both in their immediate environment and in the wider world around them. As noted earlier, these resources include the fundamentals of warmth, shelter and sustenance, human contact, and care – not just at a basic level of survival, but of a quality to provide good 'life-chances'. Other fundamentals, highly relevant for many of the world's children, include freedom from war and violence, displacement, exploitation, discrimination and other natural or human-made disasters.

In the UNCRC these needs are also identified as fundamental rights. For example, Article 6 highlights a child's right to life, and the State's obligation to ensure to the maximum extent possible the survival and development of the child; Articles 7, 8 and 30 relate to a child's right to identity and the State's obligation to preserve a child's identity; Articles 19, 32, 33, 34, 35, 36 and 37 highlight a child's right to freedom from abuse, harm and neglect; Articles 18, 25, 26, 27 and 39 outline the State's obligation to provide suitable services and in particular in Article 39, to support the recovery and reintegration of children who have suffered harm and abuse and for the review of services; Articles 23, 24, 26, 27, 28 and 29 concern children's rights to health, education; and Articles 12, 13, 14, 15, 16 and 31 highlight children's rights to freedom of thought, conscience, to freedom of association and the right to rest and leisure.

It is clear from any definition of children's needs/rights that children are not isolated islands but live in the context of relationships with other children and adults and that they also therefore need opportunities to form meaningful and positive relationships with others – so the social environment in which they grow up is important, both in the family and outside. This is frequently understood in terms of *attachment*, which is discussed further in the following section. Children need opportunities to develop their linguistic, social and cognitive skills, and this requires a rich and stimulating physical, as well as a social, environment. For some children these opportunities for learning are readily available within the family; others are more dependent on outside institutions such as school, although for all children it is best if both settings work together to offer a learning environment. As acknowledged in Article 13, UNCRC, media such as television and computers are also important sources of information and of opportunities to develop skills in using it.

Above all, as noted above, children and young people do not develop in isolation but in a *cultural* context. Robinson (2020) explores the relevance of cross-cultural child development for social work practice, noting that it is important to understand culture as both the wider culture of the society in which the child lives – its value systems, scientific beliefs, social expectations – and also to the specific culture of the social group to which the child belongs, which is best defined in terms of ethnicity and class – its traditions, beliefs and ways of doing things. Children's cultural learning comes from all the sources to which we have already referred – family, school, other social settings, communication media. It is important for children to feel that their own particular culture is valued and worthy of respect, alongside others. A starting point in all considerations regarding child development and what children need is to look at their relationships with others around them, including their close attachments. This is further considered below.

Attachment

In recent years, attachment theory has come to dominate the discussion of child development in social work. As Daniel et al. (2011, p. 22) explain:

> Attachment theory... asserts that there is a biological imperative for infants to form attachments and that they exhibit attachment behaviours to promote attachment. In this sense attachment behaviour can be viewed as

> survival behaviour. The theory relates the quality of such early attachment relationships to emotional functioning throughout life. Attachment theory also relates language, cognitive and moral development to the quality of early attachment relationships. An understanding of the theory of these developmental dimensions should therefore provide a good basis for assessing the possible effects on a child's development when attachment relationships are inadequate.

Attachment theory is not just about what happens in early childhood. As a conceptual framework, it is also relevant for work with older children and young people, and with adults, indeed it applies throughout the life course. Patterns of attachment laid down in infancy as a result of parental behaviour can tend to persist (both because parental behaviour persists anyway and because children's behaviour tends to reinforce it for better or worse). It is thought that gradually these patterns can become internalised in the child's model of self and may contribute to the developmental pathway along which the individual will travel.

In terms of the use of attachment in social work with children and families, David Howe and others have promoted its use, arguing that

> children need to secure permanent selective attachments to one or more loving and responsive caregivers if they are to achieve healthy psychological development', and that 'social workers have to consider how to maintain, strengthen or provide affectional bonds and good quality attachment experiences for children.
>
> *(Howe, 1995, p. 15)*

This is obviously of relevance in consideration of placement options and the nature and types of relationship offered between children and their carers.

Attachments and the quality of relationships are fundamental in social work practice as they influence the identity formation of children and young people in care. There is evidence that stable attachments contribute to children and young people's ability to narrate events in their lives and to construct their own life story. The development of narrative competence in recounting one's life history is particularly apparent in the teenage years and is based on processes of reciprocal memory sharing and making sense of events. It is evident that experiences of disruption, loss and change (in terms of placement, involved carers, professionals) can impact on an individual's capacity to draw events together, make sense of them and develop a narrative (Holmes, 1993; Habermas and Paha, 2001; Quinn, 2022; Marshall et al., 2020).

Other implications of an attachment perspective for social work practice with children and young people in care are noted by Fahlberg (2012) and Furnivall (2011). These include: protecting children's existing attachments where possible and sensible; supporting children to maintain existing positive attachments whilst also supporting them to develop new attachments with new carers; enabling children to make positive transitions through care and into after care by recognising, respecting and valuing their positive attachments – and by addressing damaging attachments and their impacts. For example, Fahlberg (2012) refers to situations where a child may feel a strong attachment to a parent that is not reciprocated by the parent 'bonding' with the child. Social workers may mistakenly see this an attachment that needs to be preserved, rather than as an anxious attachment that can prevent the child's needs from being met unless the failure of the parent to bond is addressed and resolved.

All of this points to the importance of professional knowledge and awareness of attachment and the impact of trauma and adverse childhood experiences on attachments. It also points to the need for practice that:

1 is attachment and trauma informed;
2 supports existing attachments rather than disrupting them (for instance by judicious use of respite care and placement moves where possible);
3 makes timely decisions regarding children's care planning;
4 understands how children's social, emotional and behavioural difficulties can arise from unstable, insecure and negative attachments;
5 offers therapeutic environments and services to children; and
6 is informed by ongoing training and support (Furnivall, 2011).

These points are further explored by Cairns and Cairns (2016), who draw on their experiences as foster carers to highlight the importance of positive relationships and within this approaches to attachment, trauma and resilience. The next sections explore relationships and the concept of resilience in further detail.

Relationships

It is evident that positive, meaningful relationships between children and young people in care and their peers, key workers, foster carers, social workers, and other professionals are fundamental. Whilst a seemingly straightforward term, 'relationships' as a construct has been explored through a variety of conceptual lenses. We find it helpful to draw attention to the work of Honneth (1995), who 'sees the foundation of positive relationships in terms of a basic moral demand for recognition of and being recognised by others' (Smith et al., 2017, p. 1614). Honneth distinguishes three modes of recognition: (1) love, or primary emotional relationships of care; (2) rights, or the respect due to everyone as a human being; and (3) solidarity, or esteem for one's value and contribution to the community'. In other words, recognition for who you are as an individual, of your equal standing as a person, and for what you can contribute. For Honneth, these forms of intersubjective recognition are crucial for our growth as individuals, and indeed as a society.

The importance of this approach for children in care is that it embraces emotional ties (love, indeed), but it also acknowledges the importance of respect for children's human rights. There is often felt to be a tension between caring for children as vulnerable and respecting their rights; Honneth's model enables us to see how the two can, and must, go hand in hand. More than that, it enables us to see children not just as needing our care or demanding our attention, but as having things to offer. In recent years, this conceptual framework regarding recognition has been applied to children's participation (Thomas, 2012), child and family social work (Houston, 2009; Smith et al., 2017; Turney, 2012), children living in residential child care (Marshall et al., 2020), and to young people leaving care (Paulsen and Thomas, 2018).

Resilience

Another concept that has become increasingly influential in thinking about work with children and young people is that of resilience. The concept emerged in around 1970 after investigators noted huge variability in children's response to experiences of multiple risks and adversities. Researchers from different backgrounds

> aimed to understand positive developmental trajectories among children who managed to hold their own or even flourish despite adversity and, ultimately, to learn how to promote healthy development among children threatened by adverse childhood experiences. Patterns of positive development in the context of adversity were broadly described as "resilience" phenomena, although investigators varied in their definitions of resilience as referring to capacity, processes, or outcomes of positive adaptation to adversity.
>
> *(Masten and Barnes, 2018, p. 98)*

Gilligan (2009, p. 6) notes that broadly defined resilience is 'a set of qualities that helps a person to withstand many of the negative effects of adversity'. He explains that resilience, although influenced by individual characteristics, develops in a social context. The importance of resilience is that 'it serves to release the natural flow of recovery and development that might other-wise be paralysed or frozen by negative experiences'. Some children are naturally more resilient than others, but there are also environmental factors than can enhance natural resilience.

Maclean (2003) identifies the 'qualities associated with resilience which develop through children's life experiences' as *self-esteem* (enhanced by acceptance and achievement); belief in one's own *self-efficacy* (enhanced by taking responsibility and making decisions); *initiative* (ability and willingness to take action); *faith and morality* (as Daniel et al. note, 'a belief in a broader value system can help the child to persist in problem solving or in surviving a set of challenging life circumstances' (1999, p. 67)); *trust* in others; *attachment* (as Maclean says, 'one sign of resilience in children is the ability to 'recruit' caring adults who take a particular interest in them'); a *secure base*, not just in terms of primary attachment but in the wider sense of a consistent and stable place to live and continuity of wider relationships; *meaningful roles* such as proficiency at school, sport, work, volunteering, caring for siblings and domestic responsibilities (provided they are not excessive); *autonomy*; *identity*; *insight*; and *humour*.

These lists are helpful in reminding us how much can be done to develop the resilience of children and young people in care, to build on their strengths rather than simply focusing on problems. Gilligan (2009) provides ideas and strategies which include providing social and emotional support, encouragement and support in education (critically important for many young people who succeed), encouragement with activities and hobbies, and promoting contacts with friends or supportive adults. We will look further at some of this later in the book, and there are further useful guides listed in the suggested reading at the end of this chapter.

Family and social circumstances of children coming into care

In thinking about the needs of children and young people in care, we must consider the needs they have in common with all children, as well as the needs that stem from their membership of a particular group. We must also consider the circumstances from which children tend to come into the care system, which have their own implications in terms of assessing their needs. To help address these issues, it is worth noting that in recent years, the amount and type of data collected on children in care has grown. There is data on the number of children in care, the reasons for being in care, the characteristics of children in care, the types of care received when in care, the outcomes for children in care including education, health, employment, criminality, and on those leaving care. There remain limits to the data collated; nonetheless the data is a good information source regarding children in care.

Regarding the numbers and characteristics of children in care, an often-quoted piece of research is that of Bebbington and Miles (1989) who carried out a survey of the family circumstances of a sample of 2,165 children in 13 local authorities who entered care in 1987. Several factors were noted as good predictors of which children were at risk of coming into state care, especially when analysed in combination. These (listed in terms of significance) were single parenthood; crowded, rented accommodation; in receipt of benefits; ethnic origin; mother under 21 years of age; large family; and poor neighbourhood (Bebbington and Miles, 1989, pp. 353–358). Hence, child of mixed ethnic origin, living with three or more other children and a single adult in privately rented accommodation with more than one person to a room, and dependent on supplementary benefit, stood a one-in-ten chance of being received into care, whilst a white child in a smaller two-parent family, in an owner-occupied home with more rooms than people, stood a chance of *one in seven thousand*.

More recent research in the UK, led by Bywaters and comprising teams of researchers across the UK (Bywaters et al., 2018, 2020), has added significant understanding to this area. Bywaters et al. (2015, p. 100) define child welfare inequality as occurring 'when children and/or their parents face unequal chances, experiences or outcomes of involvement with child welfare services that are systematically associated with structural social dis/advantage and are unjust and avoidable' (Bywaters et al., 2015, p. 100). This work has confirmed that there are large inequalities in child welfare intervention, with children living in poorer, more deprived areas being much more likely to be involved in child protection proceedings and coming into care. Bywaters et al. (2015, 2018, 2020) found that children in the most deprived 10% of neighbourhoods in the UK were at least ten times more likely to be in care than children in the least deprived 10%, that cross the UK, each step increase in deprivation brings a rise of around a third in a child's chances of being in care and that around one in 60 children is in care in England's most deprived neighbourhoods, compared with one in 660 in the least deprived area.

The research has also found that differences cannot be accounted for by socio economic factors alone. It has been found that ethnic inequalities are also important (Bywaters et al., 2018) (as further highlighted in Chapter 4) and that the impact of local policy and organisational factors (McGhee et al., 2018). For example, while Northern Ireland has some of the highest rates of deprivation, it has relatively fewer children in care compared to other UK nations (Bunting et al., 2017). Research by Wilson and Lee (2021) has explored contributory factors and highlighted the impact of cultural and family norms, local policy developments and local social work practice on figures.

Overall, the available statistics tell us several things. They tell us that children in adverse circumstances and with few resources available to them are far more likely to come into care than their contemporaries whose situations are more favourable. But they also tell us that even where children are in the least favourable circumstances as defined here, the overwhelming majority of them do *not* come into care (which means it is worth enquiring into what it is that enables these children and their families to manage at home – and at what cost). Especially importantly for our purposes here, the statistics also tell us that many of the children and young people who enter the care system bring with them a history of relative disadvantage and associated problems, which we must add to the other needs we have identified.

Abuse, neglect, harm and exploitation

An additional factor is that a high proportion of children and young people in care have been neglected, abused or exploited (Howe, 2005; Firmin and Lloyd, 2023). Indeed, in the UK, the majority (something around 60%) of children in the care system at any time are recorded as being there *because of* abuse, neglect, harm or exploitation. Articles 19, 32, 33, 34, 35, 36, 37 of the UNCRC reiterate children's right to be protected from violence, injury, abuse, harm and exploitation. In recent times, child exploitation has become an increasing focus. Often occurring outside of the immediate family, exploitation can include child criminal exploitation (children being recruited to carry drugs), child sexual exploitation (engagement in sexual activity), or other forms of activity in which adults exploit children for their own gain and in which children can be manipulated to take part with offers of money, clothes, gifts and increased social standing in their own peer group/community. This can be online and/or in person. Often the exploitation comes with threats to children's safety. This is noted in research by Montgomery-Devlin (2020) and Walsh (2023) which focuses on child criminal exploitation associated with paramilitary groups in Northern Ireland. The work by Hallett (2017) which focuses on child sexual exploitation also highlights the profound impact on children's safety and wellbeing.

Another form of abuse and harm noted in more recent literature concerns children who live in situations where there is domestic violence and abuse. The definition of domestic violence and abuse has evolved over time and now includes coercive control (NSPCC, 2023). Our understanding has also evolved over time and there is a growing appreciation that family situations characterised by violence can have direct and indirect harmful impacts on children. Children can experience physical harm as well as emotional and psychological harm by hearing, witnessing and being exposed to domestic violence. Patterns of controlling, verbally and physically violent behaviour to which children are exposed can create fear, anxiety which manifests itself in a range of internalising and externalising behaviours including disturbed sleep, poor appetite, lack of concentration, depression, tearfulness, isolation, shame, anger and relationship difficulties (Devaney, 2015). Up-to-date knowledge, policy and practice in this area are brought together in an edited collection by Devaney et al. (2021). It is essential that social workers are aware of the available research regarding the impact of domestic violence on children and how they and other professionals should respond.

Other recorded reasons for being in care (generally around 10% or less) include family dysfunction (children whose needs are not met because parenting capacity is chronically inadequate), family in acute distress, child's disability, parental illness or disability, and socially unacceptable behaviour. Research also tells us that there is an overrepresentation of children in the care system whose birth parents were in care as children, have had a child removed and go on to experience the removal of subsequent children. Research on recurrent court proceedings by Broadhurst and Mason (2014) draws attention to this issue. The fact that so many children in care, and especially those who remain in care, have a history of ill treatment or exploitation has very obvious implications in terms of their needs – implications for placement planning, for the type of care and treatment needed, and for the kind of things that may go wrong.

As noted, children who have been abused, neglected or exploited may have both physical and psychological consequences to deal with. They may have witnessed violence or had their safety threatened, their growth may have been impaired. Their self-esteem is likely to be poor. They may have difficulties with attachment or with trust and with emotional regulation. These factors can also impact on other areas of development, including educational achievement and attainment, health and wellbeing, sense of identity and belonging, future employment and social networks (Sebba et al., 2017). These and other factors will create problems for individual children and for those they live with. Unless these difficulties are successfully managed, a child's passage through care is likely to be rough and their resilience, and ability to face life successfully, further damaged (Howe, 2005; Doyle and Timms, 2014; Davidson and Bifulco, 2018).

Needs of disabled children

There are many groups of children in the care system who have particular needs in addition to the needs which all children have. Some of the issues in providing for a diverse population are discussed further in Chapter 4. At this point we want to focus briefly on children who are disabled.

It is common to distinguish between *impairment* (the actual physical, sensory, mental or intellectual issue or disorder) which causes someone to be disabled, and *disability* (the result of socially constructed barriers that stand in the way of people leading full lives). This is reflected in the UN Convention on the Rights of Persons with Disabilities, which states that "persons with disabilities include those who have long-term physical, mental, intellectual or sensory impairments which in interaction with various barriers may hinder their full and effective participation in society on an equal basis with others". This definition reflects the social model of disability by recognising both the experience of impairment and the impact of disabling barriers in society on equality of opportunity. Disabled children therefore have a range of needs, some of which are based on the nature of their impairment, others on how those around them respond to it (Adams and Leshone, 2016; Simcock and Castle, 2016).

Children with physical or sensory impairments or conditions will need a physical environment at home and school that enables them to be as autonomous as possible, and additional help in overcoming barriers to access in the wider world. Children with intellectual impairments or conditions will need support in learning to the maximum and perhaps in negotiating relationships with the outside world. Children in both groups may have difficulties in verbal and non-verbal communication, and in this case, it is critically important that they are with people who can communicate with them and that they are enabled to overcome these barriers as far as possible. Children with social, emotional and behavioural difficulties can also struggle to communicate and relate in expected ways (Cairns and Cairns, 2016). They may therefore require people who understand the long-term impacts of these difficulties and who have the knowledge and skills to relate in helpful and supportive ways.

All disabled children are very likely to face discrimination and prejudice and will need help in overcoming and challenging this (Beazley and Williams, 2014; Kelly and Byrne, 2017). Some are particularly vulnerable to abuse, whether before admission to care or after, because of factors including: dependency on others for care; challenges in communicating abusive experiences; the signs of abuse being attributed to factors other than abuse; disabled children not being taken seriously if they do communicate their abuse; and lack of opportunity to inform others. In some care settings, for example, high staff turnover may decrease opportunities for abuse to be noticed and reported. The discrimination faced by children with disabilities, their rights and their full implementation is a focus of Article 23 in the UNCRC, the United Nations Convention on the Rights of Persons with Disabilities, and General Comment No. 9 The Rights of Children with Disabilities (Committee on the Rights of the Child., 2006). In terms of tackling discrimination, it is noted that training programmes for professionals should include training on the rights of disabled children as a prerequisite for qualification.

Education and health

It is very easy when working with children and young people in care, especially in a busy, overworked department, to be preoccupied by the demands of finding and managing placements, negotiating contact arrangements, and so on – in other words, to focus on the immediate circumstances that have brought a child into the care system, and in the process fail to attend to the other needs that apply to all children in our society.

All children need good health care, and children who come from disadvantaged backgrounds, who have had problems of a nature and degree that require state care, and who may then pass through a series of more or less stable and appropriate placements, are likely to need more good health care and supervision than most (Merredew and Sampeys, 2015; Hurley, 2021). For example, basic health needs (which have often been neglected) need to be met – such as regular eye, hearing, dental and immunisation checks. Furthermore, particular and chronic conditions such as allergies, skin conditions, and illnesses often require careful attention and management. While Articles 23 and 24 of the UNCRC highlight a child's right to health and in Article 23 support for particular needs if disabled, as we see later, some research evidence suggests that despite this, children in care may actually get less good health care. Furthermore, we know from wide-ranging research that the mental health needs of children in care is a significant issue across all backgrounds (Engler et al., 2022).

All children and young people need opportunities to learn, as we have noted. In a modern complex society, this almost always means schooling. Some families are able to meet their children's needs for education outside the school system (as evidenced in a systematic review of selected aspects of home schooling carried out by Ray, 2017), but success here seems to relate to social class, educational qualifications and access to personal, material and social capital. The families whose children come into care are rarely in this category – in fact it is more likely that their children have relied on school for some of the conversation, stimulation and learning that most other children can get at home.

However, research suggests (Sebba et al., 2015; Mannay et al., 2019; Cusworth et al., 2021) that owing to a combination of personal and environmental factors evident before coming into care, children and young people when in care often fail to overcome their initial disadvantages. Personal factors can include social and emotional needs, behavioural issues, learning disability and trauma, which impact on educational attainment and achievement (Sebba et al., 2017; Sebba and Luke, 2019; Connolly et al., 2023). Environmental factors can include the impact of social structural issues such as racism, social class, social exclusion and poverty which we know impact on children's educational attainment and achievement. While Articles 28 and 29 of the UNCRC highlight a child's right to education and the benefits of education and the care system aims to provide care that helps rectify inequalities and put children on an equal footing with their peers, it does not always achieve this. There is evidence, as noted from a systematic review of children in care and their perspectives regarding education, that low staff/teacher expectations of the educational performance of children in care; multiple moves and school changes; unidentified and unaddressed learning disabilities; and social, emotional and behavioural issues make children in care highly vulnerable to failure and exclusion at school which has the effect of making things worse (Townsend et al., 2020).

We have noted that in relation to resilience, educational success can be one of the key factors that make a difference to how young people manage difficulties and overcome adversity to succeed in life (Martin and Jackson, 2002; Berridge, 2017). There is a range of research that has assessed the effectiveness of various interventions and policy initiatives designed to support the educational attainment and achievement of children in care which range from the development of personal education plans, the provision of bursaries to schools for each child looked after to provide bespoke support, access to extra-curricular activities, and support for extra tuition (Connolly et al., 2023). In terms of the most effective intervention, research indicates that direct one-to-one tuition (Connolly et al., 2023) is best. Knowing what we do about the importance of education in terms of improving long-term outcomes, it is critical that social workers prioritise this area with children when they are in foster care and/or residential care. This is a theme we will return to in the later chapters on foster and residential care.

Summary and conclusion

We have seen how a working knowledge of child development is indispensable for good practice with children and young people in care. We have looked at some of the important models and concepts, including the 'ecological' approach, developmental pathways, attachment and resilience. We have considered the family and social circumstances of children coming into care, the rights of children and the consequences of abuse and neglect and the needs of disabled children. Finally, we have thought about the health and education of children in care – and this brings us to the final message of this chapter, which is the need to respond to children and young people in a holistic way, and not to compartmentalise them. If there is one thing of value in the contemporary concept of 'children's needs', it is that a child or young person must been seen, and treated, as a whole, not as a collection of parts.

GUIDE TO FURTHER READING

A useful introduction to child development for social workers is Daniel, Wassell and Gilligan (2011). For greater detail on cultural aspects of child development, Robinson (2020) provides a useful discussion.

For more on attachment, trauma and resilience, Howe (2011), Cairns and Cairns (2016), Gilligan (2009) and Triesman (2017) provide excellent overviews.

Cocker and Allain (2019) and Sen (2018) are useful texts focusing on children in care and effective practice with this group. For further detail on the social background of children and young people in care, Bebbington and Miles (1989) is an excellent starting point which should be read in conjunction with Bywaters et al. (2020) for an up-to-date overview of this area.

Pardeck (2021) and Munro (2019) are informative texts regarding child abuse and neglect.

Horsburgh (2022) focuses on the health, education needs and long-term outcomes for children in care; Guisard-Pine et al. (2016) are useful regarding the mental health needs of children in care.

The Nuffield Family Justice Observatory website https://www.nuffieldfjo.org.uk is a rich source of information regarding public and private law proceedings and the characteristics and needs of those who come into care.

References

Adams, J. and Leshone, D. (2016) *Active social work with children with disabilities. Critical skills for social work*. Northwich: Critical Publishing Ltd.

Aldgate, J., Jones, D., Rose, W. and Jeffery, C. (eds.) (2006) *The developing world of the child*. London: Jessica Kingsley Publishing.

Beazley, S. and Williams, V. (eds.). (2014) *Childhood and disability: Key papers from disability & Society* (first edition). Abingdon, Oxfordshire: Routledge.

Bebbington, A. and Miles, J. (1989) 'The background of children who enter local authority care', *British Journal of Social Work*, *19*(5), 349–368.

Berridge, D. (2017) 'The education of children in care: Agency and resilience', *Children and Youth Services Review*, 77, 86–93.

Broadhurst, K. and Mason, C. (2014) 'Recurrent care proceedings: Part 3-birth mothers-against the odds-turning points for women who have lost children to public care', *Family Law*, 44, 1572–1576.

Bronfenbrenner, U. (1979) *The ecology of human development*. New York: Harvard University Press.

Bryer, M. (1988) *Planning in child care. A guide for team leaders and their teams*. London: BAAF

Bunting, L., McCartan, C. and Davidson, G. (2017) *Identifying and understanding inequalities in child welfare intervention rates: Comparative studies in four UK countries: Single country quantitative study report*. Northern Ireland: Queen's University Belfast.

Bywaters, P., Brady, G., Bunting, L., Daniel, B., Featherstone, B., Jones, C., Morris, K., Scourfield, J., Sparks, T. and Webb, C. (2018) 'Inequalities in English child protection practice under austerity: A universal challenge?', *Child and Family Social Work*, *23*(1), 53–61.

Bywaters, P., Brady, G., Sparks, T., Bos, E., Bunting, L., Daniel, B., Featherstone, B., Morris, K. and Scourfield, J. (2015) Exploring inequities in child welfare and child protection services: Explaining the 'inverse intervention law'. *Children and Youth Services Review*, *57*, 98–105.

Bywaters, P., Scourfield, J., Jones, C., Sparks, T., Elliott, M., Hooper, J., McCartan, C., Shapira, M., Bunting, L. and Daniel, B. (2020) 'Child welfare inequalities in the four nations of the UK', *Journal of Social Work*, *20*(2), 193–215.

Cairns, K. and Cairns, B. (2016) *Attachment, trauma, and resilience: Therapeutic caring for children*. London: CoramBAAF.

Cocker, C. and Allain, L. (2019) *Social work with looked after children. Transforming social work practice series.* Exeter: learning Matters, Sage.

Committee on the Rights of the Child. (2006) *General comment No. 9 (2006). The rights of children with disabilities.* Geneva: United Nations.

Connolly, P., Sebba, J., Winter, K., Roberts, J., Tah, P. and Millen, S. (2023) 'The effectiveness of book-gifting programmes to enhance the reading skills of children in care: A randomised controlled trial of 'Reading Together' in England', *Children and Youth Services Review, 153*, 107097.

Cusworth, L., Tracey, L., Baldwin, H. and Biehal, N. (2021) 'Home or care? A comparison of educational outcomes for maltreated children', *The British Journal of Social Work, 51*(8), 3055–3076.

Daniel, B., Wassell, S. and Gilligan, R. (2011) *Child development for child care and protection workers* (second edition). London: Jessica Kingsley Publishers.

Davidson, J. and Bifulco, A. (2018) *Child abuse and protection: Contemporary issues in research, policy, and practice.* London: Routledge.

Department of Health. (2011) *Understanding the needs of children in Northern Ireland (UNOCINI) guidance.* Belfast: Department of Health.

Department of Health, Department for Education and Employment and the Home Office. (2000) *Framework for the assessment of children in need and their families.* London: The Stationery Office.

Devaney, J. (2015) 'Research review: The impact of domestic violence on children', *Irish Probation Journal*, 12, 79–94.

Devaney, J., Bradbury-Jones, C., Macy, R.J., Øverlien, C. and Holt, S. (eds.) (2021) *The Routledge International handbook of domestic violence and abuse.* Abingdon, Oxfordshire: Routledge.

Doyle, C. and Timms, C. (2014) *Child neglect and emotional abuse: Understanding, assessment and response.* London: Sage Publications Ltd.

Engler, A.D., Sarpong, K.O., Van Horne, B.S., Greeley, C.S. and Keefe, R.J. (2022) 'A systematic review of mental health disorders of children in foster care', *Trauma, Violence, & Abuse, 23*(1), 255–264.

Fahlberg, V.I. (2012) *A child's journey through placement* (second edition). London: British Association for Adoption and Fostering (BAAF).

Firmin, C. and Lloyd, J. (2023) *Contextual safeguarding. The next chapter.* Bristol: Policy Press.

Furnivall, J. (2011) *Attachment-informed practice with looked after children and young people.* (IRISS Insights; Vol. 10). Glasgow: The Institute for Research and Innovation in Social Services (IRISS). Available here https://www.iriss.org.uk/resources/insights/attachment-informed-practice-looked-after-children-young-people (accessed 10.09.23).

Gilligan, R. (2009) *Promoting resilience.* London: CoramBAAF.

Guisard-Pine, J., Coleman-Oluwabusola, G. and McCall, S. (2016) *Supporting the mental health of children in care: Evidence-based practice.* London: Jessica Kingsley Publishers.

Habermas, T. and Paha, C. (2001) '*The development of coherence* in adolescents' life narratives', *Narrative Inquiry, 11*, 35–54. Available here https://psycnet.apa.org/doi/10.1075/ni.11.1.02hab

Hallett, S. (2017) *Making sense of child sexual exploitation: Exchange, abuse, and young people.* Bristol: Policy Press.

Holmes, J. (1993) *Bowlby and attachment theory*. London: Routledge.
Honneth, A. (1995) *The struggle for recognition: The moral grammar of social conflicts*. Blackwell, Cambridge: Polity Press.
Horsburgh, J. (2022) *Improving outcomes for looked after children*. Oxford: Blackwell Publishing Ltd.
Houston, S. (2009) 'Communication, recognition and social work: Aligning the ethical theories of Habermas and Honneth', *British Journal of Social Work*, *39*(7), 1274–1290.
Howe, D. (1995) *Attachment theory for social work practice*. Houndmills, Basingstoke, Hampshire: MacMillan Press Ltd.
Howe, D. (2005) *Child abuse and neglect: Attachment, development, and intervention*. Hampshire: Palgrave Macmillan.
Howe, D. (2011) *Attachment across the lifecourse: A brief introduction*. London: Bloomsbury Academic.
Hurley, A. (2021) *Parenting matters: Parenting a child with difficulties in learning caused by trauma*. London: CoramBAAF.
James, A. and James, A. (2012) *Key concepts in childhood studies* (second edition). London: Sage Publications Ltd.
Kellmer Pringle, M. (1974) (first edition). *The needs of children*. London: Hutchinson.
Kellmer Pringle, M. (1986) *The needs of children* (3rd edition). London: Routledge.
Kelly, B. and Byrne, B. (eds.) (2017) *Valuing disabled children and young people: Research, policy, and practice*. Abingdon: Routledge.
Maclean, K. (2003) 'Resilience. What it is and how children and young people can be helped to develop it', *Residence No 1*. Glasgow: Scottish Institute for Residential Child Care.
Mannay, D., Rees, A. and Roberts, L. (eds.) (2019) *Children and young people 'looked after'? Education, intervention, and the everyday culture of care in Wales*. Cardiff: University of Wales Press.
Marshall, G., Winter, K. and Turney, D. (2020) 'Honneth and positive identity formation in residential care', *Child and Family Social Work*, *25*(4), 733–741.
Martin, P.Y. and Jackson, S. (2002) 'Educational success for children in public care: Advice from a group of high achievers', *Child and Family Social Work*, *7*(2), 121–130.
Masten, A.S. and Barnes, A.J. (2018) 'Resilience in children: Developmental perspectives', *Children*, *5*(7), 98.
McGhee, J., Bunting, L., McCartan, C., Elliott, M., Bywaters, P. and Featherstone, B. (2018) 'Looking after children in the UK – convergence or divergence?', *British Journal of Social Work*, *48*(5), 1176–1198.
Merredew, F. and Sampeys, C. (eds.) (2015) *Promoting the health of children in public care*. London: CoramBAAF.
Montgomery-Devlin, J. (2020) *The influence of paramilitiarism in Northern Ireland on the recognition of child sexual exploitation in young males*. Belfast: Safeguarding Board Northern Ireland.
Munro, E. (2019) *Effective child protection*. London: Sage Publications.
NSPCC. (2023) *Insights on the impact of coercive control on children and young people*. London: NSPCC.
Pardeck, J. (ed.) (2021) *Child abuse and neglect: Theory, research, and practice*. London: Routledge.
Paulsen, V. and Thomas, N. (2018) 'The transition to adulthood from care as a struggle for recognition', *Child and Family Social Work*, *23*(2), 163–170.

Quinn, A.L. (2022) 'Experiences and well-being among indigenous former youth in care within Canada', *Child Abuse and Neglect, 123*, 105395.

Ray, B.D. (2017) 'A systematic review of the empirical research on selected aspects of homeschooling as a school choice', *Journal of School Choice, 11*(4), 604–621.

Robinson, L. (2020) *Cross-cultural child development for social workers: An introduction.* London: Red Globe Press.

Scottish Government. (2008) *Getting it right for every child (GIRFEC) guide.* Edinburgh: Scottish Government. Available here https://www.gov.scot/policies/girfec/girfec-resources/ (accessed 10.09.23).

Sebba, J., Berridge, D., Luke, N., Fletcher, J., Bell, K., Strand, S., Thomas, S., Sinclair, I. and O'Higgins, A. (2015) *The educational progress of looked after children in England: Linking care and educational data.* Oxford: REES Centre, Oxford University.

Sebba, J. and Luke, N. (2019) 'The educational progress and outcomes of children in care: Editorial', *Oxford Review of Education, 45*(4), 435–442.

Sebba, J., Luke, N. and Berridge, D. (2017) 'The educational progress of young people in out-of-home care', *Developing Practice: The Child, Youth and Family Work Journal, 47*, 18–35.

Sen, R. (2018) *Effective practice with looked after children.* London: Red Globe Press.

Shute, R.H. and Slee, P.T. (2015) *Child development: Theories and critical perspectives* (second edition). Abingdon, Oxfordshire: Routledge/Taylor & Francis Group.

Simcock, P. and Castle, R. (2016) *Social work and disability.* Bristol: Polity Press.

Smith, M., Cameron, C. and Reimer, D. (2017) 'From attachment to recognition for children in care', *British Journal of Social Work, 47*(6), 1606–1623.

Thomas, N. (2012) 'Love, rights and solidarity: Studying children's participation using Honneth's theory of recognition', *Childhood, 19*(4), 453–466.

Townsend, I.M., Berger, E.P. and Reupert, A.E. (2020) 'Systematic review of the educational experiences of children in care: Children's perspectives', *Children and Youth Services Review, 111*, 104835.

Triesman, K. (2017) *Working with relational and developmental trauma in children and adolescents.* London: Routledge.

Turney, D. (2012) 'A relationship-based approach to engaging involuntary clients: The contribution of recognition theory', *Child & Family Social Work, 17*(2), 149–159.

United Nations. (1989) *Convention on the rights of the child.* New York and Geneva: United Nations.

Walsh, C. (2023) 'From contextual to criminal harms: young people's understanding and experiences of the violence of criminal exploitation', Crime Prevention and Community Safety, 25(3), 282–304.

Welsh Government (2015) Social Services and Well-being (Wales) Act 2014: Part 3 Code of Practice (assessing the needs of individuals). Cardiff: Welsh Government.

Weisner, T.S. (ed.) (2005) *Discovering successful pathways in children's development: New methods in the study of childhood and family life.* Chicago: The University of Chicago Press.

Wilson, I.A. and Lee, J. (2021) 'Barriers and facilitators associated with child abuse and neglect reporting among childcare professionals: A systematic review', *Journal of Psychosocial Nursing and Mental Health Services, 59*(6), 14–22.

3

LISTENING TO CHILDREN AND YOUNG PEOPLE

CONTENTS OF CHAPTER

- Introduction
- What does listening to children and young people mean?
- Why should we listen to children and young people?
- How do we listen to and communicate with children and young people?
- The right values
- The right knowledge
- The right skills
- Dealing with specific issues that arise in communicating
- Listening to very young children in care
- Children's competence
- 'Wishes and feelings'
- Listening to children and promoting their 'best interests'
- A voice for young people in care
- Listening to children and young people collectively
- Summary and conclusion
- Guide to further reading

Introduction

> Aunt Ada and I were shown into Miss Hayhurst's office at the Ministry and after a short conversation Aunt Ada just turned and went. She didn't say 'good-bye' or even look at me, and I suddenly realised with a hopeless sense of finality that she was gone. I set up a loud wailing that rose and increased on the chance that

DOI: 10.4324/9781003503194-3

somehow, I could reach Aunt Ada and bring her back. Miss Hayhurst just went on writing as if I and my crying were non-existent. Another woman was shown in. Putting down her shopping-bag, she came straight across to me, ignoring Miss Hayhurst who had risen and was holding out her hand.

'Don't you take on now, my mawther', said the woman, kissing me. 'You'll be all right along o' me. Do you know what I got back home? Why, three old pussy cats, and look you here'. From her pocket, she brought out a little poke-bag of sweets, of the kind known as butter balls. I can still recall the salty sweet taste of them. The salt was from my tears which continued to flow, though quietly.

Then the woman turned her attention to Miss Hayhurst, and together they filled in the indispensable forms, while I studied my new foster-mother.

The King of the Barbareens (Hitchman, 1966, p. 49)

I have been here about four months, but I didn't have much choice. The very first time I went, they didn't let me visit or anything. They just took me there.

Boy aged nine

What foster homes… like they choose it, but I can say whether I like it or not. That is what every social worker has done… Well I have had most say in it really because they won't put me anywhere if I don't like it.

Boy aged twelve

These quotations give very different pictures of children's involvement in moves in foster care. Elsie's experience in 1924, as related by her adult self, Janet Hitchman, was not untypical of that period. The interviews from which the second and third quotations are drawn took place in 1996, and by then, it was much more common for children to be consulted about their placements. However, as the quote from the nine-year-old suggests, it was still by no means universal. This general picture remains true today. While research indicates that children and young people in care are more likely to be listened to and have their views taken into account, this is not always the case.

In this chapter, we will look at why listening to children and young people is important, what it means, and how it can be done ethically and effectively – not only with young people in their teens, but also with younger children. The principles defined in the UNCRC are embedded throughout. As we said in the introduction to this book, they are interrelated, interconnected and indivisible and it is therefore important when thinking of a child's right to express views and have those taken seriously, that other articles are also drawn on. As previously outlined, the UNCRC suggests that it is not possible for others to determine what is in the best interests of a child (Article 3) without first seeking the views of the child where possible and taking these into account (Article 12). In seeking the views of children and young people, we should also be mindful of related Articles that include the right to non-discrimination (Article 2), the evolving capacities of the child (Article 5), the right to life, health and development (Article 6), and a child's right to express views in any medium of their choice (Article 13). The detailed advice regarding the implementation of the Articles of the UNCRC found in the UN General Comments is also vital to take into account. Of specific relevance are General Comments: No. 7 Implementing Child Rights in Early Childhood (Committee on the Rights of the Child, 2005); No. 9 Children with Disabilities (Committee on the Rights of the Child, 2006), No. 12 The Right of the Child to be Heard (Committee on the Rights of the Child, 2009) and No. 14 The Right of the Child to have his or her Best Interests taken as a Primary Consideration (Committee on the Rights of the Child, 2013).

What does listening to children and young people mean?

When we think about listening to children and young people, it's easy to assume that this just relates to what children can tell us through the use spoken word. However, the word listen means 'to give attention to'. So, in its broadest sense, listening means to be alert to what children convey to us about their feelings, experiences, views, wishes either verbally, non-verbally, through written word and/or through any other medium of their choice. This requires us to believe and accept that all children can convey something of their feelings, thoughts and experiences to us regardless of their age, disability and language as defined in Articles 2 and 5, UNCRC and General Comment No. 7 (CRC, 2005) and General Comment No. 9 (Committee on the Rights of the Child, 2006). The onus is on us to be respectful of all children, to be open and to attune ourselves to the particular ways that each individual child might communicate with us. In this sense, listening is an ongoing, active two-way process in which we receive, impart, interpret and respond to children (Corrigan, 2014; Winter, 2010; Lefevre, 2018; Petrie, 2011).

Why should we listen to children and young people?

Listening to children and young people must be at the heart of all social work practice with children and families. There are three main arguments underlying this principle. The first argument, as we said in Chapter 1, is that children and young people are individual people and each child has a *right* to be heard and to have a say in decisions about their own lives. This is now widely accepted in principle, and is notably expressed in Article 12 of the United Nations Convention on the Rights of the Child, which says that:

> States Parties shall ensure to the child who is capable of forming his or her own views the right to express those views freely in all matters affecting the child, the views of the child being given due weight in accordance with the age and maturity of the child.

'All matters affecting the child' clearly includes matters concerning the child's personal life, such as where s/he lives or where they go to school and who they wish to have contact with and how often.

The second argument is that it is in the *interests* of children and young people that their wishes be understood and their views taken into account. There is considerable evidence from psychological research that having a sense of control over our lives is associated with other measures of well-being, both for adults and for children; even the youngest children (see Alderson and Yoshida, 2019). Many children grow up feeling that they have little control, or that important decisions about their lives are being taken without people consulting them or even explaining to them what is happening. This applies especially to children who find themselves in public care. We can help children in care to feel more in control, and thereby contribute to their self-confidence and their self-esteem, by a process of effective communication.

The third argument is that listening to children and young people actually leads to *better decisions*. It is generally the case that plans and decisions are better if they are based on the knowledge and opinions of those directly involved, and this surely applies where children are concerned. There is research evidence that allowing children to influence decisions that affect them can improve the quality of those decisions (Kosher and Ben-Arieh, 2020a, 2020b). Children, like adults, are experts in their own lives, and it would be foolish to ignore this expertise when making difficult decisions.

How do we listen to and communicate with children and young people?

Listening to children is only one aspect of communicating with children and young people. Communicating is a process that involves watching, observing, using words, sounds, signs, pictures, gestures, behaviours, to express and exchange thoughts, feelings, views and perspectives. There are quite a few theories and frameworks regarding the process of communication that all describe the process as involving a sender, a message, a medium, a channel, a receiver, a response and feedback. Lefevre (2018) in her book describes this in further detail. Of course, in reality the neat process outlined above can be messy and complicated, and some social workers feel that they do not have the skills or the tools or have not had specialist training to enable them to communicate with children.

However, one thing to remember is that communicating with children is not necessarily very different from communicating with adults. The same stages apply: the beginning of an encounter and creating the right conditions for communication to take place; the middle where issues are raised and explored; and the ending where the conversation is drawn to a close by summarising the issues raised and confirming what happens next (Winter, 2010). The same personal qualities also apply. Social workers need to show a non-judgemental approach and be warm, empathic and sensitive to the person's verbal and non-verbal language and style of communication. And the same skills also apply, with social workers being able to actively listen (through body language, eye contact, posture, tone of voice), able to ask open and closed questions, to probe, to summarise, to paraphrase and to reflect back (Koprowska, 2020; Lishman, 2020).

Obviously, from the brief discussion above, the term 'listening to children and young people' is of course a shorthand expression and we need to remember that: first, children's non-verbal communication can be just as important and revealing as the words they say; second, communication is a dialogue, and what workers say to children – especially in terms of explanation – is important as well as what children say; and third, listening to children is a precursor to action, not a substitute for it – children and young people expect us to do something about what they tell us, and soon become cynical or disillusioned if this does not happen. General Comment No. 9 (Committee on the Rights of the Child, 2006, para. 134) outlines what is necessary for all processes in which children are heard and/or in which they participate. These include the following:

- *Provide child friendly and accessible information* about yourself, why you want to listen to the child and what you will do with the information. It is easy for social workers to assume that children know who they are and why they are visiting. There are many people involved in the lives of each child in care, therefore frequent reminders are helpful, respectful to children and help put them at ease.
- *Make space and time* to be with children. Children pick up on adults who are in a rush, don't really want to be with them, and have other more important things to do or places to be. Social workers need to be aware of this and make time for children.
- *Bring materials that might assist children* to communicate. Social workers who turn up with official forms might be off-putting. It might help to create a more child-friendly and inclusive approach by bringing a tablet computer with children's games on it, or a bag with a few toys in it.
- *Inform children* so that they know that what is being discussed is relevant and also how long you can be with them (use a watch/mobile phone to indicate the time).

- *Accept that some children may not wish to communicate with you* and give them permission to end the meeting if they become uncomfortable, bored or lose concentration.
- *Remind children that there are no right or wrong answers!*
- *Summarise back and agree a plan* (and remind children that if they say they have been hurt, are being hurt or might be hurt, you may have to take further action). This helps ensure that there is accountability with participation and that participation processes are safe and sensitive to risk.
- *Keep the child up to date* with any actions you have agreed to take.
- *Ensure that you receive training* to help inform and improve your communication with children.

A huge amount of work now focuses on social workers' communication with children; we refer to some more of the available resources in the additional reading section at the end of this chapter. In terms of what makes for successful listening, the answer depends on whether you ask children or you ask their social workers. According to children, it is noted that successful listening includes:

- being genuine (being oneself and not fake)
- wanting to spend time together
- not just listening but also taking action (Whincup, 2015; Stabler et al., 2020).

From the perspectives of social workers, and writers in this area, a successful communicative encounter between a social worker and a child occurs when the professional is able to demonstrate the interplay of the right (i) values, (ii) knowledge and (iii) skills. Let's look at each briefly in turn.

The right values

Social workers must have in mind that each child is a child, a human being and not a 'case'. As a human being, each child will be able to convey, in some way, something about their circumstances, feelings and views. Children have different competencies, not necessarily lesser ones, and the ways that children choose to convey their views should be respected and their contributions valued. These values are not casually put together; they reflect the very essence of what social work is, and they also reflect a social view of childhood and a rights-informed values base. The social view of childhood is illustrated in Figure 3.1 and reflects the key principles of the sociology of childhood as discussed earlier.

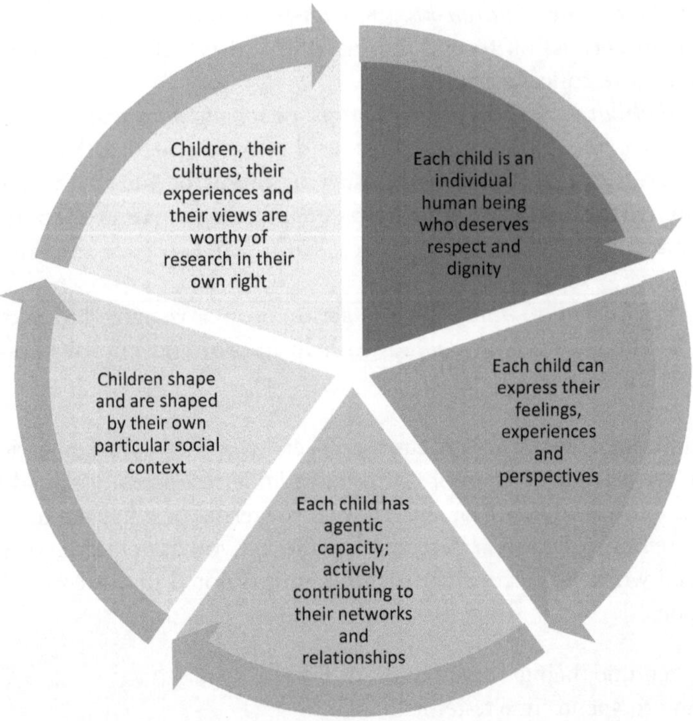

FIGURE 3.1 The key principles underpinning the sociology of childhood.

A rights informed approach reflects the UNCRC. For example, Article 2 of the UNCRC states that we are obliged to

> respect and ensure the rights […] to each child […] without discrimination of any kind, irrespective of the child's or his or her parent's legal guardian's race, colour, sex, language, religion, political or other opinion, national, ethnic or social origin, property, disability, birth or other status.

Together, the social view of childhood and a rights-informed values base could form a useful list for social workers to reflect on before they go and meet each child they are responsible for.

The right knowledge

As we reflected in Chapter 1, our work with children needs to be informed by knowledge about child development in social context and to be attuned to the individual and unique aspects of each child, their circumstances and their context. Whilst listening to and communicating with children needs to be informed by generic knowledge, it is important to avoid making generalisations about a child, but rather, it is crucial to get to know each individual child.

The right skills

There are many lists of the different types of skills required in communicating with children (see Guide to Further Reading). Rather than approach these as a checklist where every item must be ticked, it is better to approach any list as a guide. This allows you flexibility and creativity in your approach with each child – because each child is unique, each communicative encounter is unique and the processes of listening and communicating are not mechanistic, but the process is fluid, dynamic and responsive. Having said this, some of the useful skills to include in your guide include:

- Be friendly, open minded and non-intrusive (as opposed to trying to dominate the encounter with your agenda, or over-controlling it because you're worried about upsetting a child for example);
- Show empathy, warmth and a non-judgemental approach;
- Be encouraging;
- Engage in reflective listening – seeking to understand the child's view and reflecting back what's been shared to demonstrate that you have listened, heard and understood;
- Being aware of and able to use verbal and non-verbal listening and communication skills;
- Being flexible regarding methods and approaches used in communicating making sure that children's preferences and choices are honoured.

Verbal skills include questioning skills (open ended and closed questions), paraphrasing, summarising, probing and use of noises (ooohhh, aaahhh, ummm, eh, eh) for example. Non-verbal skills include: facial gestures (smiling, surprise, shock, frowning), body movements (nodding, shaking head, hand movements) and the use of body (touching, physical proximity, sitting, standing, crouching, walking – some children will move around when talking with you, they might sit close to you or far away from you, they might sit on the floor or a chair, they might move from room to room, they might play with something whilst talking with you) (see Tait and Wasu, 2012; Lefevre, 2018).

Although all of the above information is clear, it can still be hard to imagine what listening looks like in practice and to appreciate best practice unless there is access to good practice examples. In sourcing actual practice examples, we have taken a wide approach to ensure that readers have access to a broad range of resources. Regarding resources on websites that highlight actual practice examples the following are useful: *Talking and Listening to Children* (https://talkingandlisteningtochildren.co.uk), a project that involved working with social workers across the UK to highlight the ways in which they communicate with young children; *Participation for Protection* (https://www.qub.ac.uk/sites/participation-for-protection/Resources-forProfessionals/), a project which worked with professionals and young children regarding their experiences of violence, their advice on where to seek help, and their views on what services helped them best; and *REACCH, Resources for Engaging And Collaborating with Children* (https://reacch.eu) a project which highlights resources, approaches and the voice of very young children known to/in the care of social services.

There is also some published research that highlights the process of engaging with children and what they say (Alderson, 2008; Winter, 2010, 2012, 2014). In Winter (2014), the findings of a conversation with a seven-year-old male removed from home and placed in foster care are shared as highlighted in box.

Box 3.1 Views of seven-year-old male child regarding their foster placement

Interviewer:	Where you're living now in your foster placement, do you feel you have any decisions that you can make yourself?
Donal (pseudonym):	No.
Interviewer:	None at all?...
Donal:	Debbie [pseudonym for foster mother] makes these dinners like even though I don't want anything and [at home] I was allowed to choose my clothes; I was allowed to choose what [mum] would cook [and] I could choose either staying in the house or going out to the front to play.
Interviewer:	Do you not get that choice at all with your foster placement at the moment?
Donal:	No [Debbie says] you're wearing your shorts and your top.
Interviewer:	So, in, in the foster placement, you're not really involved in any decisions?
Donal:	No, she just makes the decisions. There are rules that I have to obey.

I:	... Hmm. How could they [foster-carers] treat you differently ... ?
Donal:	I don't know ... help me with whatever I need and just listen to me. I: ... Just listen to you, that's what you would want?
Donal:	I don't get to do anything .... And I have money in my savings, my savings like and she wouldn't even bring me down and buy me Playstation games.
I:	Yeah, why, would she not take you down to get them?
Donal:	Well she says that she hasn't got the time and she doesn't want to .... I think she's just like I'm just anything like a fly or something buzzing around the house.
I:	... Is that the feeling that you get by being there?
Donal:	... I'm just a pest like buzzing around the room.

Donal's account is challenging because it highlights that relatively young children can articulate deeply held feelings and views (often we assume that they cannot) and that their expressed views regarding how children perceive their transitions away from difficult situations at home and into foster care are not always positive (often we assume that the benefits of foster care will obviously far outweigh living in risky situations at home but as Donal's account reveals, alternative care may not be experienced like this for the children involved). Lastly, Donal's account is challenging because it requires highly developed communications skills to give him the space to share his feelings and treat these with respect.

Dealing with specific issues that arise in communicating

We have seen that communicating with children and young people is a core aspect of social work practice with children and young people in care. Of course, some social workers are more confident than others, but all social workers must communicate with children and young people, and it is our individual responsibility (as well as a collective organisational responsibility) to ensure that we become as skilled as we can in this work.

Children and young people may bring particular issues to such communicative encounters which can make them challenging. They may not trust their social workers because they have experienced multiple changes of social worker, and they may have felt that previous social workers did not listen to their wishes and feelings. Children might not be comfortable with straightforward verbal conversations, perhaps because their verbal skills are limited, because they are distressed or because they are simply unused to talking about such matters with an adult, especially a strange adult. Children might have social, emotional and behavioural difficulties that make it hard for them to concentrate, to stay in one place for any length of time or to express themselves in ways that are socially accepted. They may have a disability that relies on their social worker having knowledge about a specific communication aid (talking mats, speech generating devices). They may have experienced trauma. They may not use English as their first language and an interpreter maybe required. And they may naturally become upset or angry when talking about difficult issues, like we all do. Lastly, they may want to know lots of personal information about you!

On the other hand, children may be able to communicate really well through play, art, music, photos, drawings or computers and social media platforms in ways that many adults might find much more difficult. They may also find it much easier to communicate on difficult issues if the environment is right. For example, social workers have said that they have had some deep, meaningful conversations with children in cars (on the way to contact or an appointment and on the way back). This is because the car is a contained space where the social worker is not directly looking at a child (which might make it uncomfortable for them to talk) but is nonetheless listening intently. All of this indicates that social workers need to be flexible, open-minded about the most appropriate and effective ways of communicating safely with children about difficult issues (Triesman, 2017; Tait and Wasu, 2012).

To assist social workers to deal with specific issues, such as children in distress, or professional boundaries in listening to and communicating with children, there are some good supporting resources mentioned in 'Guide to Further Reading' at the end of this chapter. One early and particularly useful resource is 'Communicating with Children: Helping Children in Distress' (Richman, 2000) which can be downloaded online. Commissioned by Save the Children and written specifically for people working with 'children in situations of social crisis or conflict' (which includes refugee and displaced children, street children, as well as those who are in foster homes or residential care), it covers the communication process (beginnings, middles and ends and how to establish trust), verbal and non-verbal skills, communication about particular issues and communication in particular contexts.

More recent helpful resources have focused on listening to and communicating with children who are traumatised. Work by Tait and Wasu (2012) and Triesman (2017) contain chapters that deal with different types of situation and that outline a range of creative, innovative, and accessible approaches, strategies and resources for adults to use with children. The main free web-based resource that social workers use is the Social Workers Toolbox referred to at the end of this chapter.

Box 3.2 offers a way to remember some of the key points about communicating with children and young people. It is based on the findings of research with children in care.

Box 3.2 'TRANSACTS' – Key points in communicating with children and young people

Time – it is essential to have enough time to spend with a child; they do not necessarily want to talk 'by appointment'. Time also means working at the child's pace, allowing them to stay in control.

Relationship, trust and honesty – children communicate best with people with whom they have relationships of warmth and trust. It is important to be friendly and open, empathic and above all 'straight' with children.

Active listening – the skills of 'active listening' developed in counselling can be helpful in work with children. This means responding to cues, restating and drawing out the meaning of what the child is saying, combined with the expression of warmth, empathy and acceptance.

Non-verbal communication – an adult's tone of voice, facial expression, body language and even style of dress can affect how children communicate

Support and encouragement – children need support and active encouragement to speak up, especially when they have something difficult or negative to express. An adult may sometimes need to offer to express a child's views for them. Children don't like it when they feel they are being judged or criticised, and they don't like to be put 'on the spot'.

Activities – many children find it very boring to 'just sit and talk'. Games, writing, drawing and other activities can be used to make the process more interesting. *Life story work* can be an excellent way to involve children in reflecting on their situation (see Ryan and Walker, 1993).

Choice, information and preparation – children must have a choice about whether and how they participate in a decision-making process. They are more able to have their say if they have been prepared for the discussion and given time to think about things beforehand.

The child's agenda – it is important to give children space to talk about issues that concern them, rather than just having to respond to adults' questions.

Serious fun! – the fact that serious matters are being discussed doesn't mean that everyone has to be po-faced. Most children find this alienating; some find it threatening. If decision-making processes can be made more enjoyable, children are more likely to get involved.

(based on Thomas and O'Kane, 1998)

Listening to very young children in care

Although enabling effective participation by adolescents takes skill and commitment, the inclusion of younger children in decisions about their care poses greater challenges for social workers. One challenge is that methods of communication with younger children often rely less on verbal interaction and more on communication through other methods such as play and the use of toys, games and books. This does not mean that communicating with young children is a highly specialised skill which most of us are excused from exercising (Winter, 2010). But it does mean that social workers need to be prepared to communicate with all people, from the oldest to the youngest, in terms of real human engagement, in ways that are suitable to each child.

A second challenge is that even when social workers are personally committed to communicating with young children (or engaging in 'direct work', as it is sometimes called), there is often a lack of time and resources. Research has indicated that building relationships and communicating with young children, although an area that the social work profession is genuinely committed to, is often crowded out by high caseloads and organisational imperatives to complete case file recordings, reports and forms (Winter, 2010). Often too, there is a lack of money to invest in child friendly resources and facilities to support social workers and young children to engage effectively.

A third challenge is the issue of younger children's competence, an issue which is often raised when talking of children's participation rights. Children's competence, and how to assess it, is to some extent, an issue in social work with all children, but the younger a child is, the more sharply the question presents itself. What is meant by competence? Do social workers know how to assess the competence of younger children? Might social workers have a tendency to underestimate or be unaware of younger children's competencies? And when it comes to the crunch, are young children competent to have a view on what should happen to them?

Children's competence

Competence is a multi-faceted concept. In a review of publications that focus on children's competence and participation, Moran-Ellis and Tisdall (2019) note that the term 'competence' can refer to abilities, skills and knowledge. The knowledge could be categorised as cognitive (knowledge and understanding); technical (for example, the ability to write); social and practical; linguistic; and psychological. The term competence is also associated with legal competence. You may have heard of the term 'Gillick competence' which concerns children's ability to consent to medical treatment without the knowledge and involvement of their parents in that decision.

Competence in social work has historically been dominated by a crude view of the theories of Piaget and a model of child development based on ages and stages. In his model, it is proposed that as children grow older their patterns of thinking develop through a series of age-related stages which are 'global' – that is, at a particular age and stage of development, all a child's cognitive processes are limited to a particular pattern, until the child moves on to the next stage. Other thinkers have built on and critiqued the work of Piaget to illustrate how children's development, while having biological aspects common to all children, is also embedded in social contexts.

Children's skills and knowledge develop differently depending on their particular contexts. This was emphasised by Donaldson (1978) and others, who revised Piaget with the insight that children's thinking is embedded in social contexts, and that their understanding of a concept depends on whether the situation in which it is used makes 'human sense' to them. However, as we have said above, biological and physical changes in the structure and organisation of the brain undoubtedly continue until puberty and even beyond, and such changes must affect mental functioning, for example.

Garbarino et al. (1992, p. 41) put it well when they said:

> Recent research indicates that Piaget probably exaggerated the differences in children's thinking at different stages of development. However, there is ample evidence to demonstrate that there are important differences in how children think, know, and understand and that children are not simply ignorant or inexperienced adults. Rather than describing them as stages, it may be more useful to think of developmental differences as reflecting gradual but perceptible shifts in ways of participating in and understanding experience. Thus, it is important for adults to try to understand that a child's interpretation and understanding of a situation may be quite different from their own.

More recently, the idea of a global 'ages and stages' model has been questioned, with the awareness that children's competence can be contextual. For example, exposure to trauma, as discussed earlier in the book, can impact children's concentration, memory and emotional regulation which can negatively impact on educational achievement and attainment, for example. On the other hand, children in stressful situations where they are exposed to parental ill health or parental relationship difficulties can develop highly attuned practical, emotional and social skills as they 'read', respond and relate to the situations they are in.

As social workers, we therefore need to be aware of the fact that some children who come into care have had very adverse experiences which will affect their thinking in all sorts of ways. However, it would be wrong to assume that such experiences always impact negatively on children's competence or preclude them from taking part in decisions about their future.

The basic question therefore as to whether there are fundamental differences between children's thinking and adults' thinking, or inherent limits on what children can understand at different ages, is very hard to answer in precise terms. We have seen that it is unwise to make assumptions, such as 'children below the age of 11 cannot'. On the other hand, it is also unwise to expect children to show a full range of cognitive skills regardless of age. This complex area requires social workers to consider each child individually and to think through what is meant by competence in their particular context. Here, the sociological view regarding childhood competence might be helpful. Competence, as noted below, is seen as something that is negotiated in social context and

> the social competence of children is to be seen as a practical achievement: that is, it is not something which is accorded to children by adults [...] but it is an achievement that is bounded by structural features of the milieux in which children live their lives.
>
> *Hutchby and Moran-Ellis (1998, p. 16)*

For social workers, the implications of taking a different view of childhood competence on their practice to enable children to participate in decision making are substantial. Above all, we need to design processes of decision making in such a way as to *elicit* and *enable* children's competence. The UN-CRC and its General Comments help with this.

The UN General Comment No. 7, which focuses on very young children and rights in early childhood, says that young children are especially at risk of discrimination because they are relatively powerless and depend on others for the realisation of their rights. It describes this further saying that:

> Respect for the young child's agency – as a participant in family, community and society – is frequently overlooked, or rejected as inappropriate on the grounds of age and immaturity. In many countries and regions, traditional beliefs have emphasised young children's need for training and socialisation. They have been regarded as undeveloped, lacking even basic capacities for understanding, communicating and making choices. They have been powerless within their families and often voiceless and invisible within society.

It says that Article 12 applies to all children regardless of age:

> The Committee wishes to emphasise that Article 12 applies both to younger and to older children. As holders of rights, even the youngest children are entitled to express their views which should be "given due weight in accordance with the age and maturity of the child".
>
> *(Art. 12.1)*
>
> Young children are acutely sensitive to their surroundings and very rapidly acquire understanding of the people, places and routines in their lives, along with awareness of their own unique identity. They make choices

> and communicate their feelings, ideas and wishes in numerous ways, long before they are able to communicate through the conventions of spoken or written language.
>
> *(para 14)*

Lastly, it tells all professionals how they should behave towards children when it says:

> To achieve the right of participation requires adults to adopt a child centred attitude, listening to young children and respecting their dignity and their individual points of view.

In other words, social workers have a vitally important job to do in *empowering* children, especially younger children, to take an engaged, informed and active part in decisions about their own care. One particular area that causes social workers concern is the tension between the obligation to listen to children to ascertain their wishes and feelings and the obligation to promote their best interests, especially where there is a divergence between what children wish for and what professionals determine is in their best interests.

'Wishes and feelings'

Across the UK, child care legislation and accompanying statutory guidelines oblige social workers to ascertain and consider the 'wishes and feelings' of children in care as part of their review meetings, case conferences and wider care planning. Social workers also have a duty to ascertain the wishes and feelings of children involved in court care proceedings. According to Dillon (2021, p. 664), the term 'wishes and feelings' is contentious because it reads 'as whimsical and desire-focused' and ascertaining wishes and feelings can be approached by social workers as a tick box exercise, yet she reminds us that 'the purpose of this legislation is to create meaningful participation that can empower maltreated children and even prevent further abuse from happening'.

The wording of the phrase 'ascertaining the wishes and feelings of the child' should not be taken lightly and suggests that when we communicate with children about their care we need to have a dual focus:

- first, *on what they want* – on the child's views and thoughts about her/his situation, and in particular on what s/he would like to happen;
- second, *on how they are feeling* – and on the impact of the child's experiences on her/his happiness, security and sense of self.

In what follows, it will be important to keep this dual focus in mind. As we have already outlined, we should respond to what children have to say, include them as participants in decision-making processes, respect their *rights*.

At the same time, we must remember that they are young people in vulnerable situations and they may have undergone traumatic experiences. They may be bewildered, overwhelmed or frightened and they may not trust people around them, so we must respond to their *needs* on a *feeling* level.

Listening to children and promoting their 'best interests'

As noted above, social workers can face difficulties where a choice has to be made between giving full weight to a child's own wishes and views or making a decision that appears to be in a child's best interests but does not reflect the child's views and wishes. The problem is further explained by Archard and Skivenes (2009, p. 2):

> The problem arises because the two commitments seem to pull in different directions: promotion of a child's welfare is essentially paternalist since it asks us to do what we, but not necessarily the child, think is best for the child; whereas, listening to the child's own views asks us to consider doing what the child, but not necessarily we, thinks is best for the child.

Early research by Thomas and O' Kane (1998) outlined the nature of the problem in practical terms by exploring the clash between children's wishes and feelings and their best interests. They noted that these conflicts arose in relation to differences of opinion over placement, family contact, school and over children's leisure activities. Differences over placement usually involved conflict between a child wishing to return home and the view of social workers or carers that this was against the child's interests. Differences over contact involved children wanting more family contact, or less. Differences over school included a boy of ten with learning disability who wanted to go to a mainstream school when his carers wanted him to go to a special school, a boy of 11 whose mother wanted him to go to Catholic school when he did not, and a girl of ten who wanted to change schools because she was 'picked on', when adults thought a move would not help. Differences over leisure time mainly concerned children who wanted to go off with friends in circumstances when parents or carers thought this was inappropriate.

Some social workers and carers were very clear that although they had sought the child's wishes and feelings, the interests of their welfare meant that the decision made could not reflect these wishes. Others were less confident of their own ability to make the right decision, or more willing to allow the child a substantial role in the process. A third group went for a balance between protecting the child from harm and allowing them to learn by taking risks.

Some children were assertive about their wishes and feelings and wanted to be heard. A 12-year-old boy said, 'I don't need, well I do need sometimes, but most of the time I don't need people to say what is best for me'. Others were more self-effacing or submissive to adult judgement – for instance the ten-year-old girl who said, 'They care about you – they want you to do what is best'.

More recent research has reflected in the processes involved in ascertaining children's wishes and feelings and determining what is in their best interests. The first thing to say is that children have a right to have their best interests taken as a primary consideration under Article 3, UNCRC and supported by detailed advice on implementation which is outlined in General Comment No. 14. This General Comment reminds us that the best interests principle is a substantive right, a legal principle and a rule of procedure, and that:

> the concept of the child's best interests is flexible and adaptable. It should be adjusted and defined on an individual basis, according to the specific situation of the child or children concerned, taking into consideration their personal context, situation and needs. For individual decisions, the child's best interests must be assessed and determined in light of the specific circumstances of the particular child.
>
> *(para 32, p. 9, Committee on the Rights of the Child, 2013)*

Second, it is not possible to determine what is in the best interests of a child without taking account of the child's own views. General Comment No. 12 (Committee on the Rights of the Child, 2009), on the implementation of 'The Right of the Child to be Heard' states:

> There is no tension between Articles 3 and 12, only a complementary role of the two general principles: one establishes the objective of achieving the best interests of the child and the other provides the methodology for reaching the goal for hearing either the child or the children. In fact, there can be no correct application of Article 3 if the components of Article 12 are not respected. Likewise, Article 3 reinforces the functionality of Article 12, facilitating the essential role of children in all decisions affecting their lives.
>
> *(para. 74)*

There is therefore a balance to be achieved between these two obligations. This is easy to say but very difficult to do in practice. Lansdown (1995, p. 26) has suggested that the nature of the balance varies according to the perceived competence of the child *in relation to a particular decision*. She suggests that 'if the child lacks the competence to understand the implications of the decision, a parent should only override the child if to do so is necessary to protect the child or to promote his or her best interests', whereas if the child is competent a stronger test should apply, in that a parent should only override a competent child 'if failure to do so would result in serious harm to the child'.

In relation to 'perceived competence', Archard and Skivenes (2009, p. 20) notes that it needs to be clear who has assessed the competence of a child, how they have gone about doing this and whether they have arrived at their decision of competence independently from their assumptions about their own view as to what is in the best interests of the child. There are two points here. The first is that we need to be clear that the views expressed by children are genuinely those held by children and that they have not been coached by adults around them. The second point is that in deciding best interests, professionals may have a tendency to claim a child lacks competence because they have expressed a wish or view that contradicts the assumptions and views of the adult decision maker. Third, and final, as noted by Lansdown (1995, p. 26), when a decision is reached and children's wishes are *not* reflected in the decision, 'the child is entitled to an explanation of the reasons and acknowledgement of their concerns'.

General Comment No. 14 (Committee on the Rights of the Child, 2013, para 50, p. 12) considers it useful to draw up a list of

> 'non-exhaustive and non-hierarchical list of elements that could be included in a best-interests assessment by any decision-maker having to determine a child's best interests. The non-exhaustive nature of the elements in the list implies that it is possible to go beyond those and consider other factors relevant in the specific circumstances of the individual child or group of children. All the elements of the list must be taken into consideration and balanced in light of each situation. The list should provide concrete guidance, yet flexibility.

The elements include: the child's views; the child's identity; preservation of family environment and maintaining relations; care, protection and safety of the child; situation of vulnerability; the child's right to health and education; with each being weighed against the other.

A voice for young people in care

There have always been practitioners who are good at working directly with children, responding to their feelings, and enabling them to articulate their wishes. However, historically, many agencies and institutions have not always supported this kind of practice, and children's wishes, and feelings have sometimes been disregarded. The demand for positive action to involve children and young people in decisions about their lives in care – and even about their admission to care in the first place – gathered strength in the 1970s and 1980s with the then establishment of organisations such as Who Cares? And NAYPIC (National Association for Young People in Care).

The reform of child care law through child care legislation that was implemented across the UK in the late 1980s and early 1990s, and the UK becoming a signatory to the UNCRC, undoubtedly gave an impetus to young people's participation, and to social workers' obligations to consult with children and ascertain their wishes and feelings.

Research conducted in the 1990s indicated there was some improvement in the involvement of children and young people in decisions about their lives, as noted by their increased participation in case conferences, care planning and review meetings, court proceedings and family group conferences. For example, Thomas and O'Kane (1999) found that it was usual for teenagers to be invited to their reviews, but less common for children under 12. They also found that the use of 'looked after review' forms made it more likely that children would be invited, but that children whose parents were in conflict with the local authority were less likely to attend even when they were invited. Grimshaw and Sinclair (1997) found that children in voluntary care (accommodated) were more likely to attend their review meetings than those on care orders.

More recent legislation since 2000 has strengthened the focus on participation and the obligation on social workers to ascertain children's wishes and feelings, as noted in the creation of the role of Independent Review Officers (IROs), for example. IROs work independently of the social workers, social work teams and managers involved with children and families. Their job involves ensuring that care plans for children in care reflect their needs and their wishes and feelings by rigorously reviewing the plans and establishing a relationship with each child to ensure their views are reflected. Later legislation has extended this statutory duty, so that the role of the IRO now includes having an overview of, and monitoring, each child's whole situation, not just their review.

Another development since 2000 that has helped all children, but especially children in care, is the establishment of a Children's Commissioner in each of the four jurisdictions in the UK. The Children's Commissioners have a legal duty to promote and protect the rights of all children, with a special focus on children with challenges and difficulties, including children in care. Each Children's Commissioner is independent and free to determine their own priorities reflecting the promotion and protection of children's rights as the paramount consideration. Children's Commissioners deal with individual cases in all UK nations except Scotland, and even in Scotland, there is some element of casework, which is a recent development. In general, they work on cases where there is a human rights breach, but most of them also give advice and signpost to all callers, including children. In England, the casework is *only* for children in care (Help at Hand service). They also investigate broad issues of importance to children, respond to consultations on issues affecting children and young people and seek to influence the development of law, policy and practice.

There are several organisations and advocacy groups that work specifically with and for children in care including: Become; Coram Voice; Who Cares?

Scotland; Voice of Young People in Care (VOYPIC) (Northern Ireland); and Voices from Care Cymru (Wales). They lobby with and on behalf of children in care and provide advice, guidance, support and mentoring services. They also engage in research and host a range of material on their websites. Practices such as the involvement of young people in the selection of staff, and in arrangements for independent inspection of care services, show how things have moved on.

Despite these developments, children's participation in their case conferences, review meetings and court proceedings remains a concern. In review meetings, Diaz et al. (2018, 2019, 2020) note that barriers to children's effective participation include high caseloads, high staff turnover, lack of understanding of children's participation rights and children's own negative experiences of participation and consequent reluctance to be involved. Similar concerns are noted by Töros (2020, p. 9) who quotes children saying that being left out of decision-making processes left them feeling 'cranky and upset', 'angry', 'horrible', 'sad and bad', 'frustrated', 'left in the dark' and like 'an outsider'.

In summary, broad human rights frameworks, combined with specific child care legislation and statutory guidance, policies and procedures, enshrine the importance of the participation rights of all children. Despite this, challenges in implementing participation rights remain, especially in relation to very young children, disabled children and children from different cultural, linguistic, religious and ethnic backgrounds and children whose main language is not English. An important development to consider in this context is listening to children in care collectively.

Listening to children and young people collectively

As we noted in the introductory chapter, children and young people have the right to express their views and have these heard individually, and also collectively. We have noted how children's personal participation occurs in the context of decision-making processes such as case conferences, review meetings and court proceedings about them. However, children in care may also have views collectively about the ways in which they are treated and about the services provided for them.

Public-level participation, where decisions taken might influence policy and practice, can occur through voluntary and advocacy organisations, government departments, trusts or local authorities and research organisations. The role of a child in public level groups might be as a participant, a consultant or a peer researcher (Dixon et al., 2019) and there are many benefits from collective participation including strengthening collaborative and problem-solving skills and improvements to self-identity and self-esteem when impact on policy and practice is evidenced.

Examples include Children in Care Councils which exist in 97% of local authorities and are intended to give children in care a real say in the design, delivery and evaluation of services for them. Other examples include collective participation in consultation events and campaigns (Dixon et al., 2019) in which agencies have developed skills in communicating with children and young people as a group about issues that concern them, through questionnaires and surveys or open forums, for example. Limitations and ongoing challenges include ensuring that the interests of 'hard to reach' groups of children in care are represented (such as disabled children, very young children, refugee and migrant children who do not have English as their first language, and LGBTQIA+ children). Second, it is important to ensure that collective groups represent the full diversity of opinion within their group. Third, monitoring impact is important, since it is easy for groups to become tokenistic because of the attitudes of adults and structures which operate to marginalise input into decision making. However, as noted by Dixon et al. (2019), there are ways of overcoming these difficulties, and when it works the communication can be very rewarding for children and for professionals.

Summary and conclusion

We have looked at some of the reasons for listening to children and young people and taking account of their wishes and feelings. We have thought about some of the more effective ways of communicating with children, and we have looked at how young people in care have begun to get their voices heard. We have considered some of the issues that arise in work with younger children, and at the vexed question of children's competence. We have thought about the conflicts that arise between listening to children and promoting their 'best interests'. Finally, we have begun to think about some of the ways in which we can listen to children and young people collectively. What is perhaps most important in this aspect of social work practice is a real commitment to involving children and young people in making decisions about their own lives. Also, critically important are three principles that will be a major feature of the next chapter – namely respect, recognition and openness.

GUIDE TO FURTHER READING

There has been a substantial growth in the literature available on this topic in the last ten years, and readers will no doubt find good material themselves. Thomas (2002) and Lefevre (2018) have reviewed some of the theory. For the practice of listening to children, helpful texts include McLeod (2008), Winter (2010), Tait and Wasu (2012), Corrigan (2014), Triesman (2017), and again Lefevre (2018). There are also web-based resource packs for agencies and teams, which contain training exercises and direct work materials especially Social Workers Tool Box which has many free resources for download http://www.socialworkerstoolbox.com, including a Children's Participation Toolkit for Social Workers. Other helpful organisations include *Research in Practice* – https://www.researchinpractice.org.uk and *The British Association for Adoption and Fostering* – see www.baaf.org.uk/.

It can also be very helpful to read accounts by young people who have experienced the care system, such as *The Cornflake Kid* (Riddell, 1996), *Hackney Child* (Daniels and Livingstone, 2014) or *The Looked After Kid. My Life in a Children's Home* (Hewitt, 2014). Fictional accounts such as *The Story of Tracy Beaker* (Wilson, 1991) can illuminate a child's point of view in an accessible way.

References

Alderson, P. (2008) *Young children's rights: Exploring beliefs*. London: Jessica Kingsley Publishers.

Alderson, P. and Yoshida, T. (2019) Babies' rights, when human rights begin. In Murray, J., Swadener, B.B., Smith, K. (eds.) *The Routledge international handbook of young children's rights* (pp. 29–40). London: Perlego Publishers.

Archard, D. and Skivenes, M. (2009) 'Balancing a child's best interests and a child's views', *The International Journal of Children's Rights*, 17(1), 1–21.

Committee on the Rights of the Child (2005) *General comment No. 7: Implementing child rights in early childhood*, 20 September 2006, CRC/C/GC/7/Rev.1. Geneva, United Nations. Available here https://www.refworld.org/docid/460bc5a62.html (accessed 23.01.24).

Committee on the Rights of the Child (2006) *General comment No. 9: The rights of children with disabilities*, 27 February 2007, CRC/C/GC/9. Geneva, United Nations. Available here https://www.refworld.org/docid/461b93f72.html (accessed 23.01.24).

Committee on the Rights of the Child (2009) *General comment No. 12: The right of the child to be heard*, 25 May – 12 June 2009, CRC/C/GC/12. Geneva, United Nations. Available here https://www.refworld.org/docid/4ae562c52.html (accessed 23.01.24).

Committee on the Rights of the Child (2013) General Comment No. 14: The right of the child to have his or her best interests taken as a primary consideration, 29 May 2013, CRC/C/GC/14. Geneva, United Nations. Available here https://www.refworld.org/docid/51a84b5e4.html (accessed 23.01.24).

Corrigan, M. (2014) *Listening to children's wishes and feelings*. London: CoramBAAF.

Daniels, H. and Livingstone, M. (2014) *Hackney child. A true story of surviving poverty and the care system*. London: Simon and Schuster.

Diaz, C. (2020) *Decision making in child and family social work. Perspectives on children's participation.* Bristol: Bristol University Press.

Diaz, C., Pert, H. and Thomas, N. (2018) "Just another person in the room': Young people's views on their participation in child in care reviews', *Adoption & Fostering*, *42*(4), 369–382.

Diaz, C., Pert, H. and Thomas, N.P. (2019) 'Independent reviewing officers' and social workers' perceptions of children's participation in children in care reviews', *Journal of Children's Services*, *14*(3), 162–173.

Dillon, J. (2021) "Wishes and feelings': Misunderstandings and missed opportunities for participation in child protection proceedings', *Child and Family Social Work*, *26*(4), 664–676.

Dixon, J., Ward, J. and Blower, S. (2019) '"They sat and actually listened to what we think about the care system": The use of participation, consultation, peer research and co-production to raise the voices of young people in and leaving care in England', *Child Care in Practice*, *25*(1), 6–21.

Donaldson, M. (1978) *Children's minds.* Glasgow: Fontana/Collins.

Garbarino, J., Dubrow, N., Kostelny, K. and Pardo, C. (1992) *Children in danger: Coping with the consequences of community violence.* Hoboken, NJ: Jossey-Bass/Wiley.

Grimshaw, R. and Sinclair, R. (1997) *Planning to care: Regulation, procedure and practice under the Children Act 1989.* London: National Children's Bureau.

Hewitt, P. (2014) *The looked after kid. My life in a children's home.* Edinburgh: Mainstream Publishing.

Hitchman, J. (1966) *The King of the Barbareens.* Harmondsworth: Penguin.

Hutchby, I., I and Moran-Ellis, J. (eds.) (1998) *Children and social competence: Arenas of action.* London: Routledge.

Koprowska, J. (2020) *Communication and interpersonal skills in social work* (fifth edition). London: Sage.

Kosher, H. and Ben-Arieh, A. (2020a) 'Children's participation: A new role for children in the field of child maltreatment', *Child Abuse and Neglect*, *110*, 104429.

Kosher, H. and Ben-Arieh, A. (2020b) 'Social workers' perceptions of children's right to participation', *Child & Family Social Work*, *25*(2), 294–303.

Lansdown, G. (1995) *Taking part: Children's participation in decision making* (Vol. 1). London: Institute for Public Policy Research.

Lefevre, M. (2018) *Communicating and engaging with children and young people: making a difference* (second edition). Bristol: The Policy Press.

Lishman, J. (2020) *Communication in social work.* London: Macmillan Press, Red Globe Press.

McLeod, A. (2008) *Listening to children: A practitioner's guide.* London: Jessica Kingsley Publishers.

Moran-Ellis, J. and Tisdall, E.K.M. (2019) 'The relevance of 'competence' for enhancing or limiting children's participation: Unpicking conceptual confusion', *Global Studies of Childhood*, *9*(3), 212–223.

Participation for Protection. Available here https://www.qub.ac.uk/sites/participation-for-protection/ResourcesforProfessionals/

Petrie, P. (2011). *Communication skills for working with children and young people: Introducing social pedagogy.* London: Jessica Kingsley Publishers.

REACCH, Resources for Engaging and Collaborating with Children. Available here https://reacch.eu

Richman, N. (2000) *Communicating with children: Helping children in distress*. London: Save the Children.

Riddell, M. (1996) *The cornflake kid*. Kirmington, Ulceby, England: Partnership Publications.

Ryan, T. and Walker, R. (1993) *Life story work*. London: British Agencies for Adoption and Fostering.

Stabler, L., Wilkins, D. and Carro, H. (2020) 'What do children think about their social worker? AQ-method study of children's services', *Child and Family Social Work*, *25*(1), 118–126.

Tait, A. and Wasu, H. (2012) *Direct work with vulnerable children: Playful activities and strategies for communication*. London: Jessica Kingsley Publishers.

Talking and Listening to Children. Available here https://talkingandlisteningtochildren.co.uk

Thomas, N. (2002) *Children, family, and the state: Decision-making and child participation*. Bristol: Policy Press.

Thomas, N. and O'Kane, C. (1998) 'When children's wishes and feelings clash with their best interests', *International Journal of Children's Rights*, 6, 137.

Thomas, N. and O'Kane, C. (1999) 'Children's participation in reviews and planning meetings when they are 'looked after' in middle childhood', *Child & Family Social Work* 4(3), 221–30.

Töros, K. (2020) 'A systematic review of children's participation in child protection decision-making: Tokenistic presence or not?', *Children and Society*, *35*(3), 395–411. https://doi.org/10.1111/chso.12418

Triesman, K. (2017) *Working with relational and developmental trauma in children and adolescents*. London: Routledge.

United Nations. (1989) *Convention on the rights of the child*. New York and Geneva: United Nations.

Whincup, H. (2015) *Direct work and home supervision requirements: A qualitative study exploring experiences of direct work from the perspectives of children, young people, and social workers*. Stirling: University of Stirling.

Wilson, J. (1991) *The story of Tracey Beaker*. New York: Doubleday.

Winter, K. (2010) *Building relationships and communicating with young children: A practical guide for social workers*. Abingdon, Oxfordshire: Routledge.

Winter, K. (2012) 'Ascertaining the perspectives of young children in care: Case studies in the use of reality boxes', *Children and Society*, 26(5), 368–380.

Winter, K. (2014) 'Understanding and supporting young children's transitions into state care: Schlossberg's transition framework and child-centred practice', *British Journal of Social Work*, 44(2), 401–417.

4

CARING FOR YOUNG PEOPLE FROM DIFFERENT BACKGROUNDS

CONTENTS OF CHAPTER

- Introduction
- Working with difference and oppression
- Disability and disabled children
- Understanding 'race', 'ethnicity' and 'identity'
- Language
- Sexuality
- Poverty and class
- Working with Travellers, refugees, and asylum seekers
- The social work role and interagency working
- Summary and conclusion
- Guide to further reading

Introduction

As we outlined in Chapter 2, there is enormous diversity among children and young people who come into care reflected in differences in their background circumstances – age, ethnic background, language, culture, religion and sexuality – as well as their reasons for being in care, length of time in care, and placement arrangements. We also noted that whilst in some respects these differences reflect the diversity of the general population, there is a concern that certain groups of children and young people are over-represented in the care system – for example black children of Caribbean heritage, children of mixed heritage, children from travelling and Roma backgrounds, children with disabilities, children from poorer socio-economic backgrounds (NIHRC, 2021),

DOI: 10.4324/9781003503194-4

and also those who have escaped war, conflict including 'unaccompanied asylum seeking children', a group whose numbers have grown in recent years. In this chapter, we will explore the issues faced by some of these diverse groups and the knowledge, skills and values required by social workers. Throughout there will be an emphasis on the principles of recognition, respect, openness to difference and diversity and the role of the social worker in working with difference and oppression.

Working with difference and oppression

A core aspect therefore to social work with young people in care is the ability to work with difference and diversity. Indeed, the Global Definition of the Social Work Profession (approved by the International Federation of Social Workers in July 2014) notes that respect for diversities is central to social work. This may appear straightforward but can present challenges that social workers need to address and overcome. For example, some people might think that the easiest thing to do is to ignore difference and treat everyone the same. However, this approach reinforces prejudice, discrimination and oppression. In another challenge, certain cultural beliefs, values and traditions can violate peoples' basic human rights.

In thinking a little further about discrimination and oppression, we have noted above that children and young people who come into care are very largely drawn from groups in society who are in some degree disadvantaged or oppressed – because they are disabled, because they are from minority ethnic groups, above all because they are poor. This oppression and disadvantage presents two key challenges for social workers:

1 How do we avoid repeating this oppression in our own practice?
2 What can we do to help overcome the effects of oppression and disadvantage?

In this chapter, we will look at how these challenges present themselves in relation to particular groups. All practice with children should be grounded in a human rights approach. The UNCRC Article 2 reminds us that we are obliged to respect and ensure children's rights without discrimination of any kind, irrespective of the child's (or parent's or guardian's) race, colour, sex, language, religion, political or other opinion, national, ethnic or social origin, property, disability, birth or other status, and that we are obliged to take all appropriate measures to ensure that the child is protected against all forms of discrimination or punishment on the basis of the status, activities, expressed opinions or beliefs of the child's parents, guardians or family members. With this in mind, the key principles that we think social workers should follow in working with difference and diversity are recognition, respect and openness.[1]

Recognition is a term that we considered in the previous Chapter 2, when we introduced Honneth's particular theory of intersubjective recognition. Here, however, we are considering specifically the recognition of *difference*. Noticing difference and responding to difference is crucial. It is no part of ethical social work to pretend that everyone is the same or that differences do not matter. People are different, those differences do matter and they demand to be recognised and acknowledged if people are to have equal chances. A good example is the issue of ethnic monitoring, where unfair treatment of people of different background or skin colour has only been revealed when note is taken of these characteristics and records kept. Another example is the issue of access to public buildings, where an assumption that everyone is 'able-bodied' has the effect of excluding people who cannot physically climb stairs unaided. The act of noticing and responding to difference indicates respect.

Respect here means respecting each person as an individual for who they are. It means respecting and valuing their background, their family, their experience of life and their culture. It means accepting that other people may look different, live differently, have different abilities, hold different beliefs and values from those which are familiar to us, but that they are still entitled to our respect as human beings. It also means respecting the inherent worth and dignity of all people regardless of their social standing, social class and perceived success or not. As noted, these principles are reflected in the international definition of social work, in the professional standards of social work in the different regions of the UK, and in the codes of ethics that underpin social work associations, for example the British Association of Social Workers.

'Openness' means being prepared to learn about other people's lives and experiences, their cultures, histories, beliefs and languages. It means acknowledging and accepting that certain assumptions or biases can negatively impact the lived experiences and life chances of other people. It also means a commitment to developing new ways of understanding, new ways of responding and new ways of working together to ensure that people who have different backgrounds, needs and aspirations are not discriminated against and that any unequal life chances they may have experienced to date are acknowledged and addressed where possible.

In what follows, these principles will be applied as we further explore social work with particular groups of children and young people; in particular those who are disabled, from minority ethnic groups, of various sexual orientations, those who use minority languages, who are from disadvantaged social classes or who are poor, and/or those who have come from another country seeking refuge.

Of course, these groups are not mutually exclusive. People's individual circumstances and characteristics combine together. The term 'intersectionality' is used to draw attention to how different aspects of a person's identity (their ethnicity, gender, sexuality and so on) combine to create different types of disadvantage. Hence, some children and young people in care may be doubly or trebly disadvantaged because of their membership of minority groups (rather than a minority group).

Another important point is that when using the term 'different' we should not think in terms of 'them and us' – those who are different and those who represent 'the norm'. We are all different. We all have our own mix of physical and mental characteristics and abilities, and we all have a culture, a language, a gender, a social class and a sexual orientation. Some of these features may mean that we are disadvantaged or discriminated against. The principles of recognition, respect and openness to difference and diversity apply to everyone. The challenges of combating disadvantage and oppression apply to some more than to others.

Disability and disabled children

The meaning of disability

Disability is a field fraught with disputes about terminology (see the edited collection by Kelly and Byrne, 2017). Both how the generic term is defined and also how various types of disability are referred to have changed, usually because with increased knowledge and awareness the words previously used have come to be seen as disrespectful or demeaning. As we noted in Chapter 2, a distinction is often drawn between *disability* and *impairment*, where 'impairment' means the underlying physical or neurological factor and 'disability' refers to the effects of society's failure to accommodate to the effects of this. As for children, historically it was conventional to refer to 'children with disability', but more recently people committed to a rights approach (see Runswick-Cole et al., 2017) have used the term 'disabled children', the argument being that this is preferable as a term, because it emphasises that disability is something that is done to children (by society's response) rather than something inherent in them.

Disabled children in care

A disabled child in care is a person with an impairment who experiences disability. The *impairment* is a condition, illness or even injury that impacts on function. Impairments can be mobility focused, physical, sensory (hearing and or sight), neurological or cognitive, intellectual. Some examples of neurodevelopmental disorders include autism spectrum disorder, Prader-Willi syndrome, foetal alcohol disorder and Down syndrome. There are many others. Other impairments include various types of chronic disease which are not immediately visible to others. The *disability* refers to the fact that society disables children and young people who have impairments because of peoples' attitudes and assumptions and the way that societal structures, facilities, systems and processes prevent people with impairments from being able to take part in everyday life on an equal basis with others.

The distinction between impairment and disability is important because it reflects a human rights, social justice and social model of disability that draws attention to the disabling effects of prejudice and discrimination and highlights the need for everyone to examine their attitudes, assumptions, biases and prejudices. This is highlighted in the Preamble of the Convention on the Rights of Persons with Disabilities (CRPD) (United Nations, 2006b, p. 2) which states:

> Disability is an evolving concept and [...] results from the interaction between persons with impairments and attitudinal and environmental barriers that hinders [...] full and effective participation in society on an equal basis with others.

Government statistics and social work research make it clear that children and young people with all these impairments are represented in the population in care, and to a greater extent than in the general population, in all parts of the United Kingdom (Kelly et al., 2016; NIHRC, 2021). Reasons for the overrepresentation of disabled children in care are complex and interrelated. Disabled children are more likely to live in families experiencing their own poor mental and physical health and experiencing poverty and social isolation. This can mean some families have fewer material, economic, practical and social resources. Some disabled children have more than one impairment and require complex 'around the clock' care. Other children have impairments such as autism where receiving an expert opinion to confirm the diagnosis can be a lengthy and frustrating process. Regarding children with mental health conditions, which are also defined as a disability, rates have risen as a result of several factors: increased awareness, increased substance misuse and societal pressures – including those driven by the COVID-19 pandemic which began in 2020.

These factors, combined with the lack of access to sufficient specialist support services, can leave families becoming overwhelmed, stressed, exhausted, unwell and unable to care for their child, and entry into care often follows. It is also known that some disabled children are more likely to experience physical, sexual and emotional abuse which can lead to entry into care. Reasons for the abuse are also complex but can be associated with the assumptions made about disabled children (they don't know and they can't say). Their vulnerability is exacerbated by the fact that often they rely on multiple carers for their daily care and that the signs of abuse are overlooked because they are connected with the impairment. It is also known that when in care, children with all types of impairment are more likely to experience further abuse at the hands of their carers. The systems and processes that should be in place to ensure that disabled children have access to meaningful relationships and to spaces and places where they can inform people about their experiences, feelings and views can also be inadequate (Callus and Farrugia, 2016).

In all these ways, the experiences of disabled children and their families are inconsistent with our principles of recognition and respect and demand a response from the social work profession. We have discussed the relevance of the UNCRC, General Comment No. 9 The Rights of Children with Disabilities (United Nations, 2006a) and the CRPD (United Nations, 2006b) which outline the principles regarding how social workers (and indeed all people) should respond to disability. These issues are further explored below.

Responding to disability – 'stigma', access and inclusion

The way in which we understand disability is fundamentally important to how we treat disabled children. A contrast is frequently drawn between the 'social' and 'medical' models of disability (Oliver, 1990; Kelly and Byrne, 2017). The medical model sees disability as a disease or disorder of the individual, to be cured or ameliorated if possible, adapted to if not. With regard to the social model, we have already drawn attention to its central tenet in this chapter. It is the idea that a person does not *have* a disability, but rather disability is something *experienced* by people with impairments because of the negative assumptions, barriers and unequal opportunities in society which exclude them from participating fully in its life and activity. The Committee on the Rights of the Child's General Comment No. 9 (United Nations, 2006a, para 5, p. 2) explains this further when it states, 'The Committee emphasizes that the barrier is not the disability itself but rather a combination of social, cultural, attitudinal and physical obstacles which children with disabilities encounter in their daily lives'.

Stigma

In thinking about why people hold negative assumptions which in turn create barriers and lead to unequal opportunities, writers have applied the sociological theory of *stigma* developed by Goffman (1963). The term refers to an 'attribute that is deeply discrediting within a particular social interaction'. The person with such an attribute is 'reduced in our minds from a whole and usual person to a tainted, discounted one' (Goffman, 1963, p. 3). Since his original text, the concept has come to be widely used in relation to ill-health and disability, as well as to other attributes, including race, ethnicity, sexuality, social class and so on. The process of labelling an attribute as a stigma is clearly a relational and social structural one and hence what is defined as a stigma or not is contextual, contingent and changes over time and place.

Although it is arguable that all disabled people experience some degree of stigma, as indicated in General Comment No. 9 (Committee on the Rights of the Child, 2006, para 8, p. 3) where it states that 'Social stigma, fears, overprotection, negative attitudes, misbeliefs and prevailing prejudices against children with disabilities remain strong in many communities and lead to the marginalization and alienation of children with disabilities', Goffman (1963, p. 14) indicated that three types of attributes are likely to be defined as a stigma. These include first bodily impairments (sight, hearing, mobility), second 'blemishes of individual character', for example 'weak willed', 'dishonest' inferred from a known record of criminality, unemployment and so on), and third 'tribal stigma of race, nation and religion'. Hence, the theory predicts that people are especially likely to be stigmatised if their impairment is highly visible, if it is not well understood by the public, and if it is seen as a result of some moral failing. Indeed, as recent research illustrates, it remains the case that there are people from a range of backgrounds in the UK and elsewhere who believe that parents who have disabled children and disabled children are being punished by God for their sins.

The discussion above is primarily located at the level of the individual and contributory factors that lead to stigma being ascribed. At the individual level, tackling this involves social workers reflecting on their attitudes and assumptions. But beyond this, it is clear that societal structures, services and facilities can reproduce and reinforce stigma as well as transform approaches. So, while each individual has their part to play in challenging ignorance and discrimination, there is also a collective responsibility at the team, organisational, regional and political levels, to develop policies, practices and approaches that challenge public ignorance, address the barriers, and ensure that services are provided in ways that reduce stigma rather than adding to it. A strategic approach is in keeping with the social model of disability which demands that organisations address issues such as inaccessible buildings, inaccessible information and negative representations in publications, policies and practices.

This strategic approach is the responsibility of the whole team, organisation or service; it certainly should not be left to the disabled child or young person alone to fight for change. However, it is also important to ensure that disabled children in care and their carers are aware of their rights to representation, complaint and redress and that they have access to appropriate advocacy services to promote and protect their wellbeing and their rights. This is particularly important given the reliance of disabled children in care on services the access to, and quality of, which can be matters of concern.

Access

As noted above, a central issue is that of *access* – particularly for disabled children in care, many of whom have complex needs resulting in attendance at multiple appointments. Social workers need to be aware that we are obliged, under the UNCRC, and as detailed in General Comment No. 9 (United Nations, 2006b, para 14(b), p. 5), that 'care and assistance shall be designed to ensure that children with disabilities have effective access to and benefit from education, training, health care services, recovery services, preparation for employment and recreation opportunities'. Basic considerations therefore include whether services are *accessible*. This is seen at its most obvious in physical terms, most starkly when someone simply cannot get into a building because the entrance is not adapted to their needs. Furthermore, how do children get to their services, what transport arrangements are in place and are these safe and appropriate? Once connected with services, what are disabled children's experiences? Do professionals communicate effectively with them in ways that lead to mutual understanding? Are professionals responsive and attentive, and are services inviting and welcoming? Of course, accessibility is a test of public services in many other ways too, and these questions apply to all disabled people and all kinds of services and facilities, from the local shop to the school.

Inclusion

The term 'inclusion' is understood, conceptualised and theorised in different ways. In the context of education, inclusive education is a right as outlined in Article 24 of the UN Convention on the Rights of Persons with Disabilities (CRPD). This Article also outlines our obligations to ensure that disabled people are not excluded from education on the basis of their disability, that disabled people can access an inclusive and quality education on an equal basis with others in the communities in which they live, that a disabled person's individual requirements are provided for and that appropriate support measures are in place. The term inclusion therefore also encompasses the adaptation of *all structures, systems, processes, policies, procedures and practices* to mitigate against barriers and to ensure equality of opportunity. It is clear that with the drive for inclusion, service provision, especially in education, has come a long way. Historically, for example, children who experienced disability were educated in separate settings known as special schools. In the 1980s, in the context of the increased focus on human rights, the pressure grew for an education system based on inclusion for all, and today it is an international policy and practice imperative.

When thinking about wider service provision for disabled children in care, the same principles apply. Historically, disabled children were placed in institutional settings, largely segregated from community and family life. This approach no longer exists and disabled children either live at home receiving social services and other support services (including 'respite' in the form of short breaks), or if they do come into care, most live in foster placements. Child care legislation in England, Wales and Northern Ireland states that accommodation provided for a child who is disabled should be 'not unsuitable' to their particular needs, which may be read as indicating that ordinary accommodation should be adapted where necessary rather than providing segregated accommodation for disabled children. Part of the ethos of the Children Act 1989 is that disabled children are 'children first' and disabled second. In other words, the first question to ask when we are providing a care service is 'what does this children need as a child in the context of our legal duties and responsibilities to all children?' and only afterwards do we ask 'what in addition needs to be done to ensure that this child's disability does not put her or him at a disadvantage?'. Of course, within this framework, there remain some disabled children, who due to their complex needs require specialist residential or hospital care.

Statutory obligations under child care legislation require social services to identity all children in their area who are disabled, to provide appropriate services and to ensure that the rights of disabled children are promoted and protected. To a lesser or greater extent, this involves the use of labels such as 'special educational needs', 'challenging behaviour', 'complex needs' which while necessary to help identify appropriate services can also have the effect of reinforcing negative views and assumptions. It is important to be mindful of labels and terms that can exacerbate the discrimination faced by disabled children. For example, Middleton and Stevenson (1999, p. 75) argue that the current welfare system 'creates disadvantage for children who are physically different, and it does so by conceptualising them as having "special needs"'. She contends that only 'a fundamental review of the welfare system' (p. 76) can overcome this.

However, this does not mean that individual professionals are powerless to make a difference. In fact, there is a great deal that the practitioner can and should be doing. One is to recognise one's own 'disablist' attitudes:

> Professionals may value disabled children less than those who are not disabled, regard them as objects of pity, or fail to notice their uniqueness. Disabled children are often viewed through the lens of their disabling condition and assumptions made about them on the basis of their physical characteristics. Realisation that they hold unhelpful attitudes can be a painful journey for those who consider themselves caring, tolerant and in favour of a society based on principles of equality or social justice. This can engender guilt, which some disabled activists might encourage, but such a response is not conducive to constructive change. It is more helpful

> to develop an understanding of the mechanisms through which we learn disablist attitudes and the means by which they are reinforced. In this way we can acknowledge, resist and revise them.
>
> *Middleton and Stevenson (1999, p. 78)*

Middleton and Stevenson (1999, p. 79) also suggest that an 'unhelpful mystique' has grown up around work with disabled children, and that this can have the effect of deskilling both professionals and family members. This does not mean that skills and knowledge are not needed, but it does mean that there is no excuse for any of us dodging our responsibility to meet the needs of all children and include them in the services we provide. Middleton's ideas have been expanded upon by writers such as Davis (2004) and Burke (2008) and books edited by Kelly and Byrne (2017) and Runswick-Cole et al. (2017) (as noted earlier) are particularly helpful for social workers regarding practice issues. One thing they all highlight is the importance of good communication skills including non-verbal cues and wide-ranging methods of communication. These are considered below.

Communication skills

Holland (2011) has highlighted that disabled children who express their views non-verbally can be underestimated by professionals, many of whom are only confident with verbal means of expression. This view is supported by other writers who draw attention to the unconscious assumptions that professionals and indeed family members may hold which have the effect of underestimating and/or excluding children from opportunities to express their views (Thomas and O'Kane, 1999; Stein, 2009; Holland, 2011). As argued in this chapter, social workers require the right mindset as well as the knowledge and skills to appreciate that children may communicate non-verbally and through gestures, electronic devices, objects, sensory toys, pictures, symbols on cards and so on (Prynallt-Jones et al., 2018). Extra time might need to be planned in and, as part of this, practitioners should be encouraged to spend time with the child in their foster home, nursery, or school to understand how they communicate and to learn from the child and those who care for them every day.

Understanding 'race', 'ethnicity' and 'identity'

As noted in Article 2 UNCRC, another way in which people are different, and on the basis of which they may be subject to prejudice or unfair discrimination, relates to ethnicity. You might see the terms 'race' and 'ethnicity' used interchangeably, but there are differences in these terms.

Race is seen as biological and refers to skin colour for example. Race can be a highly misleading concept because it is associated with the idea that there are fundamental genetic differences between people, associated with skin colour. The idea that humans can be divided into several major groups between which there are profound genetic differences is now known to be wrong. Genetic differences within ethnic groups are much more significant than those between them. Contrary to popular belief, superficial physical differences including skin colour or hair type are *not* associated with differences in character, ability or temperament. The term race appears in legislation designed to end discrimination (racism) – for example the Equality Act 2010 promotes the equal treatment of people regardless of colour, national or ethnic origin, nationality and race.

It is important to note jurisdictional differences with regard to the Equality Act 2010 which applies in Wales, Scotland and England but except for a few sections does not apply in Northern Ireland, where equal opportunities and discrimination are devolved or transferred matters. The Northern Ireland Act 1998, in Section 75, places a statutory obligation on Public Authorities to carry out their functions with due regard to the need to promote equality of opportunity and good relations in respect of religious belief, political opinion, gender, race, disability, age, marital status, dependants and sexual orientation. In England, Wales and Scotland, the Equality Act 2010 replaces earlier anti-discrimination legislation including the Race Relations Act 1976. In Northern Ireland, the Race Relations (NI) Order 1997 is in force. At the time of writing, the Executive Office had opened a period of consultation on the review of the Race Relations (NI) Order 1997.

Ethnicity is the term used for the culture of a person or a group. It includes dress, customs, language, religion, family/community heritage and nationality, for example. Examples include being labelled or identified as Welsh, Scottish, Irish, Roma Traveller, African or Asian, for example. The fact that physical appearance is often a marker for such differences means that difference is hard to ignore and can have a profound effect on how people behave towards each other. Our sense of identity, of who we are, is highly bound up with ethnicity. Particularly for members of minority groups in any given society, preserving cultural beliefs and practices can be critical to the survival of this sense of identity.

Understanding the terms 'race', ethnicity and identity and their relevance to social work practice with children in care is crucial. As indicated earlier in the book, children in care are a very diverse group. Broad categories are used to describe ethnicity such as 'white', 'mixed', 'Asian' or 'Asian British', 'Black' or 'black British', 'other ethnic groups (including Chinese)' and 'other'. Within these broad groupings, there are more specific ethnic backgrounds as illustrated in Figure 4.1.

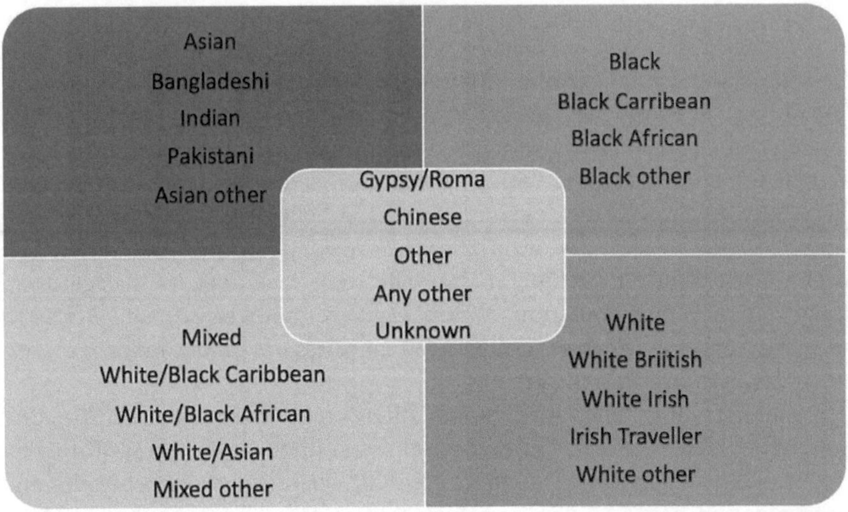

FIGURE 4.1 Broad ethnic categories and specific ethnic backgrounds.

A significant body of research (Chand and Thoburn, 2006; Barn, 2007; Bywaters et al., 2018, 2019, 2020), built up over the last four decades, indicates that children from black, Asian and minority ethnic backgrounds face discrimination at all stages in their involvement with social work services. There are variations in intervention rates with some children from certain ethnic backgrounds being overrepresented in the care system. Research by Bywaters et al. (2020), which focused on social work intervention and was based on children from 18 local authorities, found that children from 'Asian' backgrounds were almost three times *less* likely to be in care than 'white' children and almost four times less likely than 'black' children.

Bywaters et al. (2020) found other striking differences within and between minority ethnic groups. Children identified as Indian were far less likely to have experienced children's services involvement than those from Pakistani or Bangladeshi backgrounds. Within the group labelled 'black', those children described as 'black African' were less likely to be in care than white British children, except in areas of low deprivation, where they were more likely to be. By comparison, 'black Caribbean' children were more likely to be in care than 'white British' or 'Asian' children, regardless of the deprivation level of their neighbourhood. In summary, there is substantial evidence to support the claim that African-Caribbean children are over-represented in the care system while others, such as Indian and Chinese children, are under-represented. Unaccompanied asylum-seeking children (UASC) make up a small but growing group of children requiring placements too.

However, the most over-represented group of children coming into care consisted of those from mixed ethnicity backgrounds (Bywaters et al., 2018).

Ten per cent of children in care were from mixed ethnicity backgrounds, compared with 4% for Asian children and 7% for black children. It is hard to pinpoint exact specific processes that cause these differences, but it is known that the interaction 'of racism, ethnicity, socio-economic circumstances, service provision and wider social policies' are contributory factors leading to such inequalities.

Once in care, inequalities persist and that discrimination against minority ethnic groups continues. A report by the Independent Inquiry into Child Sexual Abuse (Roger et al., 2020, p. 3) highlights missed opportunities to identify when a child from a minority ethnic group is experiencing sexual abuse because of worker stereotypes and assumptions. In explaining how these assumptions impact the report states,

> First, through stereotypes and misconceptions about what is 'normal' or 'acceptable' for certain ethnic groups. These can lead to child sexual abuse going unrecognised or professionals taking no action in response. Secondly, the broader context of racism in society can make it harder for individuals in ethnic minority communities to speak up about child sexual abuse out of concern for reinforcing negative stereotypes.

A recent report researched and written by Listen Up (a Black led organisation) and commissioned by Barnardos (Barnardos and Listen Up, 2023) highlights the impact of racism through the voices and perspectives of Black and minority ethnic children and young people in the care and criminal justice system. It highlights significant challenges and barriers and the responsibility on all practitioners to interrogate and address the impact of their own stereotypes, assumptions and biases.

There are also significant difficulties recruiting minority ethnic carers and therefore difficulties finding ethnically matched placements for children. Factors are complex and include social structural issues such as poverty, poor housing, houses that are too small for larger families resulting in room sharing, language barriers cultural norms, traditions and assessments that lack cultural awareness (Chowdhury, 2021, p. 24). In practice, this means that some children from minority ethnic groups experience their connection to their culture becoming severed, disjointed or confused and there is a lack of opportunity to develop a more positive sense of their own identity.

Identity is a hard to define concept but is commonly understood to mean a strong 'sense of self' and 'sense of belonging' – knowing who you are, where you come from and feeling accepted. Self-image and self-esteem are also relevant when thinking about identity. The process of identity formation begins in childhood and is shaped by experiences, memories, relationships and interactions with friends, family and community from which a personal narrative develops about 'who I am' and 'where I come from'. The way that identity is shaped and claimed by individual people suggest that it is not fixed but can change over time, and that we all have a plurality of identities rather than one fixed ethnic and cultural identity.

As illustrated in a review of literature by Degener et al. (2022a, 2022b), the concern for minority ethnic children in care is that: (a) they are disconnected from their familial and local context which shapes and informs their growing identity; (b) they are likely to be in trans-racial, trans-cultural and trans-religious placements not reflecting their own ethnic background; (c) children do not feel a sense of belonging in their placement; (d) carers do not have sufficient training to address identity needs; (e) children's links with their ethnic and cultural backgrounds are disrupted and weakened; (f) in the longer term and into adulthood this can cause problems.

This is of concern because, as Articles 2, 7, 8, 9, 10 and 20 of the UNCRC point out, as well as the right to identity (which must be taken into account in determining best interests, as further detailed in General Comment No. 14, para 55), children and young people from minority groups also have the right to expect that care providers will be sensitive to their needs, whether those are physical needs such as for skin and hair care, or cultural needs such as provision for diet, religious festivals or particular clothing. Social workers, whose professional codes oblige them to understand diversity and promote equality and social justice, need to be at the forefront of work with children to address these issues and promote a positive sense of identity. In so doing, as Banks (1999) explains, it is necessary first to address one's own ethnic identity, history and attitudes (see Box 4.1).

As Banks (1999) says, this example illustrates the 'appalling position in which some black children can find themselves when their needs are not sensitively identified and met at the outset'. He points out that the agency is faced with a complex set of tasks if it is to address the problems created by earlier poor decision making, and that forcing a move on the basis of ethnic matching alone is simply going to make matters worse. Nargis needs bereavement counselling before anything else can happen, and she also needs to be actively involved in selecting and assessing a suitable family for her future placement. And of course, all efforts to improve practice need also to take account of the wider socio-political context and the complex power dynamic in which racism, emerging from hundreds of years of colonialism, slavery and oppression, is embedded into the very fabric of society.

So just what is required of the social worker with children and young people in care, or in any field, in relation to culture and ethnicity? Clearly they cannot be an expert in every culture that they are likely to encounter. That is not the nature of the task. Rather, practitioners should have the knowledge to appreciate that racism is a harm against children and their families and that they must respond to the needs and situations of diverse groups on the basis of the principles of respect, recognition and openness, and should be able to recognise when additional expertise is needed and to

Box 4.1 'Nargis' (adapted from Banks, 1999)

Nargis was a 14-year-old South Asian girl of mixed heritage, her mother was white English mother and her father, Pakistani. Nargis disliked her Muslim name and had chosen her own name, Susan. Nargis had come into care at the age of eight when her mother had died in childbirth. Her father's whereabouts was unknown. His family had rejected Nargis because her mother had not been married to him. Her mother's family had also rejected her because of her father's origin.

Nargis had been placed with white English short-term foster carers, who subsequently became her long-term foster carers. They lived in a white working-class area and had not been trained in meeting the needs of a black child of mixed heritage. It became apparent that Nargis had chosen the name Susan to avoid constant questioning by other children and to try and avoid racist taunts. For the same reason, she also told her friends that her background was Italian.

In addition to identity difficulties, Nargis had unresolved issues around her mother's sudden death and her abandonment by the rest of her family. The social work department was considering moving her to a South Asian family. She was resisting this because they were an older couple, not as active as Nargis would have liked and they food reflective of their own culture which Nargis did not like. She had also become attached to her white foster carers who had offered her stability at a time of great change.

(adapted from Banks, 1999, pp. 27–28)

develop their own skills, or draw on the knowledge of others, as appropriate. The concept of 'cultural competence' has been developed to help think about this task.

Cultural competence

So what is cultural competence and how is it practiced? From research into the expectations of people using services and their expectations of professionals, O'Hagan (2001) defines cultural competence as comprising:

- 'respect on initial contact';
- an appreciation of why the client's culture is so important, and awareness of components that the client may regard as crucial;
- 'genuine and friendly curiosity';
- an ability to admit ignorance and respond appropriately to one's mistakes.

O'Hagan (2001, p. 254)

O'Hagan's research was with Irish speakers in Northern Ireland, some of whom who face discrimination and prejudice within Northern Irish society. In more recent writing (Laird, 2014; Laird and Tedam, 2019), it has been acknowledged that 'cultural competence' is a broad term with different theoretical considerations, but encompassing skills, attitudes and practices of professionals and their integration into systems, processes, organisations and structures that support effective work in different cultural contexts. Reflecting this, the British Association of Social Workers Code of Ethics (BASW, 2021) states that social workers should recognise and respect ethnic and cultural diversity (including diversity *within* ethnic and cultural groups), and should promote policies, procedures and practices consistent with this goal.

With regard to the question about how to practice cultural competence, advice by various writers includes social workers being trained, practicing self-awareness and reflexivity, seeking advice from the relevant communities on specific cultural issues (Barn and Das, 2016), and lastly 'adopting a respectful, open and humble approach' (Mbarushimana and Robbins, 2015, p. 149). These issues are considered further in Chapters 7 and 8.

Language

For many people, language is a key component of culture, and respect and recognition for the different languages used by children and families are important for this reason. They are also important for practical reasons. Much of the work of social workers with children and young people and with their families, especially where children are looked after away from home, is highly sensitive and concerned with emotions and feelings. It can be very difficult for anyone to talk about such issues in a language that is not their first language or the one they normally use to talk about such matters – no matter how fluent they may be in other respects. An awareness of language is therefore crucial to effective social work practice in this area.

Minority ethnic languages

Most contemporary societies are multilingual – in fact, worldwide most people speak at least two languages. In the UK, the majority are monolingual, and this can create disadvantages for members of minority ethnic communities who have a different language. Linguistic differences between social workers, families and children are common given the diverse population. Within the UK, for instance, there are many resident speakers of Guajarati, Punjabi, Hindi, Chinese, Greek, of Somali and other African languages, of French, Spanish and Portuguese, of Vietnamese and other South East Asian languages, as well as growing numbers of speakers of Russian and East European languages. In some schools, particularly inner-city schools, many languages are used by children. In other areas it is rare to find any child whose first language is not English. This diversity is also apparent in Scotland, Northern Ireland and Wales. This makes for different demands on social workers and other professionals, and different patterns of resources with which to meet those demands (e.g. the availability of translators and interpreters may vary widely).

We are reminded in the Serious Case Reviews (SCR) of children known to social services, who died at the hands of their carers in their family homes, that language barriers can be a contributory factor in the ineffective relationships between the family and their social worker. For example, in the case of Daniel Pelka (aged 4) whose first language was Polish, and who died at home after experiencing parental abuse, the review by Coventry Safeguarding Children Board found, 'Of particular note was that without English as his first language and because of his lack of confidence Daniel's voice was not heard throughout this case' (Lock, 2013, para 14.9, p. 71). Social workers need to ensure they can access interpreters.

In research by Westlake and Jones (2018), social workers communications skills using an interpreter were focused on. They found that although social workers find these situations challenging, they can be managed well and communication can be effective, as long as the social worker was assertive and clear regarding roles, responsibilities and the process of interpretation. The research highlighted that bespoke training on this aspect of practice would be helpful. In the contemporary context, with significant migration caused by war, conflict, political persecution and/or economic hardship, social work teams and organisations (as well as individual social workers) need to be mindful of what is required to communicate effectively with families and children whose first language is not English. A useful practitioner resource on the use of interpreters has been published by Lucas (2020) as part of the Institute for Research and Innovation in Social Services (Iriss) series (available online).

Yr iaith Gymraeg

In Wales, or Cymru, the Welsh language is not only a central component, perhaps the central component, of culture for a large proportion of the population. It also has the legal status of an official language. People are entitled to conduct their official business – pay taxes and bills, use the law courts – in either Welsh or English. Public bodies have a duty to make services available through the medium of Welsh as well as English and must state publicly their policies for achieving this. This applies to social work agencies and care providers, especially local authorities, as much as to any other organisation.

The implications of this for individual practitioners can be considerable. Welsh-speaking children and families must have the choice to deal with a worker who can communicate with them in their preferred language. This means that all agencies should have at least some workers who are completely fluent in Welsh – whether this be in an area where a majority of people have Welsh as their first language, or in an area where very few people use Welsh. Welsh speaking children and families may also feel more comfortable if any worker with whom they come into contact has at least some familiarity with the language. It does not take a great deal of skill to learn to say 'Bore da' ('Good morning') or even 'Mae'n ddrwg gen i, ond dw i ddim yn siarad Gymraeg' ('I'm sorry, but I don't speak Welsh').

In other parts of the British Isles too, there are old languages that are still used – Scots Gaelic, Ulster Scots, Irish and to a much lesser extent Manx and Cornish. While some might think of Ulster Scots as a dialect, it is also recognised as a language (see for example the British government declaration in relation to the European Charter for Regional or Minority Languages). O'Hagan (2001), although not mentioning Welsh, devotes considerable attention to the resurgence of Irish in Northern Ireland and the attempts to give it greater status by the devolved Assembly. Speakers of these languages sometimes face intolerance from monoglot English speakers, including professionals in the health and welfare services, who see their insistence on using the Celtic tongue as in some way perverse or politically motivated. However, if we go back to our principles of respect, recognition and openness, we see that these principles apply to the choices that indigenous people make about preserving their culture, as much as they do to people who have moved to Britain from other continents.

Sexuality

Until recently, little attention has been paid towards LGBTQIA+ children and young people (McCormick, 2018). Their existence has not been acknowledged, their needs are not clearly defined and appropriate services may be few and far between. The lack of acknowledgement has itself created many problems; as McCormick et al. argue (2017, p. 28), 'a lack of visibility often leads to discrimination'. This lack of visibility is even more concerning given that fact that 'findings from recent research with LGBTQIA+ young adults suggest that an openness and a willingness to discuss issues of sexual orientation are strongly associated with positive outcomes'.

LGBTQIA+ children and young people in care have said they feel pressured to remain invisible and silent. As noted earlier, every child has the right to an identity. They also have the right to freedom of expression, non-discrimination, and for all decisions and actions that affect them to be made in their best interests. It is therefore a concern that for children and young people in care with lesbian, gay, bi, trans, queer, questioning, asexual and other non-cisgendered or non-heterosexual identities (referred to by the acronym LGBTQIA+), it is too often the case that these rights are not realised.

LGBTQIA+ children and young people in care face a range of issues, both in relation to their own sense of identity and in terms of the attitudes and reactions of others – including their caregivers. With regard to identity, children may sense at an early age that their sexuality may be different from their peers, and so need a social environment where they can be comfortable with this and talk about it if they wish. As they get older, they may need advice and information on legal issues as well as on taking care of themselves physically and emotionally, from people who know something about it (whether from personal experience or from training) and who are not afraid to deal with these issues in a relaxed way.

In relation to the attitudes and reactions of others, it is unfortunately all too often the case that LGBTQIA+ children and young people recount experiences of being insulted, abandoned and rejected and of being looked at differently by others who have acted in discriminatory ways (Kaasbøll et al., 2022). In other examples, children and young people's confidentiality and privacy have been violated when they have 'been outed' without their permission (i.e., their identity made known to other professionals without their consent). All of these experiences can contribute to poor mental health outcomes for this group of children and young people (Dettlaff and Washburn, 2018). In another lack of acknowledgement about their needs, the government does not collate data on the number of children and young people in care who are LGBTQIA+, although it is known from research that LGBTQIA+ are overrepresented in the care system (Dettlaff and Washburn, 2018).

LGBTQIA+ children and young people face enormous challenges accessing services, whether that be from an absence of services, a lack of knowledge of their availability, or discriminatory attitudes and behaviours on the part of carers or professionals. Such discrimination is contrary to the values and principles underpinning the social work profession and its codes of practice which every practicing social worker is required to sign up to and emulate in practice.

Addressing injustice, inequality and the barriers people experience requires a multi-layered response. At the individual level, this involves practitioners accepting children and young people as they are and for who they are, rather than trying to make them be someone they are not on the basis of assumptions, prejudices or expectations. More training, education and information should be made available and at a systemic level, the policies, procedures and practices of organisations should be examined to ensure that people are not directly or indirectly discriminated against and that their needs are addressed. There is a growing resource available to help both online and with regard to written literature, referred to at the end of this chapter.

Poverty and class

Most children and young people who come into the care system are from poorer families. We have already mentioned the seminal study by Bebbington and Miles (1989) and the more recent work by Bywaters et al. (2019, 2020), which highlights the inequalities experienced by those who come into contact with social services. Although poverty can be measured in different ways, the basic definition, according to the Joseph Rowntree Foundation (JRF) on their website, is 'when your resources are well below your minimum needs'. It could mean 'not being able to heat your home, pay your rent, or buy the essentials for your children'. It means having to make difficult decisions about money – whether to heat the house or buy food.

Some people are more at risk of poverty than others. This includes people from some minority ethnic groups, disabled people and people from care backgrounds. People experiencing poverty also face marginalisation. This means that due to a lack of available resources, some people in poverty are unable to participate fully in everyday society and can become isolated. These experiences of isolation and marginalisation are compounded by other problems associated with poverty including poorer physical and mental health, lower educational opportunities and low employment rates (with a corresponding higher rate of being in unstable, unskilled jobs).

You may hear the term 'social exclusion' used when discussing poverty and its impacts. There are different definitions of the term social exclusion, but it is commonly understood to be a multidimensional concept and to refer to 'a state in which individuals are unable to participate fully in economic, social, political and cultural life, as well as the process leading to and sustaining such a state' (United Nations, 2016). This concept is useful in thinking about some of the ways in which people who are materially poor often have limited opportunities to participate in many aspects of society, and restricted access to a range of social resources or 'social capital' (see Chapter 6). However, it is sometimes used to suggest that the remedy for social exclusion is to develop the skills and personal resources of poor people, or to seek ways to overcome the social barriers between poor families and the wider society. While these objectives may be important, they are not a substitute for tackling low income directly. This is most clearly outlined in the Anti-Poverty Practice Framework for Social Work in Northern Ireland (DoH, 2018) which highlights social workers' responsibilities to address the causes of poverty and its impacts at the level of the individual, community and at the social structural level too.

This guidance highlights that poverty is a social justice issue and that poor people are frequently subject to intense discrimination, prejudice and stigma, exacerbated by the fact that they are often seen as responsible for their own poverty. Although children are more often seen as victims – indeed the political impetus for measures to reduce poverty almost always depends on focusing on *child* poverty, for this reason – the stigma still cannot be escaped. The stigma endured because of being poor is pervasive and includes being labelled as lazy, unmotivated, making bad choices and poverty being self-inflicted. All these characteristics are associated with being poor, and this gives children from such a background a mountain to climb in terms of prejudice, invisibility, latent hostility or low expectations.

Again we need to return to our basic principles: *respect* for children and their families, no matter what their background or circumstances, and for the strategies which they adopt to survive in those circumstances; *recognition* of the reality of poverty and the barriers it creates to inclusion and participation in society; *openness* to the potential of poor children and their families to succeed, and to give as well as to receive.

Working with travellers, refugees and asylum seekers

There are other groups of children and young people who have particular experiences of discrimination and oppression. These include Traveller children and their families, unaccompanied asylum seekers and refugees, for example. Each group is considered separately below as their needs and experiences differ.

Traveller children

A recent report by the Northern Ireland Human Rights Commission (NIHRC, 2018, p. 5) notes that the term 'Gypsy, Roma, and Traveller' is often used to encompass a wide range of communities. In the report, "Traveller' is used as an umbrella term for any member of a traditional Gypsy or Traveller community living in or travelling through NI with a long-shared history, culture and traditions that includes identifying with or continuing to practice a nomadic way of life'. Children who belong to traditional travelling communities are members of an ethnic group who, as well as being victims of myth and prejudice, are often ignored or excluded by mainstream services. Even when services provide for them, they often fail to do so in a way that respects or recognises their culture and language. This is despite the fact that legislation (the Equality Act 2010, section 9) defines Gypsies and Travellers as a racial group who are therefore protected from direct discrimination (s13), indirect discrimination (s15) and harassment (s26). In Northern Ireland, the Irish Traveller community is protected under Race Relations legislation and it is illegal to discriminate against this group.

With regard to social work, there is evidence that Gypsy, Roma, and Traveller children are overrepresented in child welfare in Europe and in the UK (Allen and Hamnett, 2022). Social workers are expected to ensure that when children from Gypsy, Roma, and Traveller backgrounds come into care, they should be looked after in a way that "respects, recognises, supports and celebrates their identity", which includes their ethnic origin and cultural background (Allen and Adams, 2013). Importantly, social workers should also be aware of the diversity within these groups, especially with the quite different needs and cultural histories of Roma children compared to Traveller and Gypsy families and children. Roma children, for example, are more likely to be from families that have migrated from other European nations and to speak one or more of a range of languages. There is also diversity within Roma populations as highlighted in the census survey data (Office for National Statistics, 2021).

Professionals are therefore required to provide support to ensure that these children's needs are met, and to challenge policies, practices and procedures of their own and other organisations that contribute directly or indirectly to the ongoing discrimination of these groups.

Another group of 'new age' Travellers also are vulnerable to prejudice and exclusion, even though the cultural barriers may be less marked (Lowe and Shaw, 1993). In both cases, the fact that families do not have a conventional settled home in a fixed geographical location tends to fuel misunderstanding, as well as disqualifying them from certain facilities and services. Providing care and accommodation for Traveller children can be challenging for all these reasons, and also because when families and communities are moving on it can be difficult to maintain a stable placement with consistent family contact. A culturally sensitive approach is required which begins with engaging with families, being open minded and exploring with them what their identity means to them and how best to respect and preserve it.

Refugees, asylum seekers and unaccompanied minors

Another group who has become increasingly significant in recent years are refugees, asylum seekers, and unaccompanied minors. People seek asylum for several reasons including: fleeing war and persecution; extreme poverty; seeking employment to send money home to family and friends; escaping arranged marriages, military service; seeking to reunite with other family members. Most come from either the Middle East (countries including Syria, Afghanistan, Iran and Iraq) and from African countries such as Nigeria, Eritrea, Somalia and Gambia. Other countries include Pakistan, Egypt and European countries – Romania and Ukraine for example.

An asylum-seeker is defined as a person who has left their country, is fleeing harm and/or persecution and who is seeking asylum. All asylum seekers are seeking to be recognised as refugees. A refugee is defined as a person who 'owing to a well-founded fear of being persecuted for reasons of race, religion, nationality, membership of a particular social group or political opinion, is outside the country of their nationality and is unable or, owing to such fear, is unwilling to avail themselves of the protection of that country' (UN, Convention Relating to the Status of Refugees (1951), Article 1). Seeking refugee status can be a long and difficult process.

With regard to children and young people, some travel with their families and some have become separated from their families. They arrive in the UK alone and are known as unaccompanied minors. At end September 2022, the UK received 5,152 applications for asylum from unaccompanied children and young people. Most were between the ages of 14–17 years but a few were younger. There are also children who are trafficked into the UK by criminal gangs and who are exploited and victims of forced labour in drug gangs, sexual exploitation and other forms of labour.

Because unaccompanied children and young people usually have no-one with legal parental responsibility caring for them, they will be looked after by the local authority or the Health and Social Care Trust and accommodated under the relevant provisions of the children's legislation which exists in all jurisdictions of the UK. As children's services do not have parental responsibility for them, they may well decide to apply for an order which means they acquire parental responsibility for the unaccompanied child.

Due to the number of unaccompanied children and young people arriving in the UK, many arriving in the same location, local social services were unable to meet demand for carers and accommodation. The led to the Home Office, in July 2021, commissioning hotels to care for unaccompanied children and young people. What this does is remove them from the children in need and child protection frameworks that operate in each Local Authority. Their needs are met outside this. There are ongoing concerns regarding the suitability of the accommodation (even on an emergency basis), the safety of the children (over 200 children have gone missing, thought to be the victims of ongoing human trafficking) and their wellbeing (all children regardless of their ethnicity, religion, country of origin are placed in the same accommodation). A bulletin written in 2023 by The Refugee and Migrant Children's Consortium (a coalition of over 60 organisations working with asylum seekers and refugees) highlights these concerns in detail.

A recent social work guide (Wroe, 2019) draws attention to definitions of these groups, their lived experiences, the role of the social worker and service responses to need. Attention is drawn to the complex and difficult nature of people's situations and circumstances, and to the need for a more nuanced and bespoke response. As Boccagni and Righard (2020, p. 378) point out:

> *Being* or *becoming* an asylum seeker, or a refugee, is a critical life event. It is not the only one though, and it cannot subsume all of the identities, interests, life projects and concerns of people who are also asylum seekers or refugees.

To put it in a different way, these groups may be particularly vulnerable for a number of reasons. As indicated above, they are usually from ethnic minorities who are very different from the host community, in some cases quite unknown to the host community. Their culture and language may be very different from the host community, and they may not speak the language of the host community at all. Some have fled war, conflict, and persecution. They are likely to have been separated from their families, endured precarious and dangerous conditions while moving from country to country, and many have experienced traumatic events including exploitation, injury, death, and the fear and uncertainty of not knowing where the next meal or place of shelter will be found. In addition, they may then live in a community where they know little or nothing of where things are or how they work, their entitlement to services and resources may be restricted as a result of government action to 'crack down' on asylum seekers, and they may well be victims of racial attacks or abuse.

The social work role and interagency working

The last point above highlights the fact that responsibility to respond effectively and empathically to the needs of different groups does not lie solely with social workers. Doctors, health visitors, teachers, police, housing officials, all have their part to play in ensuring that all members of the community have fair and effective access to services and help when they need it. Indeed, in no other aspect of practice are interagency and multidisciplinary working more important than in how we deal with difference and oppression. Joint training can be vital in creating a shared understanding of the task and shared ideas on how to tackle it. It is good to see that a guide to culturally competent practice such as O'Hagan's is aimed at health and social care professionals in general, not just at social workers.

Summary and conclusion

We began the chapter with the proposition that working well with difference and oppression depends on three principles of respect, recognition and openness. We then saw how this applies in work with disabled children and young people in care, using the concepts of stigma, access and inclusion. We also saw how it operates in relation to culture and ethnicity, especially in work with black and minority ethnic children. We looked at issues of language and of sexuality, at poverty and class, and at what is involved in working with refugee children and with travellers. Finally, we considered the importance of working together across agencies if we are to counteract oppression in an effective way. Social workers cannot take on the sole responsibility for ridding society of oppression and discrimination. However, by attending carefully to our own practice, by listening to children and young people and their families, and by making alliances and working collaboratively with others, we can make a real contribution.

GUIDE TO FURTHER READING

Middleton and Stevenson (1999) is still a good starting point for thinking about work with disabled children. More recently an edited collection by Kelly and Byrne (2017) provides updated perspectives, as do Runswick-Cole et al. (2017). Graham (2007) is very helpful in thinking about work with black children and families. O'Hagan (2001) is a seminal text on dealing with culture in general, offering an interesting blend of research, theory and practice. More recently Laird (2014), Tedam (2020) and Laird and Tedam (2019) are very helpful, and Livingston et al. (2023) are useful for social work in Wales. On working with children and young people with diverse sexualities, Argüello (2019) and McCormick (2018) are must-reads. On working with traveller children, useful resources include Allen and Adams (2013); Sweeney and Matthews (2017). A useful website can be found at https://www.gypsy-traveller.org

Note

1 Note that we use these terms in a different sense elsewhere in this book – see Chapter 2 for Honneth's theory of recognition, and Chapter 9 for a particular use of 'openness' in the context of adoption.

References

Allen, D. and Adams, P. (2013) *Social work with gypsy, roma, and traveller children.* London: CoramBAAF.

Allen, D. and Hamnett, V. (2022) 'Gypsy, Roma, and Traveller children in child welfare services in England', *British Journal of Social Work*, *52*(7), 3904–3922.

Argüello, T.M. (ed.) (2019) *Queer social work: Cases for LGBTQ+ affirmative practice.* New York: Columbia University Press.

Banks, N. (1999) Direct identity work. In Barn, R. (ed.) *Working with black children and adolescents in need.* London: British Agencies for Adoption and Fostering.

Barn, R. (2007) "Race', ethnicity, and child welfare: A fine balancing act', *British Journal of Social Work*, *37*(8), 1425–1434.

Barn, R. and Das, C. (2016) 'Family group conferences and cultural competence in social work', *The British Journal of Social Work*, *46*(4), 942–959.

Barnardos and Listen Up. (2023) *Double discrimination: Black care experienced young adults navigating the criminal justice system.* London: Barnardos.

Bebbington, A. and Miles, J. (1989) 'The background of children who enter local authority care', *British Journal of Social Work* 19(5), 349–68.

Boccagni, P. and Righard, E. (2020) 'Social work with refugee and displaced populations in Europe: (Dis)Continuities, dilemmas, developments', *European Journal of Social Work*, *23*(3), 375–383.

British Association of Social Workers (BASW). (2021) *The BASW code of ethics for social work*. Birmingham: BASW.

Burke, P. (2008) *Disability and impairment: Working with children and families*. London: Jessica Kingsley Publishers.

Bywaters, P., Brady, G., Bunting, L., Daniel, B., Featherstone, B., Jones, C., Morris, K., Scourfield, J., Sparks, T. and Webb, C. (2018) 'Inequalities in English child protection practice under austerity: A universal challenge?', *Child & Family Social Work*, *23*(1), 53–61.

Bywaters, P., Scourfield, J., Jones, C., Sparks, T., Elliott, M., Hooper, J., McCartan, C., Shapira, M., Bunting, L. and Daniel, B. (2020) 'Child welfare inequalities in the four nations of the UK', *Journal of Social Work*, *20*(2), 193–215.

Bywaters, P., Scourfield, J., Webb, C., Morris, K., Featherstone, B., Brady, G., Jones, C. and Sparks, T. (2019) 'Paradoxical evidence on ethnic inequities in child welfare: Towards a research agenda', *Children and Youth Services Review*, *96*, 145–154.

Callus, A.M. and Farrugia, R. (2016) *The disabled child's participation rights*. Abingdon: Routledge.

Chand, A. and Thoburn, J. (2006) 'Child protection referrals and minority ethnic children and families', *Child and Family Social Work*, *11*(4), 168–177.

Chowdhury, C. (2021) "They want to give our children to white people and Christian people': Somali perspectives on the shortage of Somali substitute carers', *Adoption & Fostering*, *45*(1), 22–36.

Committee on the Rights of the Child. (2006) *General comment No. 9 (2006). The rights of children with disabilities* (forty-third session), CRC/C/GC/9. Geneva: United Nations.

Davis, J.M. (2004) Disability and childhood: Deconstructing the stereotypes. Chapter21, pp 142–148 in Swain, J., French, S., Barnes, C. and Thomas, C. (eds) *Disabling barriers. Enabling environments*. London: Sage Publications Ltd.

Degener, C.J., van Bergen, D.D. and Grietens, H.W. (2022a) '"Being one, but not being the same": A dyadic comparative analysis on ethnic socialization in transcultural foster families in the Netherlands', *Child and Family Social Work*, 27(2), 143–151.

Degener, C.J., van Bergen, D.D. and Grietens, H.W. (2022b) 'The ethnic identity of transracially placed foster children with an ethnic minority background: A systematic literature review', *Children and Society*, *36*(2), 201–219.

Dettlaff, A.J. and Washburn, M. (2018) 'Lesbian, gay, and bisexual (LGB) youth within in welfare: Prevalence, risk and outcomes', *Child Abuse and Neglect*, *80*, 183–193.

Equality Act 2010 Available here https://www.legislation.gov.uk/ukpga/2010/15/contents (accessed 26.01.24)

Goffman, E. (1963). *Stigma. Notes on the management of spoiled identity*. London: Penguin Books.

Graham, M. (2007) 'Giving voice to black children: An analysis of social agency', *British Journal of Social Work*, *37*(8), 1305–1317.

Holland, S. (2011) *Child and family assessment in social work practice* (second edition). London: SAGE Publications Ltd.

Kaasbøll, J., Pedersen, S.A. and Paulsen, V. (2022) 'What is known about the LGBTQ perspective in child welfare services: A scoping review', *Child and Family Social Work*, 27(2), 358–369.

Kelly, B. and Byrne, B. (eds.) (2017) *Valuing disabled children and young people: Research, policy, and practice*. Abingdon: Routledge.

Kelly, B., McShane, T., Davidson, G., Pinkerton, J., Gilligan, E. and Webb, P. (2016) *Transitions and outcomes for care leavers with mental health and/or intellectual disabilities: Final report*. Belfast: QUB.

Laird, S.E. (2014) *Practical social work law: Analysing court cases and inquiries*. Abingdon: Routledge.

Laird, S.E. and Tedam, P. (2019) *Cultural diversity in child protection: Cultural competence in practice*. London: Bloomsbury Publishing.

Livingston, W., Redcliffe, J. and Quinn, A. (2023) *Social work in Wales*. Bristol: Policy Press.

Lock, R. (2013) *Serious case review re Daniel Pelka: Born 15th July 2007 died 3rd March 2012*. Coventry: Coventry Safeguarding Children Board.

Lowe, R. and Shaw, W. (1993) *Travellers: Voices of the new-age nomads*. Glasgow: HarperCollins Publishers.

Lucas, S.E. (2020) *Spoken language interpreters in social work. Insight 52*. Glasgow: The Institute for Research and Innovation in Social Services (IRISS).

Mbarushimana, J.P. and Robbins, R. (2015) '"We have to work harder": Testing assumptions about the challenges for black and minority ethnic social workers in a multicultural society', *Practice*, 27(2), 135–152.

McCormick, A., Schmidt, K. and Terrazas, S. (2017) 'LGBTQ youth in the child welfare system: An overview of research, practice, and policy', *Journal of Public Child Welfare*, *11*(1), 27–39.

McCormick, A. (2018) *LGBTQ Youth in foster care: Empowering approaches for an inclusive system of care*. London: Routledge.

Middleton, L. and Stevenson, O. (1999) *Disabled children: Challenging social exclusion*. Oxford: Wiley.

Northern Ireland Human Rights Commission (NIHRC). (2018) *Out of sight, out of mind: Travellers' accommodation in Northern Ireland*. Belfast: Northern Ireland Human Rights Commission.

Northern Ireland Human Rights Commission (NIHRC). (2021) *Alternative care and children*. Belfast: Northern Ireland Human Rights Commission.

Office for National Statistics. (2021) *Roma populations, England, and Wales: Census 2021*. London: Office for National Statistics.

Office of Social Services and Department of Health. (2018) *Anti-poverty practice framework for social work in Northern Ireland*. Belfast: Office of Social Services and Department of Health.

O'Hagan, K. (2001) *Cultural competence in the caring professions*. London: Jessica Kingsley Publishers.

Oliver, M. (1990) *The politics of disablement*. Basingstoke: Macmillan.

Prynallt-Jones, K.A., Carey, M. and Doherty, P. (2018) 'Barriers facing social workers undertaking direct work with children and young people with a learning disability who communicate using non-verbal methods', *The British Journal of Social Work*, *48*(1), 88–105.

Race Relations Act 1976 Available here https://www.legislation.gov.uk/ukpga/1976/74/enacted (accessed 26.01.24).

Roger, H., Hurcombe, R., Redmond, T. and George, R. (2020) *"People don't talk about it": Child sexual abuse in ethnic minority communities.* Independent Inquiry into Child Sexual Abuse, London: Home Office.

Runswick-Cole, K., Curran, T. and Liddiard, K. (eds.) (2017) *The Palgrave handbook of disabled children's childhood studies.* London: Palgrave Macmillan.

Stein, M. (2009) *Quality matters in children's services: Messages from research.* London: Jessica Kingsley Publishers.

Sweeney, S. and Matthews, Z. (2017) *Friends, families, and travellers. A guide for professionals working with gypsies, roma, and travellers in children's services.* Brighton: Friends, Families, and Travellers.

Tedam, P. (2020) *Anti-oppressive social work practice.* Exeter: Learning Matters, Sage.

The Northern Ireland Act 1998 Available here https://www.legislation.gov.uk/ukpga/1998/47/contents (accessed 26.01.24).

Thomas, N. and O'Kane, C. (1999) 'Children's participation in reviews and planning meetings when they are 'looked after' in middle childhood', *Child and Family Social Work*, 4, 221–230.

United Nations High Commission for Refugees (UNHCR). (1951) *Convention relating to the status of refugees.* Geneva: United Nations.

United Nations. (2006a) *Preamble of the convention on the rights of persons with disabilities.* (CRPD). Geneva: United Nations.

United Nations (2006b) *Convention on the rights of persons with disabilities (CRPD).* Geneva: United Nations.

United Nations (2016) Leaving no one behind: the imperative of inclusive development. Report on the world social situation 2016. New York. United Nations. HYPERLINK https://www.un.org/esa/socdev/rwss/2016/full-report.pdf [last accessed 02.05.24]

Westlake, D. and Jones, R.K. (2018) 'Breaking down language barriers: A practice-near study of social work using interpreters', *British Journal of Social Work*, 48(5), 1388–1408.

Wroe, L. (2019) *Contextual safeguarding and 'county lines'.* Luton: University of Bedfordshire, Institute of Applied Social Research and the International Centre, Researching Child Exploitation, Violence and Trafficking.

5

LAW, POLICY AND PRACTICE IN LOOKING AFTER YOUNG PEOPLE

CONTENTS OF CHAPTER

- Introduction
- Law, policy and professional practice
- Law, family policy and national cultures
- Human rights legislation
- The law governing the care of children and young people
- The Children Act 1989 and equivalent legislation in the devolved UK nations
- Current legal frameworks in the devolved UK nations
- Private law and family disputes
- Public law and support for children and families
- Public law and intervening to remove children from families
- Newer ways of managing court proceedings
- Caring for children away from home
- The law governing adoption
- Translating law and policy into practice
- Relationships with other agencies
- Summary and conclusion
- Guide to further reading

Introduction

In all areas of social work practice, it is crucial that social workers know and understand the law (Brammer, 2020). There are many laws that impact on all our lives: laws on equality, human rights, welfare benefits, housing,

DOI: 10.4324/9781003503194-5

employment, race relations, asylum, refugee law, health and education, for example. Other laws which directly govern social work practice relate to domestic violence, mental health and mental capacity law, criminal and youth justice law, adult safeguarding as well as child care law which is the focus of this book.

Laws can appear daunting and complicated. In the UK, an additional complication is that some powers to make laws have been devolved from the central Parliament in London to the Scottish Parliament, the Senedd or Welsh Parliament, and the Northern Ireland Assembly. The precise nature of devolution varies across all those jurisdictions, but in all three cases, health, education and social care are fully devolved. The purpose of this chapter is to outline key developments and current legal frameworks regarding social work with children and families in the UK including human rights considerations. The chapter also considers specific legislation in each of the devolved nations. It begins with outlining what we mean by law and implications for the social worker role.

Law, policy and professional practice

The law governs social work practice in several ways. First, it provides a broad framework within which social work is practiced. Second, it provides the mandate by which social workers exercise their *powers and duties*. Third, it defines people's entitlements, prescribes what and how services should be provided, and gives the authority for compulsion. Whether social work services are provided by national or by local government, or by voluntary agencies, legal frameworks is of crucial importance.

Associated with the law are *powers* and *duties*. It is important to understand the difference. Duties require agencies to exercise their functions in specified ways. Powers, on the other hand, enable people or organisations to do things which they could not otherwise do; this is important for local government in the UK, because it is illegal, for example, for a local authority to spend public money on purposes for which they are not authorised. Another important point is to be aware of the difference between statutes (Acts), regulations and guidance (see Figure 5.1).

Statutes are Acts; pieces of legislation passed by Parliament in England (or the equivalent devolved structure (Senedd – the Welsh Parliament, the Scottish Parliament or the Northern Ireland Assembly) that become law. An act usually contains a main text as well as schedules and supplements. One way to become more familiar with what the law looks like is to find a printable version of a piece of legislation, which can be easily located online. You will note the formal layout, the division of the document into parts (for example Parts 1–3) and within each part sub-headings with numbered sections and clauses. All of this has the force of law.

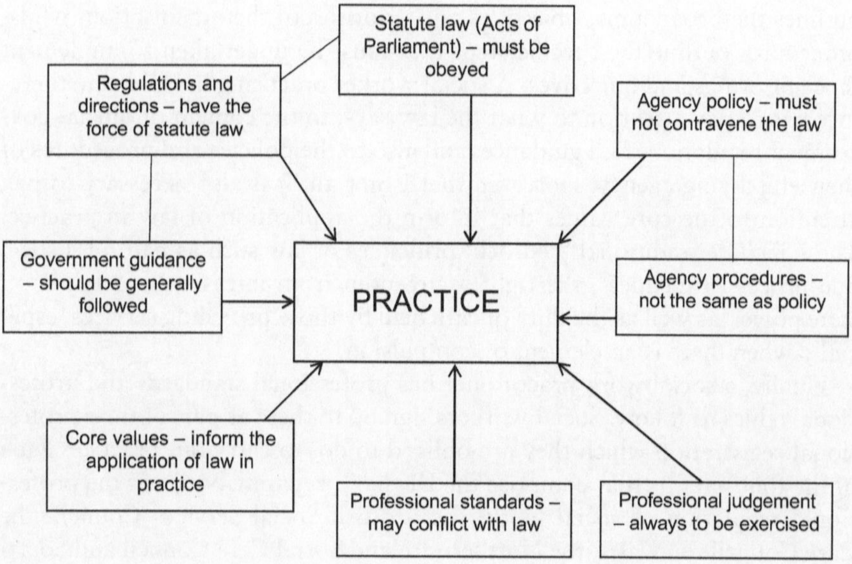

FIGURE 5.1 Law, policy and practice.

Regulations are also known as Statutory Instruments or secondary legislation and they supplement an act. They provide the detail for the enactment of a statute – i.e. detailed guidance regarding the implementation of all aspects of a piece of legislation. They also have the force of law and therefore must be followed.

Guidance can be statutory or non-statutory. If it is statutory, it means that local authorities (or in the case of Northern Ireland, the Health and Social Care Trusts) and their employees must follow it unless there are exceptional reasons for not doing so. If it is non-statutory, it is like practice guidance. In England and Wales, if directions are issued under Section 7a of the Local Authority Social Services Act 1970, the local authorities must follow them. Other 'general practice guidance' not issued under Section 7 should certainly not be ignored but does not have the same force. Child care law can be quite prescriptive, not only informing agencies and professionals what must be done, but also often specifying how it should be done, as illustrated by the amount of guidance and regulation that accompanies recent child care legislation.

Although this book is primarily concerned with child care law, it is important to acknowledge that other areas of law also have significance – for example, those relating to domestic abuse and violence, mental health, criminal and youth justice.

In implementing child care law across the UK, social work organisations also have their own policies and procedures. An organisational policy outlines the broad aims, objectives and priorities of the organisation, whilst procedures outline the specific steps that must be undertaken to implement those priorities and objectives. A social worker practising in child care therefore has to pay attention to what the law says, to the content of official government regulations and guidance, and also to the policies and procedures of their employing agency. However, that is not all. It is also necessary to pay attention to the core values that inform the application of law in practice. These include traditional 'bedrock' principles of law such as natural justice, due process, timeliness, the right to freedom from intrusion and limits on state power, as well as the duty of care held by those providing services, especially when there is an element of compulsion.

Finally, a social work practitioner has professional standards and professional ethics to follow. Social workers sign up to these as part of their professional registration which they are obliged to do, to carry out practice. Each of the four nations that comprise the UK has a separate body for the professional regulation of social work: the Scottish Social Services Council, the Care Council for Wales, the Northern Ireland Social Care Council and Social Work England. The British Association of Social Workers also maintains an independent statement of professional ethics.

Social work practice is therefore about exercising the authority that is vested in the profession through the law and doing this in ways that uphold the values and ethics of the social work profession, which include respect for the dignity and inherent worth of each individual and individual rights to justice and self-determination. In this context, it is not surprising to note that there can be tensions between ethics, values and the law and that the exercise of professional judgment is critical in navigating these sensitive situations and complex decisions, especially when children and young people might be coming into care and/or are in care.

We consider that the key professional obligations of the social worker operating under the law are:

1. to use the law to promote ethical and effective practice;
2. to have regard not just to the letter of the law but to its underlying principles; and
3. to challenge oppression and discrimination.

Law, family policy and national cultures

As indicated earlier, legal systems differ in the provision they make for children's welfare and for parenting. These differences may reflect wider differences in the legal framework in different countries. They also reflect differences in social policy towards children and families, and differences in national cultures. Some cultures make no provision for legal adoption.

Some legal systems make it very difficult to remove parents' rights over their children, while others will only allow children to come into care if parental rights are removed.

Featherstone et al. (2014) outline the complexity of family policy and the changing relationship between the state and the family, itself reflecting changes in political, social and economic contexts. Some countries have family policies that are explicit and comprehensive with clear over-arching goals, others less so. Walsh et al. (2019, p. 1051) have recently argued that in the UK, there is 'no discrete family policy' but that a core theme across all four nations is 'individualism (and the idea that) that all family adults have equal agency in assuring the well-being of their families'. They go on to highlight that 'policy related to family is therefore routinely pro-employment in nature and links private choice, parental responsibility, childcare, child well-being and family responsibilities' (Walsh et al., 2019, p. 1051).

Family policy has often been characterised by an emphasis on early intervention and prevention of harm, which comes in many guises. For example, there has been a growth in the number of parenting programmes designed to support and educate parents with the aim of improving outcomes and preventing difficult home situations deteriorating and further social work intervention being necessary (Canavan et al., 2016; MacDonald and Dunn, 2023). There has also been a growth in the number of early childhood care schemes, which combine the care of children and the extension of pre-school placements for children with an emphasis on preparing children for school.

Whilst these programmes do benefit children and families, there is some concern that intervention into family life is legitimised either by an emphasis on parental employment, or by discourses about troubled or troublesome families, rather than by focusing on what is good for children (Winter, 2009; Winter et al., 2022). As mentioned in Chapter 1, Fox Harding (1997) argued that child welfare policy in the UK is characterised by four competing value positions: laissez-faire, state paternalism, parents' rights and children's rights. It could be argued that current family policy actually has aspects of all four value positions inherent in its aims, objectives and aspirations.

In this chapter, we review the law relating to the care of children in the UK, highlighting the different arrangements in England, Wales, Scotland and Northern Ireland. There will be occasional mention of legislation in the Irish Republic, in other parts of Europe and in other English-speaking countries of the world. (Other English-speaking countries tend to have broadly similar legal systems and often similar approaches to decision-making about children, even when their family policies may be markedly different; whereas frameworks and approaches in continental Europe tend to be rather different, and less adversarial.)

We begin by outlining the broader legal provisions for human rights which shape and inform child care laws, regulations and guidance.

Human rights legislation

The Human Rights Act 1998 made the rights outlined in the European Convention on Human Rights (ECHR) enforceable in domestic law in the UK. This defines fundamental rights to which we all are entitled. Of particular relevance to child and family social work is Article 6 (the right to a fair trial). It states:

> Everyone is entitled to a fair and public hearing within a reasonable time by an independent and impartial tribunal established by law.

Also important is Article 8 (the right to respect for private and family life, home and correspondence). This states:

> There shall be no interference by a public authority with the exercise of this right except such as is in accordance with the law and is necessary in a democratic society in the interests of national security, public safety or the economic well-being of the country, for the prevention of disorder or crime, for the protection of health or morals, or for the protection of the rights and freedoms of others.

The practice of children's legislation should reflect and embody these rights. There are examples of cases heard in the European Court of Human Rights where these fundamental rights have been ignored, overlooked or interfered with.

The UNCRC, comprising 54 articles, establishes children as a group requiring separate and special provisions with regard to their human rights; and creates a set of standards and principles with which the practices of its signatories ('States Parties') should comply and against which legislation, policy and practice should be evaluated. These are often characterised as rights to protection, provision, and participation.

With regard to the UNCRC, the Social Services and Well-being (Wales) Act sets out a

> duty upon persons carrying out functions under the SSWA 2014 in relation to children with needs for care and support, child carers with needs for support and persons in respect of whom functions are carried out under Part 6 of the Act (looked after and accommodated children).

The duty, in this case, is 'to have due regard to Part 1 of the United Nations Convention on the Rights of the Child'. This clearly places children's human rights at the centre of expectations on social workers and others working with children in need of care and support. This piece of legislation is currently one of the strongest human rights duties in the UK in the areas of social work with children. As noted elsewhere, Scotland has also been making efforts for the UNCRC to become embedded into domestic law.

Other relevant legislation that social workers should be aware of, and has been considered in other chapters, includes equality legislation, race relations legislation, mental health and mental capacity legislation.

The law governing the care of children and young people

Whatever the national context, modern legal systems dealing with the care of children and young people usually make provision for the following:

- the circumstances in which children are to be cared for voluntarily;
- the circumstances in which children may be removed from home compulsorily;
- the arrangements to be made for children who are looked after away from home;
- services designed to support children in their own families;
- arrangements for after-care; and
- arrangements for adoption.

While it is not the aim of this book to give a history of child care policy either in the UK or more widely (the Guide to Further Reading at the end of the chapter gives some suggestions for finding out about this), it is worth drawing attention to a couple of key historical moments which have governed the ways in which children's services are provided. The first was the enactment of the Children Act 1948. The Children Act 1948 applied in England, Wales and Scotland; the Northern Ireland equivalent was the Children and Young Persons Act (Northern Ireland) 1950. This legislation, as part of the post-war settlement of the 'welfare state', established a principle that care could be provided at the request of, and by agreement with, families who were unable temporarily to look after their own children, with a view to their eventual return. It also introduced a principle that the care provided should as far as possible be similar to the care given to children living with their own families.

The Children Act 1948 followed an inquiry into the supervision of children in foster care, in particular the case of Denis O'Neill, who had been placed in foster care far from his home and died because of neglect and ill-treatment by his foster carers. In response, the new legislation placed a strong emphasis on the supervision and monitoring of children's welfare. This emphasis continued through the post-war years, in particular from the mid-1970s onwards with a series of official, public inquiries into the deaths of children in care or under supervision. These publications resulted in a criticism of social work with children and families as offering too little too late, while on the other hand social workers were also being criticised for intervening too much and too early in cases such as the removal of children from their families in Cleveland on what eventually appeared to be baseless allegations of sexual abuse. The core question of when and whether to intervene is at the heart of social work practice in this area, and of public policy. It was one of the questions which was sought to be resolved in the Children Act 1989, as we shall see in the following section.

This comprehensive reform of the law was intended, among other things, to balance the dual concerns represented by 'too much, too soon' and 'too little, too late', by making clearer the circumstances in which intervention to remove children was legitimate and by ensuring that support services for families were provided. Some argue that the balance is still not right, and that negative stereotypes about parents underpin services characterised by legalistic responses and increased surveillance of families – see for example Featherstone et al. (2014). The approach taken in other European countries is different; there is often a greater emphasis on preventative and therapeutic services, even where children may be being seriously harmed, rather than taking legal action against families. Even when the courts do become involved, this may be in a more conciliatory way than the adversarial approach that is dominant in the UK and other English-speaking countries. There is a greater emphasis on residential care, and on links between social work and education, via 'social pedagogy'. Although social work theory and practice in the past have tended to look more to the English-speaking world to share ideas, it is important to learn from our European neighbours too. The second historical moment which has governed the ways in which children's services are provided was the Children Act 1989 in England and Wales, and the equivalent legislation in Scotland, the Children (Scotland) Act 1995 and the Children (Northern Ireland) Order 1995 in Northern Ireland.

The Children Act 1989 and equivalent legislation in the devolved UK nations

The Children Act 1989 was, according to the Lord Chancellor at the time, 'the most comprehensive and far-reaching reform of child law which has come before Parliament in living memory'.[1] There have of course been many new laws since then, but it remains the foundation of child care law in England and Wales, and its basic principles are still applied to a large extent throughout the UK.

The act applies to England and Wales and came into force in 1991. The Children (Scotland) Act 1995 and the Children (Northern Ireland) Order 1995 were based on similar principles, although Scotland has always had its own legal system, and in this particular context uses the 'children's hearing system', currently governed by the Children's Hearings (Scotland) Act 2011.

The Children (Northern Ireland) Order 1995 is in many respects identical to the Children Act, but also includes provisions relating to child employment, unmarried parents and guardianship.[2]

Several shared core principles underpin the legislation introduced in this period. They may be summarised as

- Prevention
- Parental responsibility
- Presumption of no order
- Paramountcy
- Participation

First, the aim is to prevent children coming into care as long as to do so is in their best interests. This means that the state has an obligation to support parents to care for children at home.

Second, the state has an obligation to respect the role of parents. Parental responsibility cannot be taken away from a parent except by a legal process such as adoption, freeing for adoption or a permanence order (in Scotland). Parents who separate or divorce, or whose children go into care, retain their responsibility, and their right, to remain involved in their children's lives.

The presumption of no order means that the court should not make any order regarding the care of children unless this is positively better for the child than making no order at all. There is also a 'presumption of contact', which means that contact is normally in the interests of children and should be positively promoted when a child is separated from parents and other family members, unless there are good and specific reasons to the contrary.

In considering cases, the court is governed by the paramountcy principle, which is that the child's welfare overrides all other considerations. In determining this, the court must have regard to the 'welfare checklist', summarised here as:

a the wishes and feelings of the child;
b the child's physical, emotional and educational needs;
c the likely effect on the child of any change in their circumstances;
d the child's age, sex, background and any characteristics considered relevant;
e any harm which the child has suffered or is at risk of suffering;
f how capable the parents and others are of meeting the child's needs; and
g the range of powers available to the court.[3]

Another important aspect of court decision making is that the state must give due regard to the participation of children and parents in court processes, including receiving information, being consulted on plans and having their views recorded). Professionals who overlook these rights can be found to be in breach of the Human Rights Act 1998.

The Children Act 1989 brought together in one statutory framework the public law regarding state services to children and child protection and the private law that governs family life and disputes over children's upbringing. This made it possible for courts to make decisions about children in complex cases without some of the confusion that arose in the past and ensured that where children are placed compulsorily in state care this is done under the same rules and principles in all cases. At the same time, the Act reformed the duties and powers of local authorities to children and families and the ways in which services were provided, especially when children are looked after away from home.

While the core principles of the child care legislation of the 1990s remain relevant today, the legislation in all jurisdictions has been amended and updated since then. Brief updates on the current legal and policy frameworks in the devolved four nations are provided next, before then moving on to consider the main themes of the legislation including: private law and family disputes; public law and support for children and families; public law and intervening to remove children from their families; caring for children away from home and adoption.

Current legal frameworks in the devolved UK nations

In *England*, the Children and Young Persons Act 2008 extends the legal framework and obligations for children in care in England and Wales. It aims to improve the stability of placements and the educational experience and attainment of children and young people in care and leaving care. Provisions included the requirement for Independent Reviewing Officers (previously introduced on an optional basis) whose role is to chair reviews and planning meetings and scrutinise care plans for looked after children, for schools to have a designated member of staff with the responsibility to promote the educational achievement of children in care, and a duty to provide further education and training to children and young people in its care. The Children and Families Act 2014 addresses many broad issues relating to children and families, but in particular it enabled children to stay with their foster carers until they are 21 years old, rather than having to move at 18 years. The Children and Social Work Act 2017 introduced the principles of corporate parenting referred to in an earlier chapter. There is also new guidance and regulations on care planning (The Care Planning, Placement and Case Review (England) (Amendment) Regulations 2021).

In *Wales*, the Social Services and Well-being (Wales) Act 2014 is concerned with the well-being of all those who need care and support – adults, children and carers of all ages. It defines well-being, introduces outcomes against which improved well-being is to be measured, and outlines the duties of local authorities in relation to these. Although the Children Act 1989 still applies, the more recent Social Services and Well-being (Wales) Act 2014 replaces Part III of the Children Act 1989 and is enacted by the Senedd. This Act provides for the assessment of needs for care and support, the provision of services and related financial arrangements. Part Six deals with duties to looked after children, including arrangements for their accommodation, care planning, review, family contact and leaving care, supported by the Care Planning, Placement and Case Review (Wales) Regulations 2015 and the Care Leavers (Wales) Regulations 2015.

In *Northern Ireland*, as noted, new legislation passed in 2022 is currently being implemented. Some regulations and guidance have been previously amended, for example guidance on children in private fostering arrangements (DHSSPS, 2011), the Standards for Leaving Care Services (DHSSPS, 2012) and minimum standards for kinship care (DHSSPS, 2019), but naturally, given the implementation of the new legislation, further new regulations and guidance are expected.

The Adoption and Children Act (Northern Ireland) 2022 updates adoption legislation and extends and strengthens the services and provisions of the Children (Northern Ireland) Order 1995. For example, its provisions include extending the supports available for adults formerly in care, if they are engaged in training and education, from 24 years to 25 years. It also places a scheme that enables young people to live with their foster carers until they are 21 years old, on a statutory footing and introduces another route to permanency – the special guardianship order. At the time of writing, in 2023, the new Act is being implemented.

In *Scotland*, the Children and Young People (Scotland) Act 2014 sets out the duties of corporate parenting and introduces further provisions to better ensure permanence planning for looked after children. It was followed by the strategy document 'Getting It Right For Looked After Children and Young People' (Scottish Government, 2015), part of the overarching strategy *Getting It Right for Every Child*, which the 2014 Act put on a statutory basis.

Having outlined the devolved nations' specific legal frameworks, we now consider the main themes covered by the legislation and the governance of those, beginning first with private law and family disputes.

Private law and family disputes

The Children Act 1989, together with the Children (Northern Ireland) Order 1995 and the Children (Scotland) Act 1995, provides for disputes between parents and other relatives to be settled under the principles outlined above. The assumption is that children's upbringing will in most cases be a matter of agreement between those involved, without the need for legal intervention. In the last few years, there has been a concerted effort by courts to encourage families to settle disputes involving children outside of court, for several reasons. First, there are significant financial costs either to the family or to the state if the family acquire legal aid. Second, there are significant emotional and psychological costs to the children because decisions may not be reached quickly and in acrimonious situations children can become embroiled in the relationship difficulties of their parents, causing stress and other impacts. Third, the volume of business received by courts has increased meaning delays in hearings.

As a result, it is now expected that where possible families have undergone mediation in an attempt to reach agreement so that there is no need for their case to come to court. The court therefore only becomes involved if the parties cannot agree and one of them applies for an order to be made. In England, Wales and Northern Ireland, the following orders are available.

- *A residence order*, which determines with whom the child is to live, or a *contact order*, which requires that person to allow contact between the child and someone else (in England and Wales these orders are now combined as a 'child arrangements order');
- *A prohibited steps order*, which prevents the person with the care of the child from doing certain things which they might otherwise do in their role as a parent;
- *A specific issue order*, which enables the court to resolve a specific issue by a particular order, without disturbing other arrangements for the child's upbringing.

These orders are also available to a court in care proceedings, which means that they can sometimes be used as alternatives to committing a child to care (see below). A broadly similar range of orders are available in Scotland, although the terminology is different.

It is also important to note that these provisions, especially regarding residence and contact, interface strongly with legislation regarding domestic violence and abuse. For example, in Northern Ireland, the Family Homes and Domestic Violence (Northern Ireland) Order 1998 updated Article 12 of the Children (NI) Order 1995 by making it a legal requirement, when the court is considering making a residence or contact order in favour of a prohibited person, 'the court shall consider whether the child has suffered or is at risk of suffering any harm through seeing or hearing ill-treatment of another person by the prohibited person'. The same legislation also updated Article 57, Children (NI) Order 1995, to give the courts the power to add an exclusion requirement into the making of an interim care order. This excludes a person when there are grounds to believe that a child has suffered or is likely to suffer significant harm in the presence of the person, if not excluded. Harm includes exposure to domestic violence and abuse.

In England and Wales, the Domestic Abuse Act 2021 explicitly recognises children as victims of domestic violence if they see, hear or experience the effects of the abuse and gives the courts powers to respond. In Scotland, as noted by Burman et al. (2022, p. 5),

> Growing awareness of the nature and impact of domestic abuse is reflected to some extent in the explicit statutory obligations, introduced by the Family Law (Scotland) Act 2006, on the civil courts to consider domestic abuse in the context of actions for child contact.

Public law and support for children and families

In keeping with the principles of the Human Rights Act 1998 and the UNCRC (1989), UK child care law makes explicit the obligation to provide family support services (including financial support, practical support and other types of service) to children defined in the Children Act 1989 and the Children (NI) Order 1995 as a 'child in need'. This refers to any child who is unlikely to achieve or maintain a reasonable standard of health or development without the provision of services by the local authority, or whose health or development is likely to be significantly impaired without the provision of services, or who is disabled, is 'in need' for the purposes of the legislation.

Local authorities (or Health and Social Care Trusts in Northern Ireland) have a range of duties in relation to every child in need, and to their family. There is a general duty to safeguard and promote the welfare of such children, and 'so far as is consistent with that duty', to promote their upbringing by their families, by providing a range and level of services appropriate to their needs. The importance of the family is recognised in the Preamble to the UNCRC, where it is described as 'the fundamental group of society and the natural environment for the growth and well-being of all its members and particularly children'. The UNCRC also recognises the importance of parents, who are described as having 'primary responsibility' for their child's development (Article 18) and 'to secure, within their abilities and financial capacities, the conditions of living necessary for the child's development' (Article 27). Their role is outlined in Articles 5 and 7 for example. The UNCRC also acknowledges that parents may need support to meet their responsibilities and duties and that "the family […] should be afforded the necessary protection and assistance so that it can fully assume its responsibilities within the community" (Preamble).

These provisions are reflected in UK child care law, with duties that include assessing children's needs, preventing neglect and abuse, providing a range of specific services and providing accommodation if it is necessary for the child's welfare. The focus on children in need and family support, with a clear definition of a 'child in need', was one of a number of changes in concepts and terminology. The legislation drew a distinction between 'care' following a court order and 'accommodation' provided with parental consent and on a voluntary basis. Under this arrangement, a parent retains full parental responsibility and can take back the full parenting role when they wish to. It was hoped that this would make it clear that providing accommodation could be a positive and constructive way to support children and families, rather than a last resort. In so doing it sought to reduce the perceived stigma of reception into care, by changing the terminology and by dealing with parents' understandable fears that if they put their children in care voluntarily it might be hard to get them back. These aspirations clearly reflect both the Human Rights Act 1998 (respect for private and family life) and the Articles of the UNCRC that underscore the importance of the role of parent(s) and the obligation to provide support. Accommodation of children is a positive and supportive option, for example, where a parent might need to go to hospital for an operation or where short breaks are provided for parent(s)/carer(s) when they are caring for a child with additional needs and require respite, for example.

Under Section 20 of the Children Act 1989 in England, Section 21 of the Children (Northern Ireland) Order 1995, Section 25 of the Children (Scotland) Act 1995 and Section 76 of the Social Services and Well-Being (Wales) Act 2014, a local authority (or Health and Social Care Trust in Northern Ireland) has a duty to provide accommodation for any child in need in their area who appears to require it because there is no one with parental responsibility, because the child is lost or abandoned, or because the person with parental responsibility is prevented 'for whatever reason' from providing suitable accommodation or care. This normally requires the agreement of someone with parental responsibility, but a child who is aged 16 years or over can agree to be accommodated in his or her own right.

Another route to accommodation, under the Children (Scotland) Act 1995, is the kinship care order (KCO) Section 11. Under this order, the court grants the kinship carers parental rights and responsibilities, which are shared between the parents and the kinship carers. The Sheriff before making this decision will seek to determine that all parties are agreed.

More broadly, other routes that might lead to a child being accommodated are if they are remanded by the court, are subject to an emergency protection order (see below) or have been taken into police protection. In these cases, it is not necessary for the child or parents to agree to accommodation being provided – they have little choice. There is also a power given to local authorities to provide accommodation for any child if this would safeguard or promote the child's welfare. Voluntary organisations may also accommodate children, in which case their duties are the same as those of a local authority.

Public law and intervening to remove children from families

The legislation also clearly defines the basis on which children can be removed from their parents, enabling children to be protected when they are at risk of harm, as well as when they have actually suffered harm. This includes provision for emergency intervention and assessment of children thought to be at risk. Orders made under this part of the act include emergency protection orders and assessment orders. They are short-term orders and do not mean that a child is 'in care', although the child may be accommodated for a short period.

In Scotland, in emergency situations, a child protection order (CPO) is applied for under the Children's Hearings (Scotland) Act 2011. The local authority applies to a sheriff for the CPO. The CPO is similar to the emergency protection order in England and Wales, in that it only lasts for a few days, is followed by an interim hearing to make longer term plans and can involve removing a child to a place of safety or keeping them where they are or demanding that the child is 'produced' if they cannot be located because of parental non-cooperation.

In England and Wales, Part IV of the Children Act 1989, and for Northern Ireland, Part V of the Children (Northern Ireland) Order 1995 relate to 'care and supervision' of children. These set out the circumstances in which children may be removed from their families or the powers of parents restricted, and the process by which this may be done. This can only happen if the court is satisfied that the child is suffering or likely to suffer significant harm and that the harm is attributable to the care given to the child not being what it would be reasonable to expect a parent to give to him, or to the child being beyond control. 'Harm' is defined as ill-treatment or the impairment of health or development.

Once these threshold criteria have been established, care proceedings become 'family proceedings' and the court has several options at its disposal regarding the future care of a child. Options include the making of a care order; this involves the local authority or Health and Social Care Trust acquiring parental responsibility (which they share with the actual parents) and making a plan for the care of the child. This could include the child remaining at home, being placed in foster care or residential care, or being adopted. A care order can remain in place until a child is 18 years old. It can be revoked by the court if no longer deemed necessary or replaced by another order.

In Scotland, under the Children's Hearings (Scotland) Act 2011, a compulsory supervision order (CSO) can be applied for. The Children's Hearing Act decides the suitability of this, having listened to all the facts and established agreement between all involved parties that the Grounds for Referral (similar to threshold criteria) have been accepted. Once the CSO is made, it can last a year without being reviewed, but it can also be revoked and reviewed within three months of it being made, if so requested. Parental rights and responsibilities remain with the parents, but this order grants the Local Authority the mandate to oversee and intervene with the exercise of these.

All the legal options outlined above reflect the principles of the UNCRC, in particular Article 3 (best interest of the child), Article 6 (a child's right to life, survival and development), Article 9 (a child should not be separated from parents unless deemed in their best interests) and Article 19 (a child's right to protection from violence, injury, abuse, neglect, maltreatment or exploitation).

Children's representation in public law proceedings

In public law proceedings in all jurisdictions, children have access to legal representation. In Northern Ireland, Children's Court Guardians are appointed in all cases that come before court. The Children's Court Guardians work for the Children's Court Guardian Agency for Northern Ireland and are independent of social services. Similarly in Wales, CAFCASS Cymru and in England, CAFCASS, provide representation for children involved in the court system. In Scotland, there is no equivalent system, but the role of the Children's Reporter is central in speaking with children, representing their views and ensuring the progress of the case. Children can sometimes also access free legal help and can access the Scottish Child Law Centre. In England and Wales, to ensure timely progress of a child's case through court, the Public Law Outline sets out the duties Local Authorities have when thinking of making an application regarding a child. Importantly, the Public Law Outline sets out to ensure partnership with parents, making it a duty for Local Authorities to ensure that they have shared their concerns with parents in a clear and accessible way and given time and support for parents to address the concerns. This is known as pre-proceedings work. The Public Law Outline also sets out to protect parents and children by a timeline for the completion of the case in the court process which should occur within 26 weeks. In Northern Ireland, the equivalent is the Case Management in Public Law proceedings outline, which also stresses the vital role played by pre-proceedings work but this does not specify a time limited for the progress of the case through court.

Newer ways of managing court proceedings

Associated with court proceedings, there have been recent attempts to change usual ways of doing things and to prevent admissions to care through court proceedings. One development is the Family Drug and Alcohol Courts (FDAC). First piloted in London in 2008, the aim of these courts is to provide a package of regularly reviewed multi-disciplinary support (including psychiatry, mental health, and social work, for example) to parents as part of pre-proceedings and/or during an application for a care order, to enable the parents to address addiction issues whilst continuing to care for their children in this supported environment. The FDAC multi-disciplinary team works independently of the Local Authority social work team and the supervision of their work is Judge led. This approach both minimises risk to the child(ren) whilst simultaneously providing the best possible interventions to support parents to address addiction issues that impact on their parenting capacity. It is based on a strengths-based approach characterised by a belief in the possibility that parents can overcome their difficulties. At the time of writing a report by Foundations (2023a) points out that there are 15 FDAC covering 36 Local Authorities in England and pilots in Wales and Northern Ireland have also been undertaken. A multi-site randomised controlled trial evaluation carried out concluded that 'outcomes are better among families in the FDAC group compared to the comparison group', that 'children with a primary carer in FDAC proceedings were four times more likely to be reunified with their primary carer in comparison to children with a primary carer in non-FDAC care proceedings' and that 'that parents in FDAC were four times more likely to stop misusing alcohol or drugs by the end of care proceedings relative to parents in non-FDAC care proceedings'. Qualitative data revealed that factors including a more supportive and gentle process (in court the court proceedings), a unique package of support, judge led supervision and a problem-solving approach were all significant for those involved.

Another development is Family Group Conferences. Family Group Conferences provide the opportunity for family and extended family members to come together to develop their own plan to address issues identified by professionals. Families are referred to the family group conference service in pre-proceedings (before) or during court proceedings and a coordinator is appointed. Their job is to help families plan for the conference making sure they are aware of the issues and the decisions that need to be made. Preparation steps include securing the family's agreement that a family group conference is going to be held, involving the child, agreeing who is to be invited, agreeing the practical arrangements (where, when, transport and so on), meeting people, and ensuring participants have advocates if needed. The plan is agreed by participants and its implementation reviewed. If the Family Group Conference has been held as part of court proceedings, the plan must be presented to the court for approval. The approach is designed to prevent children from coming into care and to rely more on the strengths, problem solving abilities and social, practical resources from within the families to address their own issues. A report completed by Foundations (2023) which included a randomised controlled trial (RCT), process evaluation and cost analysis, found that at the pre-proceedings stage, those families who were referred to Family Group Conferences were less likely to be in care one year later (36%) compared to those not referred (45%). They also found that the children involved had spent significantly less time in care six months later (87 days, on average) compared to those not referred (115 days, on average) and that care proceedings were less likely to have been issued (59%) compared to those not referred (72%).

Both developments are therefore significant in the management of cases that might end up in public law proceedings. Clearly for these developments to be fully embedded has significant resource implications.

Caring for children away from home

The legislation across the UK outlines the legal status of and the care options for children living away from home. Social workers will be involved with children in various types of placement, including kinship foster care, non-relative foster care, residential care, secure units, hospitals and pre-adoptive placements. The children may be the subject of different legal options including emergency protection orders, police protection orders, interim care orders, full care orders, residence orders, special guardianship orders, supervision orders, compulsory supervision orders (only in Scotland) and child protection orders (only in Scotland). These are further outlined in Chapter 7.

The legislation also outlines social workers' duties and issues regarding planning, reviewing and decision-making regarding children in care. The aim of the legislation and associated regulations and guidance is to improve the quality and rigour of planning and decision making in relation to children being looked after away from home. It establishes the rights of children and parents to participate, that is to be informed, consulted, involved and given the opportunity to express their views, and to make representations and complaints. These reforms were inspired in part by research in the 1970s and 1980s which showed how poor existing decision-making processes often were in these respects.

Underpinning much of the thinking behind the children's legislation, though not mentioned in those terms, was the idea of *partnership* – between parents, between professionals, and above all between families and agencies. Some of the basic definitions and provisions are outlined below.

Duties to 'looked after' children

A child who is either in care under some form of court order, or accommodated as a child in need, has the status of a 'looked after' child. The local authority or Trust has a duty to promote the child's welfare and to ensure that the child is provided with accommodation suitable to their needs. This accommodation may be provided by the local authority directly or by other people under supervision. Children 'looked after' can be living at home with their parents under supervision, but in general they are living with foster carers, in children's homes or supported in kinship care.

The authority has other important duties to children whom they look after: to consult the child, parents and others whose wishes and feelings are relevant before making any decision; to take account of 'the child's religious persuasion, racial origin and cultural and linguistic background' in making decisions; to place and maintain the child in a family, in a community home or in another suitable placement; to place the child near to her or his home and with her or his siblings, as far as practicable and consistent with the child's interests; to ensure that accommodation provided for a disabled child is 'not unsuitable'; to 'advise, assist and befriend' the child in order to promote her or his welfare on leaving care, and then to provide aftercare; to review the child's case at regular intervals; and to hear any complaints and representations from the child, parents or carers. A child's liberty cannot be restricted except when authorised by a court or in a specific emergency.

Planning and reviewing

The children's legislation that was introduced into the UK sought to reform the whole process of planning and decision making for children and young people in care. It does this mainly through regulations which are jurisdiction specific and which have been updated on several occasions. These require that any child being looked after should be subject to 'arrangements' and they also specify what should be included in these arrangements and how they are to be agreed. In particular, it is made clear that the arrangements must be based on a *plan* that takes account of a child's health, education, identity, self-esteem and emotional well-being and family relationships. The plan must be based on a thorough assessment and must be based on consultation with and inclusion of the views of the child and the family. Regulations also specify the arrangements for monitoring the child's progress and reviewing the plan. They spell out how often reviews are to take place, who is to be involved, and how decisions are to be recorded.

Leaving care and after care

Leaving care is acknowledged as a challenge for many young people and for many years was a neglected area of provision, only partly addressed in the Children Act 1989. This has been redressed to some extent in legislation, regulations and guidance in all four nations that aims to improve services for care leavers, by extending the duties and powers of local authorities and health and social care trusts. Following reform, the core provision in England and Wales is the Children (Leaving Care) Act 2000 (since amended and updated by the Children and Social Work Act 2017 and the Social Services and Well-being (Wales) Act 2014), while in Scotland it is the Children and Young People (Scotland) Act 2014 and in Northern Ireland, the Children (Leaving Care) Act (Northern Ireland) 2002, further amended by the Adoption and Children Act (Northern Ireland) 2022. These reforms are discussed more fully in Chapter 10.

The law governing adoption

Adoption, because it involves irrevocable changes to parenting relationships and children's status in families, is often dealt with under legislation that is separate and distinct from that governing other aspects of child welfare. This is the case in all jurisdictions in the UK.

In England and Wales, the first Adoption Act was introduced in 1926. It was reformed by the Children Act 1975 and the Adoption Act 1976, and more recently by the Adoption and Children Act 2002; in Scotland, the equivalent is the Adoption and Children (Scotland) Act 2007. This legislation puts a duty on local authorities to provide an adoption service, prescribes the adoption process, the status of adopted children, adoption support plans and permanence orders. In Northern Ireland, the Adoption and Children Act (Northern Ireland) 2022 reformed adoption services with the aim of improving the identification, assessment and support of adoptive carers. At the time of writing in 2023, it is being implemented.

Translating law and policy into practice

In opening this chapter, we emphasised the individual responsibility on social workers with children and families to understand the law relating to this area of practice, and the policies associated with it, and to use professional judgement and professional standards in applying this to actual cases within a framework of agency policy and procedure (see Figure 5.1).

This is of course not the only mechanism by which law and government policy are translated into practice. Agencies such as local authorities and charitable organisations also have systems for ensuring that their working practices reflect the law. Agencies have their own 'take' on what are the most important imperatives to follow, and sometimes on the interpretation they give to the law – as do individual social workers, inevitably.

Governments also have their own view of what are the most important priorities and on how best to apply the law in practice. In recent years, governments have increasingly adopted explicit strategies to make sure that the policy imperatives that drive legislation are implemented in agency practice. Social work and social policy in Britain have been characterised by a series of initiatives, as central government becomes more proactive in driving the direction in which services develop and the priorities that are set, and in attempting to improve the perceived quality of practice. In the chapters that follow, we will look at the practical and theoretical implications of some of these initiatives.

Relationships with other agencies

Although much of this discussion has been about social work, ours is never a service that can work in isolation from other agencies and professions. In providing care and support for children and young people, it is essential to work closely with health and education services, and also with police, probation, youth service agencies, community development agencies, housing, the benefits agency and a range of other agencies. These services also have their own distinctive legal powers and duties, and a shared understanding of these is essential to working effectively in collaboration.

As we said in Chapter 2, one of the principles underlying this book is to understand and work with children and young people in a holistic way – not, for instance putting their care, health and education needs into separate compartments. When the law supports this approach, it is helpful of course, but even when it does not, it is the responsibility of all professionals working with children and young people to see that they do their best individually and collectively to follow this holistic approach.

Summary and conclusion

We have seen how the law is a crucial underpinning for social work practice with children and families, providing the framework within which services are planned and delivered and the authority for intervention. We have also seen that the law is the result of social and political processes, and reflects prevailing assumptions – for instance, about the relationship between families and the state and about the status of children. We have looked at the assumptions underlying child care law in the UK, at the objectives of current legislation and at the framework it provides for the care of children and young people. Some of the specifics of this legislation are considered in more detail in later chapters, particularly in relation to leaving care and to adoption. Finally, we looked briefly at the process of translating law and policy into practice, and at the relationships between social work and other professions. It is important to remember that as social workers, we can never operate in isolation from the rest of society or from other agencies and disciplines. At the same time, we have to take responsibility for our own professional judgement and ethical conduct, and for the way in which we work with vulnerable young people and their families.

GUIDE TO FURTHER READING

On social work law in general there are a number of useful British texts – for example Brammer (2020), Carr and Goosey (2021) and Johns (2020). For Scotland, see Guthrie (2018) and for social work in Wales, Livingston, Redcliffe and Quinn (2023).

For child care law specifically, useful practical guides are as follows: For Scotland, Plumtree (2014), for England, Conroy-Harris and Cullen (2019), for Wales, Conroy-Harris and Cullen (2021) and for Northern Ireland, a book by Long (2018). As yet, there is no updated book featuring the latest legal developments in Northern Ireland.

For adoption law in Scotland, we recommend Smith, Stewart and Stobie (2011). For adoption law in England and Wales, we recommend Pearce and Budworth (2020). For Northern Ireland, it is Long (2002). The significant changes in adoption legislation in Northern Ireland under the new Adoption and Children Act (Northern Ireland) 2022 will undoubtedly be reflected in forthcoming publications.

For readers interested in learning more about European law and policy, Petrie et al. (2006) provide a good start point. For international perspectives, Devaney and Crosse (2023) introduces the reader to wide-ranging perspectives.

For a brief account of the development of child care services, Hayden (1999) is useful. For a more extended and analytical approach, Featherstone et al. (2014, 2018) and Fernandez and Delfabbro (2020) offer excellent insights. On the relationship between law and policy, the seminal text by Fox Harding (1997) remains a good place to start.

Notes

1 https://api.parliament.uk/historic-hansard/lords/1988/dec/06/children-bill-hl
2 Because the devolved Assembly has not functioned consistently for political reasons, proposed amendments to children's legislation which would reflect subsequent changes in the law elsewhere in the UK have, at the time of writing, been delayed.
3 Children Act 1989, Section 1(3).

References

Brammer, A. (2020) *Social work law*. London: Pearson Education Limited.

Burman, M., Friskney, R., Mair, J. and Whitecross, R. (2022) *Domestic abuse and child contact: the interface between criminal and civil proceedings*. Glasgow: University of Glasgow and Edinburgh Napier University.

Canavan, J., Pinkerton, J. and Dolan, P. (2016) *Understanding family support: Policy, practice, and theory*. London: Jessica Kingsley Publishers.

Carr, H. and Goosey, D. (2021) *Law for social workers*. Oxford: Oxford University Press.

Conroy-Harris, A. and Cullen, D. (2019) *Child care law – England*. London: Coram BAAF.

Conroy-Harris, A. and Cullen, D. (2021) *Child care law – Wales*. London: Coram BAAF.

Devaney, C. and Crosse, R. (eds.) (2023) *International perspectives on parenting support and parental participation in children and family services* (first edition). London: Routledge.

Featherstone, B., Gupta, A., Morris, K. and White, S. (2018) *Protecting children: A social model*. Bristol: Policy Press.

Featherstone, B., Morris, K. and White, S. (2014) *Re-imagining child protection: Towards humane social work with families*. Bristol: Policy Press.

Fernandez, E. and Delfabbro, P. (eds.) (2020) *Child protection and the care continuum: Theoretical, empirical and practice insights* (first edition). London: Routledge.

Foundations. What Works Centre for Children and Families (2023a) *Implications for policy and practice. Family group conferences*. Available here https://foundations.org.uk/wp-content/uploads/2023/06/Family-Group-Conferencing-Implications-for-Policy-and-practice.pdf

Foundations. What Works Centre for Children and Families (2023) *Evaluation of family drug and alcohol courts*. Available here https://foundations.org.uk/wp-content/uploads/2023/08/FDAC-report.pdf

Fox Harding, L. (1997) *Perspectives in child care policy*. Abingdon: Routledge.

Guthrie, T.G. (2018) *Social work law in Scotland* (fourth edition). London: Bloomsbury Publishing.

Hayden, C. (1999) *State child care: Looking after children?* London: Jessica Kingsley Publishers.

Johns, R. (2020) *Using the law in social work*. Exeter: Learning Matters, Sage.

Livingston, W., Redcliffe, J. and Quinn, A. (2023) *Social work in Wales*. Bristol: Policy Press.

Long, M. (2002) *The law of adoption in Northern Ireland: The annotated legislation*. Belfast: SLS Legal Publications.

Long, M. (2018) *Child care law – Northern Ireland*. London: CoramBAAF.

MacDonald, M. and Dunn, H. (2023) *Social work and family support*. Belfast: Department of Health/Office of Social Services.

Pearce, N. and Budworth, R. (2020) *Adoption law: A practical guide*. London: Wildy, Simmonds and Hill Publishing.

Petrie, P., Boddy, J., Cameron, C., Simon, A. and Wigfall, V. (2006) *Working with children in residential care: European perspectives*. Buckingham: Open University Press.

Plumtree, A. (2014) *Child care law Scotland: A summary of the law in Scotland* (sixth edition). London: CoramBAAF.

Smith, F., Stewart, R. and Stobie, A. (2011) *Adoption and Children (Scotland) Act 2007*. London: CoramBAAF.

Walsh, J., White, S., Morris, K. and Doherty, P. (2019) 'How do you solve a problem like Maria? Family complexity and institutional complications in UK social work', *European Journal of Social Work*, 22(6), 1050–1061.

Winter, K. (2009) 'Relationships matter: The problems and prospects for social workers' relationships with young children in care', *Child & Family Social Work*, *14*(4), 450–460.

Winter, K., Connolly, P., Millen, S. and Sweet, D. (2022) 'The UNCRC and family support: A case study of the early intervention support service', *Child Care in Practice*, 1–15. DOI: 10.1080/13575279.2022.2088473

6

ASSESSMENT AND PLANNING

CONTENTS OF CHAPTER

- Introduction
- Why and when do we assess?
- What do we assess?
- Processes of assessment and planning
- What is in a plan?
- Frameworks that inform assessment and planning
- Summary and conclusion
- Guide to further reading

Introduction

Assessment is acknowledged to be a core aspect of social work practice (Milner et al., 2020; Horwath and Platt, 2019; Holland, 2011). There is a growing interest about how and why social workers make the decisions they do and therefore there has been increased attention given to the reasons why assessments are undertaken, their content, the process of completing an assessment, and the factors that impact decisions made following the assessment (Milner et al., 2020; Killick and Taylor, 2024). This chapter focuses on these elements.

Social work assessments of families and children have several characteristics. First, they are not undertaken in a vacuum; they have context. To explain further, each assessment – its content, process and outcomes – is influenced by a combination of intrapersonal factors related to the child, the carers and the social worker, interpersonal factors (relationships and communication

DOI: 10.4324/9781003503194-6

between the child, family and social worker), organisational factors including social workers' time, resources and tools, and wider social structural factors. Decisions may be influenced by moral and political principles as to what is deemed appropriate for society to provide, and by economic factors that determine what resources are made available. Decisions may also be influenced by the social class and status of the child or young person, their age or gender, or the reasons why they need care.

Second, assessments are affected by the values, assumptions and biases of social workers. Various writers (Taylor, 2017; Rutter and Brown, 2019; McCafferty and Taylor, 2020; McCafferty, 2022) emphasise the need for social workers to be clear about their intentions, explicit about their assumptions and systematic in their approach to data collection, to think theoretically and clarify and test hypotheses rigorously, to be honest about their values and to engage with all individuals and listen to how they understand their own worlds.

Third, assessments are dynamic, contextual and contingent and evolve over time. An assessment needs to be continually updated for it to be effective. Given the contextual and subjective nature of assessments, their success relies a lot on social workers' ability and skills – to do assessments *with* children and carers rather than *about* or *on* them.

Fourth, there are established assessment frameworks to guide social work practice in this area. The main one (described in further detail later in the chapter), developed over 20 years ago, is the 'Framework for the Assessment of Children in Need and their Families' (Department of Health et al., 2000), with its focus on child development domains and the wider context of the child. It was accompanied by practice tools (Department of Health et al., 2000) and is still used today.

In focusing on assessment, the purpose of this chapter is to provide a generic overview of the process of assessment, the steps involved and to address basic questions such as:

- Why and when we assess – roles and responsibilities to assess.
- What we assess – content of assessments and associated models.
- How we assess – the stages, processes and frameworks.
- What outcomes we are hoping to achieve – impact of assessments.

We will maintain a strong emphasis on the involvement of children and young people in decisions about their care, as well as on social workers' partnerships with families and with a range of professionals and service providers. This chapter forms the foundation for subsequent chapters which consider detailed aspects of the assessment process in relation to specific aspects of the journey into care, being in care and leaving care.

Why and when do we assess?

In children's legislation in the UK, it is required that assessments are carried out where there is a concern about risk to the child of abuse or neglect, and a concern about the welfare, safety and wellbeing of the child concerned. These assessments must be carried out whether or not the family concerned has agreed. Other assessments can be carried out because families are seeking help, support and advice from social services and request or agree to an assessment. Some of these assessments are carried out by social workers, but other professionals from health and education can also take the lead.

Social worker assessments with families and children therefore have two purposes; to identify risks and to identify needs. With regard to risk, sometimes these are all too apparent and decisions have to be taken quickly without waiting for a full assessment. Sometimes key information pertaining to the assessment of risk/need is not available when we need it, and so has to be fitted into the picture later. This might impact on how long it takes a social worker to complete an assessment. That said, regulatory frameworks indicate that assessments should be completed in a timely fashion. Where there is a concern about child abuse and neglect, the assessment should be carried out within ten days. Where the assessment is on the basis of informing support needs, these should be carried out within 45 days.

What do we assess?

Assessment is a dynamic process that involves constantly testing assumptions and hypotheses regarding both needs and risks in the light of emerging understanding. The official government guidance in England and Wales (2018, para 51, p. 27) states:

> Assessment should be a dynamic process, which analyses and responds to the changing nature and level of need and/or risk faced by the child from within and outside their family.

This means that assessment should focus on the child, their family and the wider context in which the family is situated including their neighbourhood, community and wider society.

Reflecting this, the official guidance on social work assessments in England and Wales notes the myriad of risks that children and young people may be exposed to:

> Children may be vulnerable to neglect and abuse or exploitation from within their family and from individuals they come across in their day-to-day lives. These threats can take a variety of different forms, including: sexual,

> physical and emotional abuse; neglect; domestic abuse, including controlling or coercive behaviour; exploitation by criminal gangs and organised crime groups; trafficking; online abuse; sexual exploitation and the influences of extremism leading to radicalisation.
>
> *HM Government (2018, para 12, p. 9)*

Risks and needs are therefore dynamic, contextual and contingent. They can be chronic and they can also cause instant and extreme impact on a child's development and wellbeing. For example, substance misuse combined with domestic violence and abuse can cause instant and extreme impact on the needs of a new born baby because of the threats to physical safety from the violence and also the child's lack of consistent, regular access to food caused by erratic parental response to the child's hunger. Risks can also have a longer-term and cumulative impact on children's needs, their health and development, such as lack of stimulation.

As highlighted above, when assessing the significance and impact of risk, it is important to consider it *within the context* of the *specific needs* of *this individual child*. For example, while the identified risk might be parental alcohol dependency, the relevance and significance of this will vary depending on the individual child. Here the age of the child, any known disability, the main language of the child, their degree of connectedness with family, neighbourhood and community can all influence the severity, significance and impact of the risk. Hence, as noted in an earlier chapter, by using a specific framework that defines children's needs, it should be possible to evaluate how, and how well, these needs are currently being met within the family and the community. And, of course, to highlight any unmet need.

It is clear that the process of assessing needs and risks involves not just identifying the need/risks but weighing up their significance, analysing information – looking beyond the 'what' to explore the 'why' and the 'how'. Whilst we do not start an assessment by assuming that alternative care arrangements will need to be made, and whilst we have an appreciation of family, neighbourhood and community support (Canavan et al., 2016), we also need to be mindful that families can be dangerous places for some children and that not everything is as it might first appear.

Having considered broad key messages in this section (reflecting key texts such as Holland, 2011; Horwath and Platt, 2019; Dyke, 2023), we will now consider in more detail the process of what we are assessing, how and why, under the following themes:

- the individual child or young person;
- strengths and resources of the immediate and extended family;
- strengths and resources of the community or neighbourhood;
- social structural issues;

- ability of the family and community to meet the child's needs; and
- ability of agencies to meet the child's needs.

The individual child or young person

Every assessment of risk or need starts with a consideration of the individual child or young person who is its subject – their situation, personality, preferences, views, experiences, characteristics and needs. As highlighted in previous chapters, children – like adults – are experts on their own lives; they usually know more about their own lives than anyone else, and they have usually spent more time thinking about their own lives than has anyone else. This is consistent with an approach to assessment that seeks to do it *with* children rather than *to* them. Indeed, in the recent English guidance regarding assessments (HM Government, 2018), it is stated that:

> high quality assessments are child centred…(and) involve children, ensuring that their voice is heard and provide appropriate support to enable this where the child has specific communication needs.
>
> *(para 58, pp. 28–29)*

Hence, from the start, it is important to be clear that putting children at the centre of assessments is a basic expectation, not a luxury 'add-on' (O'Reilly and Dolan, 2016). Because the focus is on the child, the child should be involved in the assessment throughout. This requires us to establish meaningful relationships with children and ensure we promote and protect their rights as per the fundamental requirements of the UNCRC. In order to participate, children require information about what it is they are being asked to be involved in. The approach to every child will need to be bespoke to them and be clear, jargon-free and take account of their preferences, their capacities and competencies to understand and be involved. Even very young children require an explanation about what you are doing and why.

Reflecting the unique characteristics of each child, the social worker should be prepared to engage the services of an interpreter if needed (Chand, 2005; Kriz and Skivenes, 2010). The importance of this has been highlighted in inquiries and serious case reviews regarding the death of children at home known to social services. For example, the Victoria Climbié Inquiry (Laming, 2003) and the Serious Case Review into the death of Daniel Pelka (Lock, 2013) noted that both children did not speak English as their first language (Williams and Graham, 20216). Other issues that might impact on communication include a child's age, neurodiversity, other forms of disability, cultural practices/norms regarding child/adult conversations, personality and preferences.

Basic information gathered by the social worker about the child or young person should include their origins, their background and their characteristics.

This includes their full name, age and gender, main language, disability, social class, religion, nationality, immigration status and ethnicity. It is important to start by collecting this information fully and accurately, if we are to develop a rounded, and grounded, understanding of the child in their particular situation. Common mistakes that must be avoided include: misspelling a child's name(s); making assumptions about their religion, ethnicity and nationality rather than asking and seeking clarification; making assumptions about the capacities, interests of the child rather than engaging directly with them (and if necessary seeking the help of an interpreter to help engage with the child).

The child's relationships with others, both within the family and outside, also need focus. It is in these relationships that abuse is most likely to occur. Although most abuse is perpetrated by main carers or extended family members, it is important to consider all of a child's relationships, since there is also risk of abuse in institutional settings such as schools, clubs and religious organisations, or through online engagement in various forms of social media.

Assessment of relationships should include consideration of the child's patterns of attachment (see Chapter 7), which may have become disrupted and disturbed. The assessment should ask how does this child engage with the world, and in particular how does this child interact with other people? What messages have they already learned about the world and their place in it?

Furthermore, assessment of relationships should include a child's relationships with other adults/professionals, their nature, quality and what information a child might have shared with others. Any causes for concern noted by other adults in a child's life should be noted in the assessment. For example, in the National Review into the deaths of Arthur Labinjo-Hughes and Star Hobson, two children known to social services who were murdered by their parent(s)/carer(s), it is noted that Arthur, aged six years, was sharing information with his school teachers and grandparents that indicated he was fearful and had a concern for his own safety (Child Safeguarding Practice Review Panel, 2022).

Throughout our focus on the child, we must continually be asking 'What is life actually like for this child or young person?' One practical way to check how far your assessment captures what life is like is to ask the following:

> If I put myself in the shoes of this child, what events will I have witnessed, what journey will I have been on, what does the world look like, what do I need, and what do I hope for in the future?.

As noted earlier, putting children at the centre of assessments is a basic expectation, not a luxury 'add-on' (O'Reilly and Dolan, 2016).

These examples highlight that children's needs can be understood in a variety of ways but do include the educational, health, social, emotional, psychological, identity needs of the child. We saw how, in the work of Bryer (1988, p. 29), the overall needs of a child or young person were distinguished from the *priority* needs – those, as she put it, 'which must be met in order that the child's development will not be delayed or damaged'. These priority needs may well be what has caused people to consider providing substitute care, and they are likely to be in the forefront of people's minds. It is important to be as clear as possible about these priority needs, and a child's basic needs, so that whatever plan is made can address them effectively.

It is partly for this reason that the *Framework for the Assessment of Children in Need and their Families* (Department of Health et al., 2000) is built around seven developmental dimensions (health, education, identity, family and social relationships, social presentation, emotional and behavioural development and self-care skills) which reflect these holistic and 'ordinary' needs that all children have. As for priority needs, Bryer (1988, p. 29) points out that 'it is useless to identify what these needs are unless at the same time the cause of each need is identified', because the causation will have implications for the kind of care plan that is required to address the need in question. So from the beginning, our investigation of the child's situation demands theory and analysis, for instance about the effects on children and their development of different factors in their background or environment.

We will come back to the skills and methods by which to ensure that the voice and experience of each child is central to the assessment process. For now, continuing with the theme of focusing on the content of the assessment, there is a requirement to assess the child in the immediate context of their family, neighbourhood and community. The next section considers this aspect in more detail.

The strengths and resources of the immediate and extended family

As noted in earlier chapters, it is important to remember that families come in many different shapes and forms. A child's main carers may be single or a couple (of the same or different genders), may be birth carers, relative carers, or carers from outside of the family; they may be part of reconstituted families or intergenerational households. There may be lodgers, or siblings and partners who come and go. Family pets are also often defined by families as being 'part of the family', and so account should be taken of them too.

Opinions differ on the relative impact of the family and other social institutions, such as schools and peer groups, on children and young people's lives and development. However, the family is where children spend most of their lives, especially when young, and where they receive most of their day-to-day care. The family therefore has massive potential to do good or harm to a child, and an understanding of the strengths and the resources of the family and of what it has to offer the child is a critically important part of our assessment.

In reviewing the present and past, knowledge of the family structure and functioning will be key to explaining the child or young person's situation and to understanding any difficulties. A *family genogram or family tree* helps establish who is who in the household. This can help identify transient partners or people in the household that no-one was aware of.

It may also help identify the role of non-resident parents, usually fathers. Following this, a family *history* will provide an indispensable background for the rest of our assessment. What have been the key events in the lives of family members? What is their educational and economic background? What kind of health and other problems have there been? It is particularly important to collect this information in respect of the child's parents or carers, but we also need to understand what has been happening with other family members – brothers and sisters, grandparents, aunts and uncles.

In the same way when we look at family *functioning* – who has what roles, how the family relates together, what the dynamics are and how well the needs of family members are met – it is important to look broadly and with an open mind. As noted, there are many different family patterns, and different family members may be important to the child either because they provide care or because of their emotional relationships with the child. It is therefore important to consider everyone, and not just focus on the parents – or as often happens, the mother/main female carer. As noted above, it is also important to seek out the perspectives and role of non-resident parents, usually the fathers. A report published by the NSPCC (2022) which focuses on learning from case reviews focuses on 'unseen men' and highlights that there has been a lack of attention given to fathers with two consequences: either the risk posed by their abusive behaviour has not been considered or their protective and nurturing capacities have been overlooked.

Having established who's who and what roles they have within the family, it is then important to consider the quality of *parenting* being provided to the child. The information we have obtained concerning the family history and functioning should inform our assessment of parenting. There are differing definitions of parenting. In social work assessments, the commonly used definition of parenting is based on the Assessment Framework (referred to earlier) which defines parenting as the ability/capacity to offer a child basic care, safety, emotional warmth, stimulation, guidance and boundaries, and stability.

The association between issues affecting parents and the quality of care received by children has been well researched. Notable and recent research, as indicated in earlier chapters, has highlighted the impact of poverty, social, economic and demographic factors on parenting and other research highlights the challenges associated with mental and physical ill-health, substance misuse, and domestic violence and abuse. It is essential for social workers to have a well-developed understanding of contemporary knowledge regarding parenting and its challenges, and in particular to fully appreciate the impact of poverty and broader social disadvantage on parenting (Skinner et al., 2022).

Our assessment of parenting is important for two reasons. First, it helps us to understand the child as they are at present, informs our understanding of the circumstances in which the child lives, and offers insight into the risks facing children, their needs and their experiences. Second, information about parenting informs the development of future plans with and for children. Our analysis of this information helps establish what contribution the family can be expected to make. If we are considering leaving or placing the child with the family, we need to know whether they can provide what is needed and what support will be required. If the plan involves the child living elsewhere, we still need to know whether we should be aiming for their eventual return to the family, and what contact arrangements are realistic.

A key consideration here is what the parenting is in reality like for this child, and whether it is *good enough* or can become good enough. In assessing this, we must take account of all those issues of standards and comparability that we discussed in Chapter 1. That means that we must be aware of cultural variations in patterns of child care, and sensitive to the cultural variations in expectations of children at different ages. It also means that our judgement will in the last analysis be guided by generally accepted standards in our society, as well as by the law. A basic question should be 'what care and upbringing does any child or young person living in this society have a right to expect, and what does that mean in practice for *this* child or young person?'

In considering both the parents and the wider family, we should be thinking about what they can offer the child, bearing in mind what we have learned about the child's needs (see below), and also thinking about any danger or risks that they may present to the child. At the same time, we must not forget that family members have needs of their own. The fact that our primary obligation is to 'safeguard and promote the welfare' (in the words of children's legislation across the UK) of a particular child does not mean we should not also consider the interests and the wishes of other family members, both children and adults. Difficult issues can arise when more than one child in a family is in need of care, and an assessment of the quality of sibling relationships will be essential in tackling these. As noted earlier, the content of a social worker assessment considers the child in their family and the family within the community. This aspect of the assessment is considered next.

The strengths and resources of the community

Children live in families located in neighbourhoods and communities. There have been times in the history of social work when there has been a tendency to neglect this dimension in favour of a concentration on the individual or the family. In recent years, there has been an increased emphasis on the wider community and its impact on children's welfare, captured in 'ecological' approaches that attempt to integrate individual, family, community and wider social structural issues into our understanding (HM Government, 2018).

Often an important element of family functioning relates to relationships with and support received from neighbours, local community groups and extended family. The informal and formal networks that provide family support have been extensively written about, for example in the work of Canavan et al. (2016) who highlight the importance of a clear assessment of the positive and negative potential of the family's social networks. These writers also remind us of the value of 'natural support systems' and of informal sources of support that are based on choice and give opportunities for reciprocation. As noted by Canavan et al. (2016), these supports are sometimes described as *social capital* (derived from the sociological work of Putnam, 2000).

Just as with our assessment of parenting, making an assessment of the strengths and resources of the community is important because it may help us to understand the child as they are at present, and because it may help in planning for the future to establish what contribution the community could make, especially if we are considering leaving or placing the child at home, but also in relation to continuing contact or eventual return.

In this part of the assessment we should be asking:

- What physical resources are available in the local and wider community to support the child and the family? This includes economic opportunities, educational and recreational facilities, transport and shopping, as well as childcare resources such as mother and toddler groups, childminders, affordable nurseries, baby-sitting services, youth clubs and activities.
- What social supports are available to the child and family? Are there good networks around and are they in practice accessible to this child and this family? If not, can this be addressed?
- How well integrated are the child and family into their community and neighbourhood? Are their patterns of social relationships helpful to them or are they in themselves problematic?
- Are there community opportunities to improve a family's housing and income?

The child, family and social structural issues

As indicated above, a social worker assessment is not complete without information about social, economic and demographic factors that impact on the family. These factors can place families under considerable strain, making the job of parenting even more challenging. In particular, there should be a focus on determining the following:

a The economic situation of the family – their sources of income, incomings and outgoings, any debt accrued, access to benefits (are the family claiming state financial aid to which they are entitled), any factors that compromise the family's ability to earn income (physical and mental ill-health, immigration status, single parenthood with no social support, for example), is there evidence of exploitation?
b The social situation of the family – are they experiencing victimisation (racist attacks, sectarian attacks) that exacerbate social isolation and cause fear, uncertainty and stress?
c Demographic characteristics of the family – what is their main language, how well do they understand English, what is their ethnicity, religion and nationality, are they refugees, asylum seekers, what is their immigration status?

All of the above impact on parenting. Experience tells us that when we do not accurately and fully capture key information in our assessments, we can misrepresent the risks posed to children. Examples include Victoria Climbie, who died in the care of her aunt and aunt's partner where the assessment process did not appropriately and/or adequately analyse her specific cultural context and led to assumptions, biases and misunderstandings in the assessment process, contributing to a failure to fully appreciate the risk to which she was exposed. In a more recent example, the case of Daniel Pelka emphasised the inadequacies in the assessment process caused by a failure to gather relevant information from all agencies and to take account of Daniel's cultural and language needs, which meant that the risks posed were not fully appreciated. Indeed, in the case of Daniel Pelka, the Serious Case Review (Lock, 2013, para 14.9, p. 71) notes that:

> without English as his first language and because of his lack of confidence Daniel's voice was not heard throughout this case […] overall there is no record of any conversations held with him by any professional about his home life, his experiences outside of school, his wishes and feelings and of his relationship with his sibling, mother and her male partners. In this way despite Daniel being the focus of concern for all of the practitioners, in reality he was rarely the focus of their interventions.

This and other examples highlight the contribution of other agencies to the social work assessment. This is considered in the next section.

The contribution of health and welfare agencies

It is important to ask critically about the ability of service agencies to meet the child's needs. There are three particular reasons why this is important. First, we do not want to make the mistake of planning alternative care for a child on the basis of an assessment which highlights the family's inability to meet the identified needs, without being confident that the alternative care arrangement will be significantly better. To illustrate: is it better to remove a ten-year-old child to a foster placement knowing that it is only available for a week and that the child will have to move again, possibly changing schools and becoming dislocated from their neighbourhood and community, or is it better to try and maintain the child at home with parents who have alcohol problems and put in place a safety and support plan?

Second, we do not want to miss the possibility that professional agencies can provide additional help and support which might enable satisfactory care to be provided in the family. Even when parents are unable to change their style of parenting very much, it may be that with enough practical support they can provide a better experience for children than being separated from their parents and sometimes from each other, and perhaps facing a series of moves in care. Third, even if the conclusion of the assessment is that on balance it is in the child's interests to be placed elsewhere, there may still be needs which can be better met by the family or the community. It is implicit in work based on concepts of 'shared care' and 'partnership' that no party has a monopoly of ability and resources to meet a child's needs.

Processes of assessment and planning

Having considered the content of an assessment that focuses on the child, the child in their family, the family in their wider community/society and the contribution of other agencies, it can be seen that the assessment is not a 'one off' event, but rather a dynamic process that involves constantly testing assumptions and hypotheses in the light of emerging understanding. This is reflected in the official government guidance in England and Wales (2018, para 51, p. 27) which states that:

> Assessment should be a dynamic process, which analyses and responds to the changing nature and level of need and/or risk faced by the child from within and outside their family.

It follows that the process of assessment may follow different patterns in different cases, depending on the situation and the people involved. Still, it is useful to have a simple framework or sequence in mind, while recognising that it will not often be followed in strict order. The sequence usually goes something like this:

- collecting information
- analysing the information
- consulting
- preparing a plan
- implementing and reviewing the plan

Collecting information

In terms of *the collection of information*, an assessment tends to follow a logical sequence, even if it does not keep strictly to this in chronological terms (because information gathering and analysis cannot be entirely sequential). We are analysing information as soon as we begin to collect it, and this initial analysis affects our view of what other information we need to collect.

It is the social worker who is also responsible for managing the collection of information from a variety of sources. Collection of information occurs in several different ways. Some of it will be available in written form, from agency records (which should always be consulted carefully), reports and correspondence. Some of it will depend on observation – for instance, of parents with children, and perhaps of the child in other settings. Much of it will be gathered by talking – and more importantly *listening* – to people, either individually or in groups, and this is a doubly important part of the process because it often in effect combines the collection of information with consultation about the analysis, and sometimes also with the discussion of possible plans.

This can cause challenges because there can be a tension between including a range of professionals in the process and making it genuinely open and accessible to children and families, who may have quite different expectations and styles of communication. The social worker has an important responsibility for ensuring that everyone can contribute appropriately to the process, so that each person's knowledge and views can become part of the overall assessment.

There are a number of practical tools which can be enormously helpful in getting information about the child and family. These are well used and available from many different sources, which is testament to their usefulness. One is the *flow chart*, which is a helpful diagrammatic way of showing key events in the history of a child or family. A second is the *ecomap*, which can be drawn to show the most important relationships and links in a child's current life. The third is the *genogram*, which is a bit like a family tree and is a graphic way of describing a set of family relationships and explaining family history. Each of these tools can make the process of collecting information much easier and more comfortable for people and can also help to draw attention to key elements of a child's situation which might otherwise be missed.

Analysing information

Analysing information is a crucial part of the assessment process (Killick and Taylor, 2024; Dyke, 2023). There is no point in collecting masses of information if there is then no attempt to make sense of it. What sometimes happens in practice is that people move straight from collecting the information to formulating a plan, without any systematic reflection. This undoubtedly means that assumptions are being made about the significance of information, but that these assumptions are not really being questioned. When things are done this way it is likely that certain pieces of information will be given a significance that is disproportionate to what is really justified – and the wrong plans will be made!

Analysing information is understood in different ways but, in essence, what social workers are trying to do is to *make sense* of the information they have collected. Making sense involves reflection and reasoning. When we reflect on the information we have gathered, we are moving beyond a description of 'what is happening here' to an explanation as to 'why things are happening here'. It is from this analytical account that decisions can then be made as to what needs to happen to address the risks and the needs. This is a process referred to as exercising professional judgement (Samsonsen and Turney, 2017).

Proper space must therefore be made for analysing all the information that has been collected. Some of this will happen as it is being collected, as we have mentioned – but then it is important to bring it all together in an organised way. It is really helpful to have a proper framework for this, one that is already understood by at least some of the people involved in the assessment, who can then explain it to others. At the conclusion of this chapter, when we review some of the systematic approaches to assessment and planning that have been developed, we will see that there are some useful analytical tools among them. Once we have collected information and analysed it, a plan needs to be drawn up. The process of planning is considered in further detail below.

The process of planning

A key moment in the overall assessment process is the move from assessment to planning. Although in practice the two processes may often be combined, there is an important conceptual distinction between the collection and analysis of information in order to produce a judgement about what needs to be done, and the formation of a consequent plan of action to achieve the objectives that follow from the assessment. In part it is a move from past and present to future – from a consideration of what is happening and why, to a contemplation of what is to be done and a prediction of what is likely to happen (which is also why we often need *contingency* plans).

There are different models of planning that are relevant to our purposes here. Models vary in a number of different ways, perhaps most interestingly in the weight they place on participation. At one extreme is a process of planning controlled by one or two professionals – perhaps the social worker and his or her supervisor – with other people being consulted at an appropriate point or points. Conversely, the process can be managed in a much more collaborative way, with what is in effect shared decision-making between a group of professionals and family members. This is likely to involve a meeting or series of meetings, and the process is likely to be managed by a chair – who may have a dual responsibility, both to conduct proceedings fairly and see that everyone has a chance to express their view, and to ensure that the eventual outcome is acceptable to the agency. At the other end of the continuum is the *family group conference*, where the immediate and extended family are the decision-takers, within certain constraints and with the advice and support of professionals.

When we are planning for a child's future, we must include the child and seek their views about the plan. Furthermore, we must attempt in the plan to build something that will work and that will last. Just as an architect designing a building, or an engineer designing an aircraft, has to specify exactly what materials to use and how to put them together, we have an equal responsibility to be specific about the components of our plan for the child and confident that they will achieve our stated objectives. However, we must also be realistic in that contexts and circumstances change continually. We must take account of the fact that things can turn out differently than we expected, which is why we also need a contingency plan alongside the main plan.

With regard to children's involvement in planning, this is a legal requirement, it is their right and there are also moral and social imperatives in that planning done *with* the child and family, rather than *to* them, is more likely to be successful – both because the plans are likely to be better in themselves and because people are more likely to support them. The same principles apply to collaboration with other agencies. Although the social work department may carry the lead responsibility for promoting the welfare of the child, it is a corporate responsibility of the local authority and one shared in some measure by the health services. Professionals in education, health and housing should therefore be part of the planning process in all cases where this is appropriate.

It is also essential that the plans are 'SMART' (specific, measurable, achievable, realistic, targeted and timely). For example, if we state in a plan that a child's health needs to be attended to, the plan should state the specifics (a child's vision, hearing, dental care, immunisations need to be checked, by whom, when, where, how often, who is responsible for getting a child to and from their appointments and what the review/follow up arrangements are). The content of plans is considered further in the following section.

What is in a plan?

The regulations state that a plan for the care of a child should include the following elements:

- the child's needs and how they are to be met;
- the aims and timescale;
- the proposed placement;
- other services to be provided;
- support in the placement and contingency plans;
- arrangements for contact and reunification;
- arrangements for health care and education.

The plan should also specify roles and responsibilities, how far it takes account of the child's wishes and feelings, and arrangements for changes to the plan, disagreements and future decision-making. This is a good summary of the key elements that need to go into a plan for the care of a child or young person and it can be seen how the SMART principles should apply to all aspects. For example, the plan should contain a clear statement of the child's *specific* needs and details about the *specific* services identified to meet that child's needs. The plan should also highlight *specific* details about who is responsible, the aims, timeframe and review arrangements. Unclear and unrealistic plans and plans that a child objects to cannot be easily or effectively implemented to achieve the desired change.

The content and structure of a plan should be guided by a framework such as those used in some of the systematic approaches to assessment and planning reviewed in the following section. Planning of course does not end with a child's admission to care. Assessment and planning are both continuing processes, and the statutory requirement to hold regular reviews is but one way of reinforcing this. The process of reviewing is considered next.

The process of reviewing

It is a legal requirement for the plan to be reviewed at intervals, to ensure it is implemented and make any changes that have become necessary. It is important to ensure that all parties are given a proper opportunity to contribute to the review, and that decisions are made in an open and transparent way – so that even if colleagues or family members do not agree with the outcomes, they understand the reasoning behind them. Enabling children and young people to participate effectively in reviews can be a challenge, because the process is often designed in ways that do not make it readily accessible, especially to younger children. Recent research highlights ongoing challenges in the area of children's involvement in their meetings when involved in social

Exercise 6.1 'Annie'

Annie is ten years old and lives with her mother and younger sister, Sarah aged four. She has little contact with her father. Annie has mild cerebral palsy which gives her some difficulty in walking and speech. She attends a mainstream school where she has until recently been doing well.

Recently, Annie's mother has had several episodes of severe depression. During these episodes, her care of the children has been very poor, and arrangements have been made on occasion for them to stay with friends. Annie's mother has now joined a therapeutic programme which she has to attend on a daily basis and which is expected to continue for up to six months. Her psychiatrist has recommended that she is unlikely to benefit from the programme unless she has a break from caring for the children for at least three months. Her sister has offered to look after Sarah but is unwilling to take on both girls. In any case, Annie is keen to continue at her school and her aunt lives 30 miles away.

Annie's mother has asked for Annie to be accommodated by the local authority.

What would be the key components of a plan for Annie?

What are her needs, including her priority needs?

What other information do you need?

services (Töros, 2020). This is despite the introduction of more systematic frameworks to assist in the assessment process. These are considered next.

Frameworks that inform assessment and planning

There are several frameworks available to be used by social workers in the assessment of needs and risks. In England and Wales, as noted earlier in the chapter, the *Framework for the Assessment of Children in Need and their Families* (Department of Health, Department for Education and Employment and Home Office, 2000) provides a systematic basis for collecting and analysing information to support professional judgements, based on three global domains (see Figure 6.1):

- A child's developmental needs
- The capacity of parents or caregivers to respond appropriately to those needs, including their capacity to keep the child safe from harm
- The impact of wider family and environmental factors on the parents and child

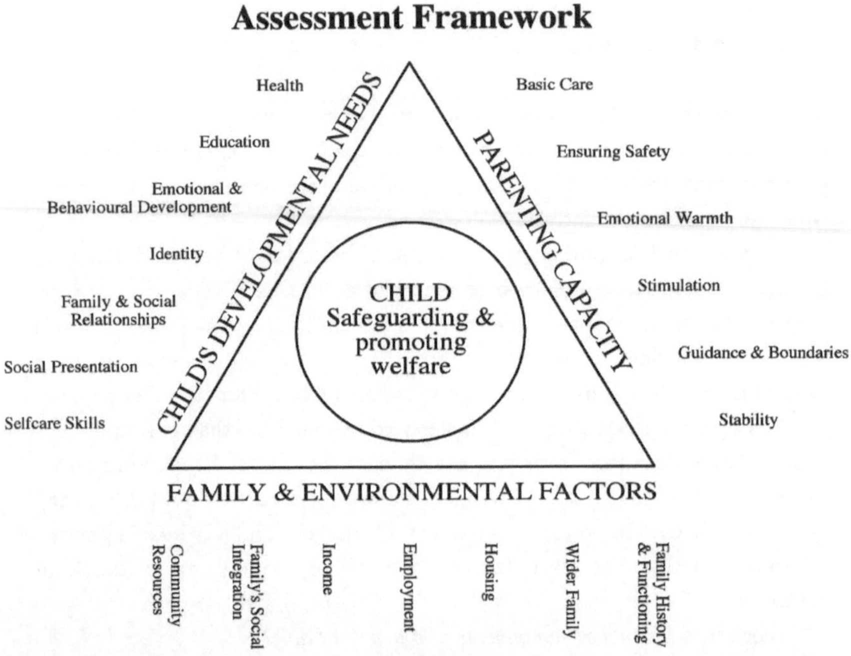

FIGURE 6.1 The three 'domains' of assessment.

Source: Department of Health, Department for Education and Employment and Home Office (2000, p. 17).

In Northern Ireland, the same framework is incorporated in *Understanding the Needs of Children in Northern Ireland* (UNOCINI).

Within these assessment frameworks, children's developmental needs are categorised under health, education, emotional and behavioural development, identity, family and social relationships, social presentation and self-care skills. A broad overview of these is outlined in Table 6.1.

In Scotland, the assessment framework is known as *Getting It Right for Every Child* (Scottish Government, 2008). It is underpinned by a conceptual framework of wellbeing rather than developmental needs. The framework is based on eight domains of wellbeing (known by the acronym SHANARRI) – all children should be safe, healthy, active, nurtured, achieving, respected, responsible and included. It is depicted as the SHANARRI wheel (see Figure 6.2).

Across the UK, *Signs of Safety* is also used. This is another model for assessing risk and need, which developed in Australia in the 1990s and is now used in child protection teams throughout the world (Turnell and Edwards, 1997; Roberts et al., 2019). The approach involves the identification of risk alongside the identification of areas of strength and times of safety where risks are reduced. The assessment of danger, strengths and safety is then reduced to

TABLE 6.1 Developmental domains

Health	The child's current health condition, their growth and development, their physical and mental well-being and their physical development and speech, language and communication development. Factors include receiving treatment when ill, management of health conditions, securing immunisations and developmental checks where appropriate, dental and optical care, diet, exercise, hospital admissions, accidents, access to sex education and impact of other habits such as substance misuse, smoking and other health risks.
Education	Access to formal education opportunities. Access to wider learning opportunities – playing, exploring, creating, experimenting, discovering, identifying, recognising, classifying.
Emotional/ social development	The child's emotional and social responses with care givers, friends, community. It includes temperament, relationships, attachments, management of feelings, coping, self-harm, phobias, psychological difficulties.
Identity	Self-awareness, self-assurance, self-confidence, coherent and accurate sense of self (who they are, family background).
Family/social relationships	Positive relationships with parents, care givers, siblings and friends, understanding of others and awareness of consequences of negative associations.
Social presentation	Awareness of social norms in interactions with others, awareness of how appearance and behaviour are perceived and the impression created ability to engage appropriately and socially with others, awareness of appropriate social boundaries, awareness of race, religion, age, gender sexuality and disability may all be affected by bullying or discriminatory behaviours.
Self-care skills	How and if children are acquiring social, practical, emotional, communication competencies to increase independence. It includes learning about and practicing discovering boundaries and limits, consequences or risk taking, social rules and norms, who to go to, when, where and how to get help.

a one-page assessment protocol comprising the following headings: what are we worried about; what's working well; and what needs to happen. Its simplicity and accessibility, together with its reliance on family members' input through family meetings, has added to its uptake by social work teams across the UK and beyond. There is a growing interest in evaluations to establish its effectiveness and impact (Baginsky et al., 2017, 2019; Roberts et al., 2019).

There are a number of tools available for assessing risk of significant harm (reviewed by Barlow et al., 2012). The key questions for social workers in practice are:

- what are the risks;
- how likely are the risks to occur;

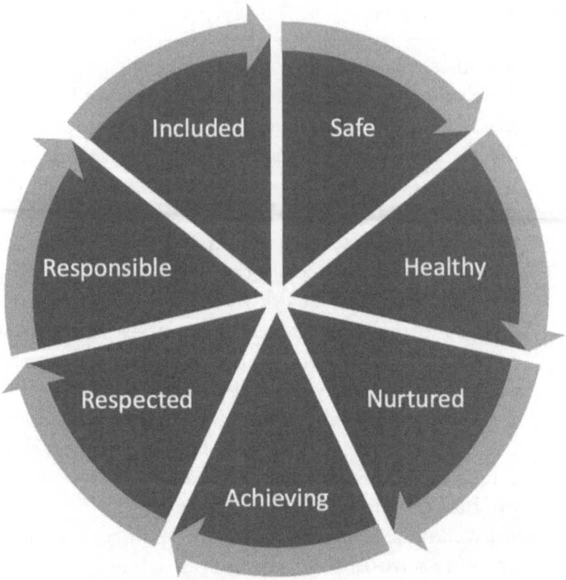

FIGURE 6.2 The SHANARRI wheel (an adaptation).

- what is the likely significance; magnitude and impact of the risk on the child's safety and wellbeing;
- are they enduring; chronic and cumulative risks or 'one off events';
- what factors might help minimise or mitigate against the risks;
- what is the strength and significance of these factors;
- what needs to change to mitigate risk; and
- when should a plan be reviewed.

Biases, assumptions and values in assessment and planning

Effective communication and relationships based on well-developed critical reflection and emotional intelligence are at the core of effective assessment. As indicated in this chapter, our own biases and assumptions influence our assessments. Being self-aware, reflective and addressing these issues is as central to social work practice as the assessment tasks we are responsible for undertaking. In terms of biases, this concerns 'mental short cuts' that can lead to systematic and predictable errors in reasoning (Kahneman and Klein, 2009; Taylor, 2017). Examples include:

- The halo effect – the tendency to trust people of a certain standing, such as lawyers or paediatricians, even in the absence of any information they may have to support their views.

- Confirmation bias – the tendency to search for, interpret, favour, and recall information in a way that confirms or supports one's prior beliefs or values.
- Availability bias – the tendency to rely on immediate examples that come to mind when evaluating a topic or concept.

Making assumptions can have the effect of generalising aspects of an individual person's experience based on stereotypes, which can lead to a totally inaccurate assessment. For example, making assumptions about children's experience based on their religion, ethnicity, disability, age, language, care experience, abuse they have encountered and so on. It is our responsibility to be honest about our biases and assumptions to mitigate their negative impact on the accuracy and relevance of the assessments we are undertaking.

The work of Ferguson regarding social worker home visits (2017, 2018) illustrates social workers' strong emotional responses in the home visits they undertake and the necessity of being able to identify and contain these in such a way that clear thinking is not hindered. Ferguson illustrates how home visits are far more than an objective task undertaken by social workers but involve a sensory experience – the sights, smells, noises, interactions and dynamics experienced in a home visit combine together to influence impressions and assessment processes. His work highlights how a combination of strong emotional responses, overpowering adults and organisational influences (high caseloads, the imperative to get a number of statutory visits undertaken in a short period of time), can result in children (the focus of the visit) being overlooked or not engaged with in a meaningful way.

These examples highlight first that it is essential for each individual to be familiar with and adhere to the core social work values that underpin standards of ethical social work practice and conduct. These emphasise that in all practice, we must respect the rights, dignity and inherent worth of each individual, treat people with respect and compassion, support their autonomy as much as is consistent with their best interests, and uphold equality, diversity and inclusion. Second, they highlight that it is essential that social workers have access to formal and informal reflective spaces and/or supervision in which they can fully reflect on the issues that impact on their practice and seek ways to address any unintentional biases in supported ways.

Summary and conclusion

We started this chapter by looking at the context and purpose of assessment with children and young people. We then considered the content of assessment in relation to the child, the family and community, and the contribution of health and welfare agencies. We examined the processes of assessment, planning, implementation and review; and we analysed what is in a plan.

Finally, we considered some systematic approaches to assessment and planning, the ways in which they can be used to support good professional practice and the importance of addressing our biases and assumptions.

While systems and practice tools can be an enormous help to good practice, they are no substitute for well-trained staff who understand what they are doing and have the time and resources to do it properly. It should also not need to be said that, however good the processes of assessment and planning, they are wasted without effective provision of services. However, there is a risk that the very necessary focus on improving assessment and planning may sometimes overshadow the need to ensure that services are available when and where they are identified as being needed and provided in a way that is acceptable to children and their families.

It is hoped that this chapter will have provided an introduction to the thinking behind good practice in assessment and planning for children in care, and an overview of this complex and challenging area of work. Many of the themes will be developed further in the following chapters.

GUIDE TO FURTHER READING

Holland (2011) is a very useful text to help think about assessment in social work in general. For an overview of assessment practice with children, both individual and collectively, Mainstone (2014) is invaluable. Dyke (2023) focuses on the construction of analytical assessments. Killick and Taylor (2024) is very helpful for developing an understanding risk and the exercise of professional judgement in decision making.

Horwath and Platt (2019) is a core text outlining fundamental knowledge regarding children's needs, parenting capacity and wider social structural factors that impact on children and families. A review of issues impacting on parenting by Cleaver et al. (2011) is very helpful, as is the review of risk assessment models by Barlow et al. (2012). Turnell and Edwards (1999) outline the core elements of the Signs of Safety approach.

As a guide to planning for children, Bryer (1988) has in some respects still not been bettered. More recently, a very helpful, accessible Guide to Planning for Children in Care by Watts (2022) has been published on the Research in Practice https://www.researchinpractice.org.uk/media/b0yh215z/2789_care_planning_for_children_-final.pdf

Kiima's book (2021) is essential reading to develop knowledge and insight regarding the cultural context of parenting.

The website of Social Workers Tool Box (https://www.socialworkerstoolbox.com) contains many practical tools and tips to assist in the assessment of children and families.

References

Baginsky, M., Moriarty, J. and Manthorpe, J. (2019) 'Signs of safety: Lessons learnt from evaluations', *Journal of Children's Services*, *14*(2), 107–123.

Baginsky, M., Moriarty, J., Manthorpe, J., Beecham, J. and Hickman, B. (2017) *Evaluation of signs of safety in 10 pilots: Research report*. London: Department for Education.

Barlow, J., Fisher, J. and Jones, D. (2012) *Systematic review of models of analysing significant harm*. Oxford: Oxford University.

Bryer, M. (1988) *Planning in child care. A guide for team leaders and their teams*. London: BAAF.

Canavan, J., Pinkerton, J. and Dolan, P. (2016) *Understanding family support: Policy, practice, and theory*. London: Jessica Kingsley Publishers.

Chand, A. (2005) 'Do you speak English? Language barriers in child protection social work with minority ethnic families', *British Journal of Social Work*, *35*(6), 807–821.

Child Safeguarding Practice Review Panel (2022) National review into the murders of Arthur Labinjo-Hughes and Star Hobson. https://www.gov.uk/government/publications/national-review-into-the-murders-of-arthur-labinjo-hughes-and-star-hobson [Accessed 30/05/2022].

Cleaver, H., Unell, I. and Aldgate, J. (2011) *Children's needs—parenting capacity. Child abuse: Parental mental illness, learning disability, substance misuse and domestic violence*. London: The Stationery Office. Available here https://assets.publishing.service.gov.uk/government/uploads/system/uploads/attachment_data/file/182095/DFE-00108-2011-Childrens_Needs_Parenting_Capacity.pdf (accessed 28.01.24).

Department of Health. (2011) *Understanding the needs of children in Northern Ireland (UNOCINI) guidance*. Belfast: Department of Health.

Department of Health, Cox, A. and Bentovim, A. (2000) *The family assessment pack of questionnaires and scales*. London: The Stationery Office.

Department of Health, Department for Education and Employment and the Home Office. (2000) *Framework for the assessment of children in need and their families*. London: The Stationery Office.

Dyke, C. (2023) *Writing analytical assessments in social work*. St Albans: Critical Publishing Ltd.

Ferguson, H. (2017) 'How children become invisible in child protection work: Findings from research into day-to-day social work practice', *British Journal of Social Work*, *47*(4), 1007–1023. https://doi.org/10.1093/bjsw/bcw065

Ferguson, H. (2018) 'Making home visits: Creativity and the embodied practices of home visiting in social work and child protection', *Qualitative Social Work*, *17*(1), 65–80. https://doi.org/10.1177/1473325016656751

HM Government. (2018) *Working together to safeguard children. A guide to inter-agency working to safeguard and promote the welfare of children*. London: Department for Education.

Holland, S. (2011) *Child and family assessment in social work practice* (second edition). London: SAGE Publications Ltd.

Horwath, J. and Platt, D. (2019) *The child's world: The essential guide to assessing vulnerable children, young people and their families*. London: Jessica Kingsley Publishers.

Kahneman, D. and Klein, G. (2009) 'Conditions for intuitive expertise: A failure to disagree', *American Psychologist*, *64*(6), 515.

Kiima, D. (2021) *Assessing culturally informed parenting in social work*. Abingdon: Routledge.

Killick, C. and Taylor, B. (2024) *Assessment, risk and decision making: An introduction*. London: SAGE Publications.

Kriz, K. and Skivenes, M. (2010) 'Lost in translation: How child welfare workers in Norway and England experience language difficulties when working with minority ethnic families', *British Journal of Social Work*, *40*(5), 1353–1367. Available here https://www.jstor.org/stable/43687535

Laming, L.H. (2003) *The Victoria Climbié inquiry*. London: The Stationery Office.

Lock, R. (2013) *Serious case review re Daniel Pelka: Born 15th July 2007 died 3rd March 2012*. Coventry: Coventry Safeguarding Children Board.

Mainstone, F. (2014) *Mastering whole family* assessment *in social work: Balancing the needs of children, adults, and their families*. London: Jessica Kingsley Publishers.

McCafferty, P. (2022) '"Do I read it? No". Knowledge utilisation in child welfare decisions', *Child Care in Practice*, *28*(3), 438–463. https://doi.org/10.1080/13575279.2020.1765149

McCafferty, P. and Taylor, B. (2020) 'Risk, decision-making and assessment in child welfare', *Child Care in Practice*, *26*(2), 107–110. http://doi.org/10.1080/13575279.2019.1703369

Milner, J., Myers, S. and O'Bryne, P. (2020) *Assessment in social work* (fifth edition). London: Red Globe Press.

National Society for the Prevention of Cruelty to Children (NSPCC). (2022) *Unseen men; learning from case reviews*. London: NSPCC.

O'Reilly, L. and Dolan, P. (2016) 'The voice of the child in social work assessments: Age-appropriate communication with children', *The British Journal of Social Work*, *46*(5), 1191–1207. https://doi.org/10.1093%2Fbjsw%2Fbcv040

Putnam, R.D. (2000) *Bowling alone: The collapse and revival of American community*. New York: Touchstone Books/Simon & Schuster.

Roberts, Y.H., Caslor, M., Turnell, A., Pearson, K. and Pecora, P.J. (2019) 'An international effort to develop a fidelity measure for signs of safety®', *Research on Social Work Practice*, *29*(5), 562–571. https://doi.org/10.1177/1049731518754724

Rutter, L. and Brown, K. (2019) *Critical thinking and professional judgement for social work*. London: Learning Matters, Sage Publications.

Samsonsen, V. and Turney, D. (2017) 'The role of professional judgement in social work assessment: A comparison between Norway and England', *European Journal of Social Work*, *20*(1), 112–124.

Scottish Government. (2008) *Getting it right for every child (GIRFEC) guide*. Edinburgh: Scottish Government. Available here https://www.gov.scot/policies/girfec/girfec-resources/ (accessed 10.09.23).

Skinner, G.C.M., Bywaters, P. and Kennedy, E. (2022) 'A review of the relationship between poverty and child abuse and neglect: Insights from scoping reviews, systematic reviews, and meta-analyses', *Child Abuse Review*, *32*(2), e2795. https://doi.org/10.1002/car.2795

Taylor, B. (2017) *Decision making, assessment and risk in social work* (third edition). London: SAGE Publications Ltd.

Töros, K. (2020) 'A systematic review of children's participation in child protection decision-making: Tokenistic presence or not?', *Children and Society*, *35*(3), 395–411. https://doi.org/10.1111/chso.12418

Turnell, A. and Edwards, S. (1997) 'Aspiring to partnership. The signs of safety approach to child protection', *Child Abuse Review: Journal of the British Association for the Study and Prevention of Child Abuse and Neglect*, 6(3), 179–190.

Turnell, A., & Edwards, S. (1999). *Signs of safety: A solution and safety oriented approach to child protection casework*. New York: Norton.

Watts R. (2022) *Care planning for children in proceedings*: Frontline Briefing (2022).

Williams, C. and Graham, M. J. (2016) *Social work in a diverse society*. Bristol: Policy Press.

7

PLACEMENT AND CONTACT

CONTENTS OF CHAPTER

- Introduction
- Issues in choosing placements for children
- Types of alternative homes (placements)
- Relating children's needs to the capacity of placements to respond
- Who decides?
- Making a placement – transitions and practical issues
- Implications of attachment and resilience
- Sibling relationships and placement
- Issues in family contact
- Difficulties with contact
- Purpose of contact
- Making arrangements for contact
- Summary and conclusion
- Guide to further reading

Introduction

Most social workers refer to 'placements' when they talk about finding alternative homes for children who cannot continue to live in their family. However, 'placement' is a technical term – we should remind ourselves that what we are talking about is finding a home, whether permanent or temporary, for a child. This is probably one of the most important decisions that social workers regularly take. The right home can ensure that a child is happy and fulfilled and create a sound basis for their development into adulthood.

DOI: 10.4324/9781003503194-7

The wrong home can leave a child unhappy or emotionally 'stuck', trigger educational or other developmental difficulties, or lead to a pattern of instability and movement that may last through childhood and beyond.

This chapter will begin with a general discussion of the issues in choosing new or alternative homes for children. In so doing, it will draw attention to the UN Guidelines for the Alternative Care of Children (a resolution adopted by the UN General Assembly in 2009), which form a set of detailed guidelines to enhance the implementation of the UNCRC principles regarding children who live away from their family homes. The chapter then reviews the types of alternative care available. Subsequent chapters consider differing homes or placements in greater detail. Throughout this chapter, we will consider how best to relate children's needs to the capacity of the carers in the new or alternative home and explore the question of 'who decides' about placement. Applying UNCRC principles throughout, we will then look particularly at three areas: the implications of what we know about attachment and resilience, the strengths and weaknesses of children living with extended family members (known as kinship placements), and the issues of sibling relationships.

Whether children continue living with members of their family or are looked after by strangers, contact with separated family and friends can be crucial to their welfare. The second part of this chapter will concentrate on this aspect of looking after children. We will look specifically at the issues involved in family contact, the purposes of contact and the principles that should guide the making of arrangements for contact. In the final section of the chapter, we look at some of the practical issues in arranging placements and helping children to make successful moves.

Issues in choosing placements for children

In an ideal world, social workers will always put much thought and consideration into deciding on the most suitable new home for a child coming into care. Often, however, there is not a lot of time because the situation is urgent and an immediate alternative home needs to be found. Aside from a lack of time, there is also a lack of choice. Social workers frequently recount experiences of having to make multiple phone calls to their local authority fostering/placement teams; they also may have to contact independent fostering agencies and other local authorities to see what options are available.

It seems that the demand for new homes for children coming into care outstrips availability. According to recent English Department for Education annual statistical returns (which are available on the Department for Education website), and similar Northern Irish data (Department of Health, 2022), although the total number of available placements has risen, so too has the number of children coming into care; currently this is expanding at a much greater rate than the increase in the number of placements. In addition, although the total number of available alternative placements may have risen, there is still a lack of ethnically, culturally, linguistically and religiously diverse placements to meet the needs of different groups of children. There is also a lack of placements for disabled children with complex needs and for children with severe social, emotional and behavioural issues. The lack of matched placements can have an impact on short- and longer-term developmental outcomes especially identity, feelings of connectedness and 'sense of self' (Degener et al., 2022a, 2022b). For all these reasons, finding new homes for children coming into care is a complex and challenging area of practice.

Governing practice in this area are several requirements which are outlined in child care law and the associated regulations. The basic start point is that wherever possible children should remain within their own families and communities, so long as this is consistent with the best interests of the child. If this is not possible, the alternative home for a child should:

- be near their main family home;
- not disrupt their education by changing school;
- allow siblings to stay together;
- be suitable to a child's particular needs – especially if the child is disabled; and
- be within the local authority area in which the child usually lives.

It is not always possible to meet all these requirements, and difficult decisions or compromises may have to be made. The varied issues that need to be taken into account when assessing and placing a child are outlined in the UN Guidelines for the Alternative Care for Children (United Nations, 2010) and include the child's immediate safety and wellbeing, their longer-term care and development and 'the child's personal and developmental characteristics, ethnic, cultural, linguistic and religious background, family and social environment, medical history and any special needs'. The process should be based on consultation with the child, birth parents, other carers and professionals. Some key questions that need to be asked are:

- What sort of placement are we seeking for this child?
- What type of care will meet the child's priority needs?
- What are the main tasks required of the carers in order to meet the aims of care?
- What is the expected length of stay in care?
- Proposed contact between child and birth parents/other family members?
- Would a residential or foster care setting be better, and why?
- What particular considerations might affect the choice of placement, e.g. background of child, need for particular location?
- Is it possible to meet all these requirements within the prescribed timetable?
- If not, which criteria will be given priority?

- What options are there?
- Which option offers the most acceptable compromise?
- Who is involved in the decision about choice of placement?
- What are the child's wishes and feelings, and what is their understanding of the situation?
- Have the new carers been given sufficient information about the child and the task they are being asked to do?

Many children who come into care have experienced trauma through neglect or abuse, and they may have deep-seated social, emotional and psychological problems (see report by the Children's Commissioner for England in 2021, for example). These problems may create initial barriers that can make the process of finding a placement difficult. On the other hand, such problems may not emerge until the child is settled and feels relatively secure, so that a placement which initially appeared trouble-free begins to come under greater stress.

As noted above, social workers may be faced with little choice in finding an alternative home for a child or young person and may have to decide to accept an option knowing that it comes with limitations. This may mean accepting an emergency option for a child, knowing that it is only available for a very short time and that a more long-term option needs to be found. For every child, a decision has to made as to whether accepting the alternative home offered will be better for the child than not accepting it and perhaps not offering an alternative home at all.

The explicit philosophy of many agencies and indeed governments is that the choice of an alternative home for a child or young person, should be 'needs-led' not 'resource-led'. Few would disagree with this as a philosophy but making it a reality can be more difficult. Even where placement resources are well provided, it is rarely possible to start with a 'blank sheet' for each child; and the first task for a placing social worker is to be well informed about what placement resources are generally available.

Types of alternative homes (placements)

The word 'placement' refers to a range of alternative living arrangements and sometimes the term 'alternative care' rather than 'placement' is used. As we highlighted in the introduction, children in care often prefer to use the term 'home'. Different types of home or alternative care are defined in the UN Guidelines for the Alternative Care of Children (UN, 2009). Very broadly, they include:

i Kinship care: family-based care within the child's extended family or with close friends of the family known to the child, whether formal or informal in nature;

ii Foster care: situations where children are placed by a competent authority for the purpose of alternative care in the domestic environment of a family other than the children's own family that has been selected, qualified, approved and supervised for providing such care;
iii Other forms of family-based or family-like care placements;
iv Residential care: care provided in any non-family-based group setting, such as places of safety for emergency care, transit centres in emergency situations, and all other short- and long-term residential care facilities, including group homes;
v Supervised independent living arrangements for children (United Nations, 2009, p. 6).

The list above begins with the least intrusive option, where the child lives with extended family or friends. The most radical option, of course, is when the child is adopted by a new family. This is sometimes referred to as the 'continuum of care' (Figure 7.1) and reflects the principle that alternative care arrangements for children should begin with considering all family/extended family options before considering other options.

Foster care arrangements (kinship and non-relative carers) are seen as the next preferred option because they most closely emulate a family environment in which children have the best possibility of experiencing warm, consistent, safe and nurturing relationships with the main carers over a period of time. Much of the thinking here is based on the importance of attachment relationships. Residential care is often portrayed as the least preferred option for most (not all) children largely because of the high turnover in the group of children who live in children's homes and the staff who look after them. Other concerns relate to the cost, quality of care (under the spotlight

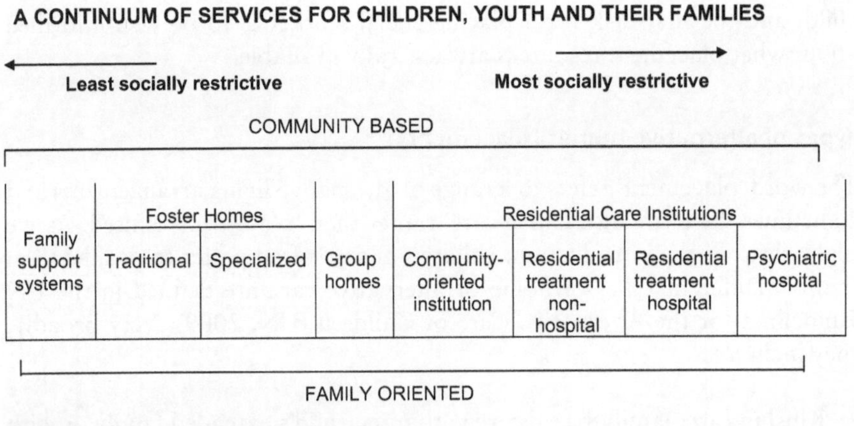

FIGURE 7.1 The 'continuum of care'.

Source: Plumer (1992, p. 199).

given inquiries into the historical abuse of some children living in some care homes) and the effectiveness of the care arrangements in improving outcomes. That said, it is important to note that many children's homes offer high quality care and enable children to feel settled and connected to their carers. Furthermore, some other children speak very positively about the care they have received. The next section explores these different placement types in more detail.

Children's own families

The overwhelming majority of children and young people remain with their families of origin throughout their childhood. This is of course the preferred way to bring up children in most societies. As noted in previous chapters, this is reflected in the UNCRC and accompanying documentation. In the UN Guidelines for the Alternative Care of Children (United Nations 2010) it is stated:

> The family being the fundamental group of society and the natural environment for the growth, well-being and protection of children, efforts should primarily be directed to enabling the child to remain in or return to the care of his/her parents, or when appropriate, other close family members. The State should ensure that families have access to forms of support in the caregiving role.

Keeping children with, or returning them to, their own families should be the aim in every case where this is consistent with the child's interests, and this is emphasised by much of the legislation we work with. This means, as noted throughout this book, that a range of accessible family support services are required offering differing types of support including financial, practical and material support (Frost et al., 2015; Winter et al., 2022; Dunn and MacDonald, 2023).

Where children and young people are already in alternative care, it means working together to return children home if possible and providing ongoing help to support the return home. There is good evidence that the right kind of family support services can be very effective in enabling children to remain successfully at home (Frost et al., 2015; Canavan et al., 2016; Dunn and MacDonald, 2023). Furthermore, research by Bennett et al. (2021) in England draws attention to what happens when investment in support services is reduced. They found that 'the rising rates of older children entering care has partly been driven by cuts to prevention services catering to their needs'. The authors recommend reinvestment in support services and making this provision statutory.

A proportion of children and young people remain legally in care while actually placed with their own parents. Recent data (Department for Education,

2022; Department of Health, 2022; Scottish Government, 2022) indicates that in the UK the proportion of the total 'children in care' population who were living with their parents in 2019 was 7% in England, 11% in Northern Ireland, 16% in Wales and 25% in Scotland. The differences partly reflect differences in legal frameworks, particularly in Scotland with the children's hearings system.

Short breaks (formerly known as respite)

One of the ways in which children and families can be supported to remain together is by the provision of respite care through 'short breaks'. Primarily targeted at disabled children and those with challenging emotional, social and behavioural issues, the purpose is to give families a break from caring for a child *and* to provide the child with the opportunity to expand their social networks and experiences outside of the family home. Specific provision for short breaks is made within children's legislation and is accompanied by regulations and guidance in each of the devolved nations of the UK. In England, to ensure that Local Authorities are meeting their obligations, the government launched the Short Breaks Innovation Fund in 2022 and it provides funding for new projects, to test approaches and determine how best to improve services in this area.

Short breaks are varied. They can include care at home for a few hours (provided by someone who comes to your home to care for your child for a few hours), day care elsewhere (nurseries, clubs, playgroups, activities, summer schemes), residential breaks (in children's homes) and overnight stays in respite foster care for example. Care may be planned well in advance to take place at regular intervals, or it may be possible for families to request it as and when they need it. Some organisations, especially charities such as Action for Children, Contact, Fostering Network, Barnardos, offer programmes which include the provision of flexible and informal short breaks as part of a broader package of support and intervention. Fostering Network, for example, offer a programme called 'Step Up Step Down' which involves highly trained foster families offering support to families with children 'on the edge of care' with the level and type of support being 'stepped up' when families are struggling (and which can include overnight stays and short breaks) and 'stepped down' when the crisis has passed.

These types of programme are noted to reduce the numbers of children and young people coming into care and illustrate that short breaks are often designed primarily to help parents and carers. If parents feel supported and find life easier to manage, this is likely to be good for children too. With regard to parents' perspectives, many fear the sudden 'cutting off' of this provision at the age of 18, despite the young person's needs remaining unchanged, and the need for proactive planning in advance of this for continued support (see, for example: Dont-Hold-Back.pdf (childcomwales.org.uk).

However, it is always important to be mindful of children's own experiences of short breaks and ensure that the experience of going away is a positive, safe, and rewarding one for the child. Research by Welsh et al. (2014), which explored the responses of disabled children and their parents in a survey regarding short break provision, revealed that disabled children identified positive experiences and experiences largely focused on the activities themselves. For parents, their answers tended to focus more on the potential longer-term benefits on developmental outcomes rather than the activity itself. This and other related research (Kelly et al., 2016), reflective of their rights under the UNCRC, highlight the centrality of including disabled children in the design and evaluation of services, so that these are delivered with them rather than just to them.

Short-term foster care

Most children and young people coming into care live in some form of short-term family placement. This could be a kinship arrangement (living with relatives or friends) or a non-relative foster care arrangement (where the child is placed with foster Local Authority/Trust foster carers or foster carers approved by one of the independent fostering providers, such as Barnardo's, Foster Care Associates, Kindercare Fostering NI, National Fostering Agency, for example). It is worth noting that in recent years, the number of independent foster care agencies has increased and in England, currently stands at over 280.

An important point for families and social workers is to be aware of the fact that there is more than one way to define 'short term'; and that while eight weeks is a commonly used threshold, some short-term placements are described as such even though they have been provided for six months and even beyond (HM Government, 2022. Placements of over six months duration generally become known as long-term placements.

Short-term foster placements may be used in a number of different ways – for example:

- in an emergency;
- for assessment;
- for a defined short-term need, such as a parent's illness;
- to provide care for a child while a longer-term placement is sought.

The carer's tasks in short- and long-term foster care are very different, as we shall see in the next chapter. Although the matching of personalities that is frequently considered in the planning of permanent placements may be absent here, careful planning is still needed for a short-term placement to ensure that children's needs are well enough met, and that the placement can be stable for the period during which it is needed. Of crucial importance is the quality of relationship between the child and the carers.

One area of concern regarding short-term placements relates to a child's opportunity to form attachments to new carers. Research by Turner et al. (2023) focuses on foster carers' emotional investment in children and commitment to developing enduring relationships with children within the context of short-term foster care arrangements. The researchers found that foster carers who perceived themselves to have a positive influence on children through a positive perception of their short-term role showed a commitment to emotionally invest in children, but it was not clear, if foster carers experienced social services delay in moving a child on, whether commitment and emotional investment might be negatively impacted.

Long-term foster care

A recent review of literature and thematic analysis (Carlson et al., 2020) indicates that most children return home, and that most of these return home within a six-month period. This means that only a relatively small number of children and young people in care at any one time are in a long-term foster placement. That said, the authors also note that there is evidence to suggest a real risk of breakdown following return because of a lack of family support.

As with short-term arrangements, long-term placements can also be with family and friends or with local authority or agency carers. Again, there is more than one way to define 'long term'; sometimes a distinction is made between *long-term* placements that may be expected to continue for many months or even a few years but with an eventual end in sight, and *permanent* placements which are expected to continue through the young person's childhood – and even beyond (see Chapter 9).

Specialist foster care

Specialist fostering refers to a variety of forms of care based around the needs of particular groups of children and young people and supported by specialist training. The varieties of specialist foster care include providing a home to:

- young people who may display unusually challenging behaviour;
- disabled children and young people (some of whom may also display challenging behaviour);

- children and young people who have been remanded by the courts or detained by the police;
- 'mother and baby' placements, for situations where both child and parent need care and supervision;
- unaccompanied asylum-seeking children.

Specialist schemes typically offer higher allowances combined with a professional fee. Carers may be (but are not necessarily) more highly trained and better qualified and may take on aspects of work with the child or young person more commonly undertaken by a social worker. These schemes are discussed further in the next chapter.

Kinship care

As noted above, more and more children are fostered in homes provided by relatives (grandparents, aunts, uncles, older siblings) and/or friends of the family. These arrangements are referred to as 'kinship care'. Arrangements can be informal (an arrangement made between a birth parent and the carer) or formal (on a legal order or placed following as assessment as foster carers by the Local Authority or Health and Social Care Trust). Whilst research shows that overall children placed in kinship arrangements experience greater stability and better outcomes than if placed with Local Authority/Agency/Trust foster carers (Winokur et al., 2018; Hélie et al., 2017, 2022), the arrangements are not without their challenges. Challenges include the characteristics of kinship carers – around half are grandparents, often single, often on low incomes and sometimes with health issues (Houston et al., 2018). This should not and does not preclude children living in kinship care – relationships with grandparents, and indeed other family members, can still be beneficial for children even when there are difficulties. It does mean however that social services, in line with their duties and responsibilities, must provide support financially, materially and practically. Other challenges include tensions in the family relationships, which may impact on the management of contact arrangements, for example.

Residential care

The number of children and young people in residential care has decreased over time. As noted earlier, this is due to a combination of factors including concerns about the cost of such provision, queries about the quality of care (especially in a context where evidence of the abuse and harm of children in residential care has come to light), and questions about its effectiveness – namely, does it help improve children's long-term outcomes (Frost et al., 2020). Naturally, these debates are complex and there is a range of evidence that supports multiple perspectives. For social workers, it is important to note that residential care remains a positive option for some children and young people, especially for teenagers and for children and young people with highly specialised needs. Although less likely to be used for younger children, there are still specialist residential care units for young children such as Children's House (Barnardos) in Northern Ireland, for example.

The trend of other organisations, rather than Local Authorities and/or Health and Social Care Trusts, providing residential homes for children, has increased in recent years. Indeed, research by Bach-Mortensen et al. (2022) indicates that in England, most residential child care is provided by private 'for-profit' companies. Their research found that 'for-profit' children's homes are generally rated as lower quality, violate more requirements and receive more recommendations for improvements compared with Local Authority provision. This is a serious concern, because with the overall decline in available places, it can be difficult to find a home for a child in residential care that is close to their local community and birth family and can offer what they need. Local children's homes each have their own statement of purpose that delineates who they care for, why and for how long, but it is often the case that residential children's homes take a range of young people who may have very different needs, usually for relatively short periods. Some local authorities, and a growing number of private providers, offer specialised residential care services – for children with complex trauma or mental health issues, those who are disabled or those who have been victims of sexual exploitation. These homes provide education, care and therapeutic input.

Secure accommodation

Secure children's homes (known as SCH) or secure accommodation is a type of residential placement for children and young people who need to be kept under conditions of security, either for their own protection or for the protection of other people. This may include, for example, a child who is at risk of self-harm, or who is involved in criminal sexual behaviour, or is extremely violent. Because this type of placement is an infringement on a person's liberty, an order that enables a Local Authority or Health and Social Care Trust to place a child can only be granted by the court, must be reviewed at regular intervals and the aim is always to ensure that the secure placement remains in place only for as long as it is needed. A recent report by What Works for Children's Social Care (WWCSC, 2020) highlighted that most children referred were already in care when the application for a secure accommodation order was made. Despite the vulnerabilities of those for whom a secure accommodation order was sought, two out of five could not be placed and were placed in alternative accommodation without their needs having been addressed. This suggests that they and those around them might be at heightened risk.

Adoption

Adoption removes a child or young person permanently from her/his family of origin, and because parental responsibility is transferred to the adoptive carers, means that a child leaves care system. It is an emotive and controversial area nationally and internationally (Pösö et al., 2021), given the interference with rights to private and family life and its situation in particular historical, political, social, economic and religious contexts where dominant discourses resulted in oppressive practices (e.g., the forced adoption abroad of unmarried mothers' babies). Even though contemporary adoption may involve some continuing contact with the child's family of origin, the fact remains that in law the birth parents cease to be parents, and new people become the child's parents. In this sense, adoption is a very radical step to take; however, for some children, especially those aged five years and under, it can be the most effective way to provide the security and stability they need. These issues are explored further in Chapter 9.

Relating children's needs to the capacity of placements to respond

Having a good picture of the range of placements available and of what each can offer, helps develop a sense of what kind of placement might be most appropriate for a particular child. However, this needs to be combined with the identification of the child or young person's overall and priority needs, in order to establish what kind of placement, and which particular placement, will best meet these needs. Factors that need to be borne in mind include whether the child needs short-term or long-term care, and whether or not the child's family is expected to resume the responsibility for care. It will be necessary to consider general characteristics of the child such as their age, gender, ethnic, religious and cultural background, as well as individual characteristics of the child and their personal history. It can sometimes be useful to look at this in terms of the 'messages' the child or young person has received from their previous upbringing and the 'messages' that are likely to be helpful to them in the future.

In Boxes 7.1–7.3 we give three examples of how these different aspects of placement choice may work out in practice.

Box 7.1 Kelly

Kelly is 15 years old and profoundly deaf. Her parents, who both have mild learning disabilities, are having difficulty managing her behaviour. She has stayed away from home several times without permission, on one occasion apparently staying with a 30-year-old man. Kelly and her parents agree that she should be accommodated. She has an 11-year-old brother who is settled at home.

The plan for Kelly may well be for an initial admission to care as a basis for work to enable the family to resume living together successfully. However, it has to be acknowledged that this may not work and that Kelly may need care until she is an adult. Young people in similar situations are often admitted to group care, or to a specialist fostering scheme. In Kelly's case, close attention to her individual needs and wishes will be necessary to determine the most appropriate placement. It will need to be one where carers are able to exercise appropriate control without driving Kelly further into rebellion. The 'messages' that she has received from her experience at home may well be to do with her being uncontrollable or not worth caring about – this will need further exploration, as will the ability of a proposed placement to give more helpful messages. Kelly's links with the Deaf community also need to be explored – in particular whether this community can offer a suitable placement. This may well be a case where a 'family group conference' would be helpful.

Box 7.2 Asha

Asha is two years old and has been removed from home on an emergency protection order because of severe neglect. She is undernourished and has a cleft palate which has not been properly treated. Asha's father is Bangladeshi and her mother is white British. The family have only been in contact with services for a short time, and it is not clear whether with support they will be able to resume caring for Asha. Asha has two older sisters who are now also being cared for.

It is not possible to say with certainty at this stage whether Asha needs a permanent substitute family, but it is clearly a strong possibility. The primary need at this point is for a placement that will provide safety and good physical care for her while she gets the treatment she needs and the family's resources are assessed. Beyond that there are some difficult issues here in placement choice. Clearly there are advantages for Asha in finding a placement that could if necessary keep her on a permanent basis; but a permanent placement should also be one that can meet her needs as a child of mixed heritage, and a placement now should if possible be one where her sisters could also be accommodated if this becomes necessary. Since all these criteria are unlikely to be met in one placement, difficult choices are likely to have to be made. A team approach to planning is likely to be invaluable in this case, as well as some clear thinking about attachment issues.

Box 7.3 Tomos and Gwilym

Tomos and Gwilym are aged eight and ten, and need accommodation while their father, a widower, has hospital treatment for depression. The prognosis is good and it is expected that they will return home within two to three months. The boys both speak Welsh as their first language, as does their father.

Tomos and Gwilym clearly need as a priority a placement close to home that will preserve their links with family, neighbourhood and school. Kinship care ought to be the first option here, but there may also be neighbours or parents of school friends who can offer care to these boys. A placement with family or neighbours may also well be Welsh-speaking, which is highly desirable for the reasons we saw in Chapter 4. Some might argue for a degree of scepticism about the positive prognosis in this case – but at this stage the aim must surely be to work for a speedy return of the boys to their father, perhaps from carers who can provide some ongoing support to the three of them. Tomos and Gwilym are likely to be worried about their father and anxious about the future, and so the quality of emotional support may be a key issue in choosing a placement. (They may also need help in grieving for their mother.)

Who decides?

Choosing a placement is not just down to an individual social worker, but rather is always a matter for discussion and negotiation involving a number of different people. This can include family placement workers, residential care staff, managers and supervisors. It may also include professionals from agencies such as education and health as advisers – and sometimes as contributors to decisions about funding. The decision may involve panels or committees. Sometimes the court may have a part to play in deciding on a placement. Once a potential placement has been identified, those likely to be involved in providing the care will need to be consulted. Above all, the decision must include the child and family, because the views of the child or young person and their family are crucial in determining how successful a placement might be. The UN Guidelines for the Alternative Care of Children (UN, 2009, para 6, p. 3) remind us that:

> All decisions, initiatives and approaches […] they should respect fully the child's right to be consulted and to have his/her views duly taken into account in accordance with his/her evolving capacities, and on the basis of his/her access to all necessary information. Every effort should be made to enable such consultation and information provision to be carried out in the child's preferred language.

As with all our planning processes, there is more than one way of including people in decision making, and 'one big meeting' is not necessarily the most effective way. The social worker may need to spend some time talking to children, parents and professionals individually about how they view the different options for placement. In the case of the child, and perhaps other members of the family too, this may need to involve further preparation including visits to proposed placements, face-to-face meetings with possible carers or viewing together a book or a video they have made about themselves and their home.

Including the child and family effectively in the decision can be difficult when the negotiations required are complex, or when there is pressure to resolve the situation quickly. For this reason, it is better if decision-making processes within the agency can be kept as simple as possible, and as much information as possible provided to children, young people and their families. This is essential to help avoid unplanned, uninformed placement moves for children which can disrupt attachments, be experienced as traumatic and have negative impacts in the short and the longer term.

Making a placement – transitions and practical issues

Having identified a placement, practicalities include completing the paperwork associated with the process of planning in relation to the placement and building in whatever detailed arrangements are needed for the day-to-day care of the child or young person, as well as the plans for contact. This includes attention to the arrangements for attendance at school attendance, health appointments, clubs, religious events, social events and dates for meetings.

Moving from a family home into a placement (or between placements) is a significant transition for a child or young person. There are theories and frameworks that explain and explore the processes by which people adjust to transitions in their lives. A useful model in the context of children's transitions into and out of care is Schlossberg's transition model. Its tenets and application are explored in work by Winter (2014, p. 404) who notes that, 'Schlossberg defines a transition as 'any event, or non-event that results in changed relationships, routines, assumptions or roles' (Schlossberg et al., 1995, p. 27). The conceptual model comprises three main elements:

- approaching transitions (the context, type and anticipated impact of the transition);
- taking stock of coping resources which includes the situation (what is happening); the self (to whom is it happening); the support (what support is available) and strategies (how does this person cope); and
- taking charge (working with a person on the above aspects of transition can help with the process) (Schlossberg et al., 1995, p. 26).

Applying the above to practice, social workers must ensure that the child and parents understand exactly what is going to happen, and why. Relevant, accessible information needs to be provided. Social workers must ensure that they listen to the child to make sure that they have an idea as to how the child is thinking and feeling about what is planned. They must also listen to parents and/or other family members/significant carers. If appropriate, one strategy to assist a child to cope is some form of introduction to the carers – via audio or video link, or even a photo album if an actual visit is not possible. This might help allay any fears, for example. Another very important aspect of assisting a child to cope might involve the social worker being very clear about when and how often they will be visiting, how they can be reliably contacted and that they will respond in a timely fashion. This might help the child, parents and carers avoid feelings of having been abandoned.

Despite these strategies, children may have enduring feelings of loss and abandonment. They also often blame themselves for being in care; 'it's my fault', 'I did something bad or naughty'. It is therefore important that the reasons for their entry into care are re-visited often to reinforce the facts and deal with any misperceptions. Carers might also be struggling to develop a relationship with a child, and parents may be experiencing overwhelming feelings of loss or anger. All these feelings demand that further supports are identified and made available.

It's morning. As you awaken, you look around you. It is an unfamiliar room. You slept little last night. You've always been warned about strangers and here you are, with no one else you know, in the midst of them.

You hear people up and about. What are you supposed to do? Lie in bed until someone comes and tells you to get up? Get up, get dressed, and go downstairs on your own? Did anyone tell you last night what was expected? Your memory is fuzzy.

Where are your parents? When will you see them? Do they know where you are? One question after another engulfs you. Pulling the covers over your head, you try to block them out.

What could be done to make this transition easier? Would you be less frightened if the adults were known to you? Would even having your own teddy bear to hug be of any comfort?

Implications of attachment and resilience

Thinking further about attachment, it was noted in Chapter 2 how attachment theory can be useful in helping us to think about a child or young person's history and their future needs. In choosing a placement and making the arrangements, it is important to take into account the patterns of attachment the child has developed and how these are likely to be affected by the placement.

The key tasks in relation to attachment will vary according to the child and the situation. In most cases it will be important to ensure that existing attachments are not weakened or threatened unnecessarily by the new arrangements; indeed, in many cases one of our aims will be to strengthen these existing attachments. As indicated earlier, recent research by Turner et al. (2023) highlights that the task of a short-term carer can be difficult – on the one hand, to enable the child to settle in the placement and feel secure, but on the other hand to ensure that existing relationships are not challenged or replaced. In other cases, the aim will be to help the child make healthy new attachments. Here, the choice of carer is particularly important, because it must be someone to whom the child or young person is likely to make a good attachment and who is ready to accept this.

Social workers should support placements in ways that allow children to acquire more experience, more skills and resources in making attachments. Recently, there has been a renewed emphasis on attachment-aware practice by all professionals working with children and young people coming into, living in and leaving care. This work reflects the key principles of Bowlby on attachments and includes writers such as Fahlberg (1994), Shemmings (2005) and Schofield and Beek (2014). Schofield and Beek's work on the Secure Base Model has at its heart carers' availability to support children and young people to build meaningful, effective relationships and to provide a secure base for children through different dimensions of care.

Sibling relationships and placement

For most of us, our relationships with our brothers and sisters are the most enduring of all. For many children and young people in care, relationships with siblings can be crucial to their sense of stability and belonging. Personal accounts of life in care often reveal that separation from siblings is one of the most painful experiences. Whilst difficult issues can sometimes arise when decisions have to be made about the placement of sibling groups – perhaps because children are admitted at different times, or because a placement that is particularly suited to the special needs of one child cannot cater for a brother or sister – overall there should be no excuse for brothers and sisters to be separated on admission into care except in rare cases when it is genuinely in their best interests. If separation has to occur, clear and robust contact arrangements should be put in place.

Issues in family contact

There is a general assumption in social work with children and families – and in the law and guidance – that children in care should be in contact with their family and friends (Smith and Logan, 2013). The UN Guidelines for the Alternative Care of Children (UN, 2009, para. 17, p. 4) remind us of the importance of family and of siblings when it states:

> Siblings with existing bonds should in principle not be separated by placements in alternative care unless there is a clear risk of abuse or other justification in the best interests of the child. In any case, every effort should be made to enable siblings to maintain contact with each other, unless this is against their wishes or interests.

Research (Nesmith, 2013; Wojciak et al., 2023) shows the positive effects on children and young people of continuing contact with people who are important to them but with whom they do not live, and the negative consequences of losing such contact. The assumption is also based on attachment theory and what it says about the value of affectional bonds in giving us a sense of identity – of who we are, what we are like, and where we belong. Furthermore, the assumption seems to reflect a general value position which stresses that it is part of the natural order of things, reflective of the family as the basic building block of society, that children ought to remain in contact with people who are significant to them, and that loss of contact is inherently a bad thing.

In child care law, there is an emphasis on maintaining links with family as long as this is consistent with the best interests of the child. as noted above, this is reinforced by the United Nations Convention on the Rights of the Child, which asserts 'the right of the child who is separated from one or both parents to maintain personal relations and direct contact with both parents on a regular basis, except if it is contrary to the child's best interests' (Article 9). This applies to children whose parents reside in different states (Article 10) and to children deprived of liberty (Article 37). The Council of Europe 'Convention on Contact concerning Children' (Council of Europe, 2003), opened for signature on 15 May 2003 and signed by 12 member states, also provides for children and parents to have a right to regular contact, which can be restricted only in the interests of the child. It also provides for children to be informed and consulted, and for contact orders and agreements to be enforced across national boundaries.

'Contact' does not just mean face to face contact. With the growth in social media and online platforms, keeping in contact is increasingly likely to mean using some form of digital technology (Singer and Brodzinsky, 2020; MacDonald et al., 2023). Contact can also mean letters or telephone calls, and even indirect messages *via* a third party. Contact arrangements can and should include many different members of the child or young person's network – brothers and sisters, aunts and uncles, grandparents, friends and neighbours. In many cases, these arrangements can be very informal, and the main social work task may be to encourage and support them rather than actively manage them. For some children contact with siblings, aunts, uncles or grandparents, or friends and neighbours may be more important than with parents. For children and young people who have experienced moves in care, contact with previous carers can be especially important; it is easy for these relationships to be neglected if social workers are not alert to the importance of keeping them alive. For some children, especially those who are lonely, isolated or abused, continuing contact with a pet may the most important issue. Whatever the means through which contact takes place, social workers can be involved in managing the difficulties that sometimes emerge, as explored further below.

Difficulties with contact

Contact can be challenging for family members. For parents, it can be upsetting because it can be hard to see your child getting better care from other people. Contact can hold a mirror to parents regarding their own struggles and so evoke feelings of guilt, shame and inadequacy. It can also evoke strong feelings of loss – loss of their child and loss of control. It can evoke feelings of anxiety, especially where their child is developing new attachments and birth parents can feel as if their child does not love them, need them or want to be with them anymore. Alongside this, there are the sheer practical difficulties for many families of keeping up contact arrangements – transport, childcare, time off work – and the need to manage the contact so as not to disrupt unnecessarily the child's other activities or the lives of the carers. For all these reasons, children's family contact arrangements can dwindle with time and do require active support from carers, social workers and often a great deal of sensitivity to make them work well.

Contact can also be a difficult experience for children. Pain associated with separation may be brought to the surface by contact, and this must be handled sensitively. Children and young people may pick up on their parents' own feelings, as described above, and this can make a child feel sad, upset, angry or guilty. If the parent misuses the contact time (see below) or lacks the resources to make it a good experience, then it may become something that the child seeks to avoid or deals with by 'acting out'. To avoid these obstacles to successful contact, attention needs to be paid both to the quality of the experience and to the messages that are being communicated to the child in relation to contact.

Other difficulties may include the fact that contact brings with it the potential for harm. The dynamics involved in abusive situations from which a child has been removed, can be repeated in contact time. These situations demand very careful handling, because it may still be important for the child to maintain a relationship with such a parent, but this must be managed in a way that keeps the child safe. Part of the answer may lie in closely supervised contact, an artificial situation but one which may sometimes be in the best all-round interests of the child. Supervised contact may also be necessary if the parents are having to learn skills or demonstrate their ability to provide good care.

Social workers need to keep a clear head and a clear focus on what is best for the child or young person, and to pay careful attention to what the child is saying both verbally and non-verbally. Signs of distress from a child or young person should never be ignored, but it should not be assumed that the appropriate response is to stop the contact. Sometimes the distress may be a signal that something that is happening around the contact needs to be looked at, and sometimes it simply means that the child needs to be supported through an experience which is arousing painful feelings. As noted, some of the distress can be managed by supervising the contact meetings. It can also be managed by clarifying the purpose of contact, as we explore further below.

Purpose of contact

One of the first things a social worker should do in making plans and arrangements for contact is to ensure that everyone is sufficiently clear as to the purpose of contact for *this* child in *these* circumstances. If the care plan states that the aim is to return the child home as soon as possible, the purpose of the contact will probably be to maintain active everyday relationships between children, parents and other family members, and also with neighbours, school friends and so on, in order to keep as much continuity as possible. If the care plan notes that there are significant concerns that the parents need to address before any rehabilitation can be considered, the purpose of the contact may also involve an assessment of parenting capacity and the feasibility of change.

If there is no plan for rehabilitation, the purpose of contact is likely to be to help children and young people preserve a sense of identity and continuity in their lives – which is especially important bearing in mind that most children and young people leaving care do eventually return to their families of origin in one way or another. Even in the case of adoption, we know through all the research involving adults adopted as children and now involved in searching for birth family, that ongoing contact of some type with the birth family can be a vital part of understanding one's identity and heritage.

In each case, however, being clear about the purpose of contact should help us to think clearly about what kind of contact will best meet the needs of the child, and of the other people involved. Too often debates about contact, especially when the courts are involved, start with discussion of *how often* and then perhaps *where*, when from the child's point of view, and that of the parents and carers, the most important question may be *what kind of contact*. Fixed intervals and set times may be useful in the short term, especially if there are tensions between the adults in the situation, but in the longer run, children need arrangements that are flexible and responsive to changes in their lives – more like ordinary relationships between children and significant people in their lives, such as grandparents. Importantly, it may not be the quantity of contact that is important, so much as the quality. If we think of our own personal lives, we may well have family relatives who we don't see very, often but with whom we still have meaningful and significant relationships. This is no different for children and young people in care and the aim should be to make sure that contact is high quality. The next section outlines some practical ways to help enhance quality of contact.

Making arrangements for contact

When making arrangements for contact, it helps to think about the 'what', 'when', 'where' and 'how' of contact. In terms of 'what' contact, plans should take account of the fact that the length and frequency may need to be flexible rather than rigidly set at a certain time and for a certain time period each week, or month. It may be that it better suits the child, parents and carers to have a degree of flexibility, so that the times and type of contact can be adjusted to suit all involved. It might be that the preference for contact is via an online platform (Singer and Brodzinsky, 2020). It is also likely that children's and carers' needs, circumstances and preferences change over time. This means that while basic parameters can be set, there should be flexibility within these parameters.

With regard to when and where contact takes place, plans are often agreed to reflect organisational needs rather than the needs of the family and children. Times may be set to reflect the availability of certain buildings or certain staff, and often there is less focus on what best suits the child, parents, and carers. With new born babies where part of the contact is the assessment of parenting capacity, times of contact will need to be adjusted to the developing feeding pattern of the baby, so that the parent can be involved in feeding and changing their own child. Transport times should coincide with a baby's resting times, so that those doing the transport are not left in a situation where they have a very hungry, distressed baby in the car on the way to contact. Online contact meetings, as indicated, allow for a greater degree of flexibility (Singer and Brodzinsky, 2020).

Where contact takes place can be hugely important. Venues that are child, parent and carer-friendly should be sought. Sometimes social services buildings are sparsely equipped for contact between children and parents. Contact centres equipped for the purpose may be more appropriate. However, the environment can feel artificial, and parents may feel under surveillance by social workers and experience the anxiety, worry and sense of failure that this can evoke. The role of social workers in supporting parents and children during these times is vital. Sometimes a more creative approach is needed. For young children, it might be nice to go to the park and be pushed in a swing by their parent, or to go to the shops and be bought something to eat.

In terms of *how* contact takes place, clarity about the role of the social worker is vital. Is it to remain in the background assessing the relational dynamics and parenting in contact, or is it to support through intervening and giving advice or role modelling appropriate responses where necessary? If the contact involves an assessment component, what frameworks are being used, are parents and children aware and informed about them, and do they have an opportunity to self-reflect on what went well and what did not go well in the contact today. Are parents and children able to make an active contribution to identifying areas for improvement? Also of course, for families whose first language is not English or who have particular cultural or religious needs or who are disabled, these factors are an essential part of planning the 'what, where, when, and how' of contact.

So how can a social worker contribute to making contact more authentic? Strategies can include allowing parents, carers and children maximum autonomy to determine their own pattern of contact arrangements, tailored to their specific circumstances. For other families who need more support, it may mean providing a framework of activities that will help build and sustain relationships, or offering a support worker to help with visits. In other cases, the substitute carers may be able to take an active role in facilitating contact. There is no universal recipe – the keynote has to be flexibility and adaptability, based on the starting point of 'what will make it a good experience for everyone involved?' Written contact plans are important to make sure that everyone has a clear understanding of what is happening – but they should not be unnecessarily rigid.

Exercise 7.1 Annie again

Return to the example of Annie in the previous chapter. This time, ask:

What are the issues involved in choosing a placement for Annie?

What guidance is most relevant?

What research is most relevant?

What are the realistic options?

What arrangements would you make for contact? Why?

Summary and conclusion

> Entrance into the foster system is often sudden and without preparation. Once in the child care system, the child's traumatic separation from his or her birth family is frequently allowed to drift into permanent estrangement. Worse still, the maintenance of a bond between the child in interim care and his or her birth family is sometimes actively discouraged. The child's feelings of loss are frequently ignored or glossed over. Contacts between parents and child may be limited or prevented. Children's emotional reactions to visits with their birth families may be misunderstood and misinterpreted. Foster carers may not receive the help they need in dealing with the increased behavioural problems precipitated by the visits. However, the truth is that minimising the trauma of separations and losses and working to facilitate the development of new attachments are complementary, rather than competitive, tasks.
>
> *Fahlberg (2012, pp. 167–168)*

The passage from Fahlberg (2012), quoted above, brings together many of the themes of this chapter: the importance of attachment and the intense feelings that can be associated with separation; the value of working actively to maintain contact between a child and significant people; the need for listening carefully to the child and understanding her or his reactions. The chapter has also considered the types of placement that may be available, relating children's needs to the placements on offer, and explored issues of family contact for young people in care. The final point that needs adding is the extent to which good placement practice usually starts by asking 'what can we do to keep this child as close to home, in every sense, as possible?'

GUIDE TO FURTHER READING

On a child's journey through placement, Fahlberg (1994, second edition, 2012) is a book everyone should have. Burns et al. (2017) review the decision-making processes and policies for the removal into state care of children in different countries, and Cameron and Petrie (2009) consider the issues related to securing positive outcomes for children once they are in care. With regard to different types of placement, Frost et al. (2020) and Smith (2013) are very good starting points regarding residential care. Pitcher (2013) considers kinship care, Farmer and Moyes (2008) compare kinship and foster care arrangements. Rose (2002) considers secure accommodation. Regarding the various pathways once in care, books by Iwaniec (2006), Ward et al. (2006) and McSherry et al. (2013) are very helpful. On contact issues, Macaskill (2002) and Beckett (2021) are helpful. The NSPCC website offers accessible information on key provisions in each devolved area of the UK.

References

Bach-Mortensen, A.M., Goodair, B. and Barlow, J. (2022) 'Outsourcing and children's social care: A longitudinal analysis of inspection outcomes among English children's homes and local authorities', *Social Science & Medicine*, *313*, 115323.

Beckett, S. (2021) *Beyond together or apart. Planning for, assessing and placing sibling groups*. London: CoramBAAF.

Bennett, D.L., Webb, C.J., Mason, K.E., Schlüter, D.K., Fahy, K., Alexiou, A., Wickham, S., Barr, B. and Taylor-Robinson, D. (2021) 'Funding for preventative children's services and rates of children becoming looked after: A natural experiment using longitudinal area-level data in England', *Children and Youth Services Review*, *131*, 106289.

Burns, K., Pösö, T. and Skivenes, M. (eds.) (2017) *Child welfare removals by the state: A cross-country analysis of decision-making systems*. Oxford: Oxford University Press.

Cameron, C. and Petrie, P. (2009) 'Social pedagogy and its prospects in England's children's services', *European Journal of Social Education*, *16/17*, 49–61.

Canavan, J., Pinkerton, J. and Dolan, P. (2016) *Understanding family support: Policy, practice, and theory*. London: Jessica Kingsley Publishers.

Carlson, L., Hutton, S., Priest, H. and Melia, Y. (2020) 'Reunification of looked-after children with their birth parents in the United Kingdom: A literature review and thematic synthesis', *Child and Family Social Work*, *25*(1), 192–205.

Children's Commissioner for England. (2021) *Children's commissioner. Children in care findings from the big ask*. London: Children's Commissioner for England. Available here https://assets.childrenscommissioner.gov.uk/wpuploads/2021/10/cco-children-in-care-findings-from-the-big-ask.pdf (accessed 27.01.24).

Children's Commissioner for Wales. (2018) *Don't hold back. Transitions to adulthood for young people with learning disabilities*. Port Talbot: The Children's Commissioner for Wales. Available here Dont-Hold-Back.pdf (childcomwales.org.uk) (accessed 27.01.24).

Children's Commissioner for Wales. (2022) *The right way. A children's rights approach for social care in Wales*. Port Talbot: The Children's Commissioner for Wales.

Council of Europe. (2003) *Convention on contact concerning children*. Strasbourg: Council of Europe.

Degener, C.J., van Bergen, D.D. and Grietens, H.W. (2022a) '"Being one, but not being the same": A dyadic comparative analysis on ethnic socialization in transcultural foster families in the Netherlands', *Child and Family Social Work*, *27*(2), 143–151.

Degener, C.J., van Bergen, D.D. and Grietens, H.W. (2022b) 'The ethnic identity of transracially placed foster children with an ethnic minority background: A systematic literature review', *Children and Society*, *36*(2), 201–219.

Department for Education. (2022). *Children looked after in England including adoptions, reporting year 2022*. Available here https://explore-education-statistics.service.gov.uk/find-statistics/children-looked-after-in-england-including-adoptions

Department of Health/Northern Ireland Statistics and Research Agency. (2022) *Children's social care statistics for Northern Ireland 2021/2022*. Belfast: Department of Health.

Dunn, H. and MacDonald, M. (2023) *Reflections: Family support*. Department of Health, Belfast: N Ireland.

Fahlberg, V.I. (1994) *A child's journey through placement.* London: British Association for Adoption and Fostering (BAAF).
Fahlberg, V.I. (2012) *A child's journey through placement* (second edition). London: British Association for Adoption and Fostering (BAAF).
Farmer, E. and Moyes, S. (2008). *Kinship care: Fostering effective family and friends placements.* London: Jessica Kingsley Publications.
Frost, N., Abbott, S. and Race, T. (2015) *Family support: Prevention, early intervention, and early help.* Chichester: John Wiley & Sons.
Frost, N., Mills, S. and Stein, M. (2020) *Understanding residential child care.* London: Routledge.
Hélie, S., Poirier, M.A., Esposito, T. and Turcotte, D. (2017) 'Placement stability, cumulative time in care, and permanency: Using administrative data from CPS to track placement trajectories', *International Journal of Environmental Research and Public Health, 14*(11), 1405.
Hélie, S., Poirier, M.A., Lavergne, C., Dorval, A. and Lamothe, J. (2022) 'Factors associated with reunification and placement move for children placed in kinship care under the age of thirteen', *Child Abuse and Neglect, 130*, 105357.
HM Government. (2022) *National statistics: Children's social care in England 2021.* Available here https://www.gov.uk/government/statistics/childrens-social-care-data-in-england-2021/main-findings-childrens-social-care-in-england-2021 (accessed 27.01.24).
Houston, S., Hayes, D. and MacDonald, M. (2018) 'Hearing the voices of kinship foster carers in Northern Ireland: An inquiry into characteristics, needs and experiences', *Families, Relationships and Societies*, 7(2), 227–247.
Iwaniec, D. (ed.) (2006) *The child's journey through care: Placement stability, care planning, and achieving permanency.* Chichester: John Wiley and Sons.
Kelly, B., McShane, T., Davidson, G., Pinkerton, J., Gilligan, E. and Webb, P. (2016) *Transitions and outcomes for care leavers with mental health and/or intellectual disabilities: Final report.* Belfast: QUB.
Macaskill, C. (2002) *Safe contact? Children in permanent placement and contact with birth relatives.* Lyme Regis: Russell House Publishing Ltd.
MacDonald, M., Wright, A.C., Taylor-Beswick, A., Gillespie, K. and Collings, S. (2023) 'Digital relationality, rights, resilience: Conceptualising a digital social ecology for children's birth family relationships when in care or adopted', *The British Journal of Social Work, 53*(1), 216–235.
McSherry, D., Malet, M.F. and Weatherall, K. (2013) *Comparing long-term placements for young children in care: The care pathways and outcomes study-Northern Ireland.* London: British Association for Adoption and Fostering.
Nesmith, A. (2013) 'Parent–child visits in foster care: Reaching shared goals and expectations to better prepare children and parents for visits', *Child and Adolescent Social Work Journal, 30*, 237–255.
Pitcher, D. (ed.) (2013) *Inside kinship care: Understanding family dynamics and providing effective support.* London: Jessica Kingsley Publishers.
Pösö, T., Skivenes, M. and Thoburn, J. (2021) *Adoption from care: International perspectives on children's rights, family preservation and State Intervention.* Bristol: Policy Press.
Plumer, E. (1992) *When you place a child ....* Springfield: Charles Thomas.
Rose, J. (2002) *Working with young people in secure accommodation.* Milton Park: Taylor and Francis Ltd.

Schofield, G. and Beek, M. (2014) *The secure base model: Promoting attachment and resilience in foster care and adoption*. London: BAAF.
Schlossberg, N.K., Waters, E.B. and Goodman, J. (1995) *Counselling adults in transition: Linking practice with theory*. New York: Springer.
Scottish Government. (2022) *Children's social work statistics 2020/2021*. Edinburgh: The Scottish Government. Available here https://www.gov.scot/binaries/content/documents/govscot/publications/statistics/2022/03/childrens-social-work-statistics-scotland-2020-21/documents/childrens-social-work-statistics-2020-21/childrens-social-work-statistics-2020-21/govscot%3Adocument/childrens-social-work-statistics-2020-21.pdf (accessed 27.01.24).
Shemmings, D. (2005) *Adult attachment theory*. Norwich: University of East Anglia, Social Work Monographs.
Singer, J. and Brodzinsky, D. (2020) 'Virtual parent-child visitation in support of family reunification in the time of COVID-19', *Developmental Child Welfare*, 2(3), 153–171.
Smith, C. and Logan, J. (2013) *After adoption: Direct contact and relationships*. London: Routledge.
Smith, M. (2013) *Residential child care in practice: Making a difference (social work in practice)*. Bristol: Policy Press.
Turner, F., Kainth, G., MacDonald, S., O'Connor, R., Crawford, K. and Minnis, H. (2023) '"I will commit to this child as much as I can for the time that they are with me:" A qualitative examination of how foster carer commitment relates to short-term foster care for young children following abuse and neglect', *Child Abuse and Neglect*, *135*, 105983.
United Nations. (2010) *Guidelines for the alternative care of children. A/RES/64/142 (Sixty-fourth session)*. Geneva: United Nations. Available here https://www.refworld.org/docid/4c3acd162.html (accessed 27.01.24).
Ward, H., Munro, E. and Dearden, C. (2006) *Babies and young children in care: Life pathways, decision-making and practice*. London: Jessica Kingsley Publishers.
Welsh, R., Dyer, S., Evans, D. and Fereday, J. (2014) 'Identifying benefits and barriers to respite for carers of children with complex health needs: A qualitative study', *Contemporary Nurse*, *48*(1), 98–108.
What Works for Children's Social Care (WWCSC). (2020). *Unlocking the facts: Children referred to secure children's homes*. Available here https://whatworks-csc.org.uk/wp-content/uploads/WWCSC_Unlocking_the_Facts_SCH_summary_report_Dec2020_Acc.pdf (accessed 27.01.24).
Winokur, M.A., Holtan, A. and Batchelder, K.E. (2018) 'Systematic review of kinship care effects on safety, permanency, and well-being outcomes', *Research on Social Work Practice*, *28*(1), 19–32.
Winter, K. (2014) 'Understanding and supporting young children's transitions into state care: Schlossberg's transition framework and child-centred practice', *British Journal of Social Work*, *44*(2), 401–417.
Winter, K., Connolly, P., Millen, S. and Sweet, D. (2022) 'The UNCRC and family support: A case study of the early intervention support service', *Child Care in Practice*, 1–15. DOI: 10.1080/13575279.2022.2088473
Wojciak, A.S., Tomfohrde, O., Simpson, J.E. and Waid, J. (2023) 'Sibling separation: Learning from those with former foster care experiences', *The British Journal of Social Work*, *53*(4), 2198–2216.

8

RESIDENTIAL AND FOSTER CARE

CONTENTS OF CHAPTER

- Introduction
- Characteristics of foster care
- Working in foster care
- Characteristics of residential care
- Working in residential care
- The relationship between residential and foster care
- Supporting children and young people in residential and foster care
- Summary and conclusion
- Guide to further reading

Introduction

In this chapter, we will look in more detail at the main types of care provision for children and young people – residential or group care, and foster care or family placement. We will look first at the distinctive characteristics of each of these two broad categories of placement, with some reference to the historical background. We will then consider what skills are involved in each type of care, what factors are linked with success or failure and what are the respective roles of social workers and carers. This will prepare the ground for going on to consider what might be the advantages and disadvantages of one care type over the other. After this, we will look specifically at the role of the field social worker and at the supervision and inspection of placements. The chapter will conclude with a discussion of abuse in care and how it can be prevented, and of the place of therapeutic work in care.

DOI: 10.4324/9781003503194-8

Characteristics of foster care

Definition

The Cambridge dictionary definition of foster care is 'to take care of a child as if [they] were your own, usually for a limited time, without being the child's legal parent'. Whilst some fostering arrangements do indeed involve the carers having no legal parental responsibility for the child, legislation has changed and there are an increasing number of carers who can and do apply to court for shared parental responsibility with the birth parent(s). That said, regardless of the legal status of the child, the expectation on foster carers is that they provide a child with a level of physical, material, emotional, social, and psychological care, to the same standards as if the child were their own. In other words, foster carers are seen as providing loving, nurturing, well-resourced and safe family homes for children not their own.

Background

Foster care has existed in the UK for a long time. Up until the nineteenth century, it was common for families to place their older children in other people's houses to learn a trade, or as a domestic servant. The use of 'wet-nursing', where children are breastfed by an unrelated woman for hire, was also prevalent. In the nineteenth century, children began to be removed from Poor Law workhouses and placed by Churches or philanthropic agencies in families, and even sent abroad for this purpose (for further detail on the history of foster care, see chapter in Guishard-Pine et al., 2016).

State intervention regarding foster care – that is, the introduction of legislation and regulation of provision – came to the fore after the Second World War after many children had been dislocated from their families and communities to live with other families as part of the mass evacuations from towns and cities to rural areas. Family placement was seen as the preferred option, rather than residential institutions. To counter concerns about the safety and wellbeing of children in alterative family care that followed the death of Denis O'Neill in poorly supervised foster care (O'Neill, 2020), a framework of regulation and supervision was introduced (Hayden, 1999). Since then legislation, regulations and guidance have continued to develop, reflecting both the complexity and diversity of contemporary foster care provision and also reflecting a response to some of the core challenges and concerns.

Today, foster care is provided by Local Authority (or Health and Social Care Trust) foster carers, as well as by independent providers, some of which operate for profit. A range of carers is needed to provide different types of placement including: short-term (emergency, remand, assessment); shared care (short breaks); medium-term (preparation for adoption, leaving care or returning home) and long-term (care into adulthood). There are different types of foster carer (non-relative carers and family kinship carers). There are also bespoke programmes such as Mockingbird, for example. As outlined in an evaluation report by Ott et al. (2021), Mockingbird is a type of family support model based on replicating extended family relationships and involves creating micro support communities involving six to ten foster/kinship families. The families train together and offer practical, peer support and guidance to each other, including respite care for example, with the aim of strengthening foster families in positive ways to maximise placement stability for children in care. With this diverse provision comes the need for accessible processes and procedures to assess and approve potential foster carers. Carers also require access to a fostering social worker, training programmes, support from other foster carers (peer support programmes), financial support and advocacy services such as those provided by Fostering Network or the various kinship care charities in the UK.

Under the current regulations across the UK, local authorities have a duty to maintain and support a range of foster homes chosen to reflect the needs of children in their area. Carers have to be approved for specified types of care and can only be used for the purposes for which they are approved – although the regulations make provision for emergency placements. The approval of carers must be reviewed at regular intervals, separately from the review of a child placed there, and it is explicit that on at least some of the regular visits to a placement by the child's social worker, the child should be seen apart from the carers and their views and experiences actively sought.

Newer types of foster care

In addition to the main types of foster care outlined above, there have been recent developments in specialised types of foster care. Especially noteworthy are 'parent and child' placements, specialist therapeutic placements and placements for unaccompanied and asylum-seeking children.

'Parent and child' placements include those provided for assessment of parenting capacity, pre-birth support placements to help parents prepare for the arrival of a baby, and parenting support placements for parents who need help in learning how to parent. These types of placement can sometimes be the best way to maintain parent-child attachment and support the development of parenting skills, through role modelling, direct instruction, guidance, advice and support. 'Parent and child' placements can be useful when there are concerns regarding parental self-care, abuse of previous children, learning disability, use of drugs or alcohol, for example. The eventual aim of this is for the parent and child to return to independent living.

Therapeutic foster care is provided for children requiring high levels of specialist input following exposure to trauma, neglect, abuse, instability, and disruption. Issues that some children and young people face include social, emotional behavioural and/or mental health difficulties, manifesting as anxiety, depression, nightmares, self-harm, verbal and physical aggression and inability to form relationships with people. This type of foster care is sometimes called therapeutically led care (TLC) or wrap-around care. Acknowledging the challenges of caring for children and young people with these difficulties, foster carers are trained in particular therapeutic techniques which are often premised on the importance of being attachment-aware and trauma-informed. Carers may also have access to a trained therapist for advice and support.

What sort of people foster?

In England, the most recent Ofsted (Office for Standards in Education, Children's Services and Skills, 2022) report noted that just over 40% of all foster carers are aged 40–49 years old, and approximately 25% are aged 50–59 years old. Of the total number of fostering households, 18% are 'family or friends' placements. Just over 80% of all foster carers are white. There are more minority ethnic foster carers in the Independent Fostering Agency sector compared with the Local Authorities. Furthermore, changes in the law mean that Local Authorities and Independent Fostering Agencies now welcome applications from couples or single people whatever their gender identity or sexual orientation. Overall there are declines in the number of placements available, but increased demand overall and for particular groups of children, especially for refugee and asylum-seeking children and young people. Similar themes are reflected in reports produced by the Care Inspectorate in Scotland, Welsh Government Statistics and Research, and the Northern Ireland Health Department.

Other shared issues across the four jurisdictions include the large difference in numbers between those expressing an interest in fostering and those actually applying, and the gap between the numbers applying and those that are finally approved. Once approved, some foster carers note challenges in accessing training, support from a link worker, adequate financial support or respite provision. More broadly, there are concerns regarding recruitment and retention. Challenges are exacerbated by the fact that the higher fees paid by independent fostering agencies, as well as better access to training and support, means that potential carers are more attracted to apply to the IFA sector. Overall the number of applications to and placements provided by Local Authorities is declining. Across all nations, there is a need for increased foster care placements, and within this specialist foster placements, reflecting both the overall increase in numbers of children and young people coming into care and their particular and often complex needs.

What sort of children and young people are fostered?

Most children coming into care are placed in foster care, including placements with relatives and friends and whether provided by Local Authorities or Independent Fostering Agencies. An analysis by the Office for National Statistics using data from the 2021 census showed that, compared with the child population as a whole, children in care were more likely to come from a lone parent household, to have experienced deprivation across one or more domains (health, education, housing, employment) and to have been abused or neglected. Some groups of children were over-represented, in particular those with African and African-Caribbean heritage.

In addition, children and young people coming into care were more likely to have been excluded from school due to behavioural and emotional issues, including verbal abuse, threatening behaviour, persistent disruptive behaviour and physical assault. There is no doubt that some children and young people enter the care system with severe problems and the effects of physical, sexual and emotional abuse, emotional and behavioural disorders, mental health issues, and/or alcohol and drug misuse are encountered routinely in modern foster care (Guishard-Pine et al., 2016; Schofield and Beek, 2014). Other complexities include the numbers of children and young people who have been exploited sexually or in other ways, including involvement in 'county lines' drug dealing, or have been subjected to bullying, harassment and intimidation, often on social media (Hallet, 2017). Known as contextual safeguarding (which acknowledges the risks that exist for children outside of the family home), Firmin and Lloyd (2023) highlight the complexities involved and the implications for social work practice in working with children with these types of experience.

Working in foster care

Skills needed by foster carers

Given the complexities outlined above, it is increasingly recognised that foster care is a skilled task, which should arguably be regarded as professional. In addition to carers who can deal with all the difficulties presented by children and young people, there is also a need for more carers from ethnically, culturally and religiously diverse backgrounds, so that children have the opportunity to live in households that better reflect their own backgrounds. Furthermore, foster carers will be working at some level, in partnership with parents and this is reflected in the move away from the term 'foster parent' to the term 'foster carer'. Whichever particular fostering task they take on, foster carers have to be able to:

- make warm and effective relationships with children and young people;
- provide good physical and psychological care for them;
- enable children to feel at home, without disrupting their existing attachments;
- prioritise the needs of children and young people with a range of problems, without causing harm to the foster carers' own children; and
- work in partnership with social workers and other professionals.

Clearly this demands a lot in terms of skills and personal resources, and good preparation and training is critically important if foster carers are to be successful. National standards, provided in various forms across the UK and beyond, outline both the expectations of foster carers and the expectations of local authorities and other agencies who recruit, support and train them. In the context of widespread difficulty recruiting and retaining carers, recent reports (for example the Social Care Review by Josh MacAlister in England, 2022) highlight that an overhaul of the system is long overdue and that it should focus on better regional coordination, collaboration and oversight across local authorities and providers and greater investment in recruitment and retention through the provision of enhanced support, especially financial support.

Success and failure in foster care

Given the range of reasons that children come into foster care and the different types of foster care placement available, it is hard to predict which placements might break down and why. That said, research on placement instability has highlighted a constellation of factors that can lead to breakdown. These can be classified as child-centred factors (the characteristics and needs of the child), carer-centred factors (the knowledge, skills, values of the carers) and wider structural factors (such as access to material, practical and financial support).

Regarding child factors, research suggests that the older the child at placement, the more evident are externalising behaviour problems such as verbal or physical aggression, and the higher the rate of disruptive behaviour at school, the more likely it is that a foster placement will break down. In relation to carer characteristics, kinship foster placements are generally less likely to break down, perhaps because these placements provide vital connections and continuities for children (including in terms of their cultural, religious, ethnic and linguistic heritage). Research has also found that overall, regardless of the type of foster carer, those with high-quality and effective parenting skills experienced less placement breakdown (Vanderwill et al., 2021).

Roles and relationships in foster care

In practice, a foster placement works better when there is a successful partnership between the carers, parents, the child's social worker, the foster carers' own social worker and the child, and where appropriate other professionals too (Elvin and Barrow, 2017). With a number of professionals involved, there is scope for confusion about roles and responsibilities. There is also vulnerability in these working relationships because social workers can change quite often. To mitigate this, regular review and planning meetings help to keep communication shared, open and transparent, to develop shared plans with shared accountability and to help foster a 'team approach' to the care of the child. A child's own views and feelings are central to these meetings (Brady et al., 2019; Brady and Gilligan, 2019).

A good working relationship with social workers is essential for successful fostering. The chance to develop these relationships, as noted above, is impacted by high social worker turnover. In the latest 'State of the Nation' report by Fostering Network (2021), about a quarter of foster carers said they received insufficient information from the child's social workers. What carers value most are qualities such as reliability (including simple things like returning phone calls and visiting when promised), warmth and friendliness, keeping carers informed and useful practical knowledge.

Children and carers views of foster care

Given that the UNCRC stresses the importance of family as the 'fundamental group in society' and given that it also focuses on the protection of children, the provision of alternative care for those children who cannot live at home

Exercise 8.1 Annie in short-term care

Annie has been placed with a family in her home town. Mr and Mrs Farmer have two children of their own, boys aged eight and six. Annie is able to attend the same school, and has some contact with her mother and with Sarah, who is living with their aunt.

Mr and Mrs Farmer are fond of Annie but find her quite 'clingy'. She appears jealous of the attention they give to their own boys.

What skills do Mr and Mrs Farmer need in order to give good care to Annie and to their own children?

What support are they likely to need?

What issues are likely to arise when the placement is reviewed, and how might they be dealt with?

and their participation rights, it is essential that social workers are familiar with children's views about and experiences of foster care in relative and non-relative family placements. There is a growing body of research exploring both children's and carers' perspectives.

With regard to foster children's views, a systematic review (Ie et al., 2022) of articles written between 1990 and 2020, which explored foster children's views of family, found that children's feelings about family referred almost exclusively to birth family; although if living in kinship arrangements, they felt no difference between their birth family and their kinship family. Children expressed loyalty towards birth family even if they had experienced abuse. However, alongside this biological relatedness, children also expressed positive feelings about foster families and the 'nurturing, warm, and supportive environment the foster family provided'. This positive sense of belonging was strengthened by 'doing family' and involvement in family activities alongside being able to actively chose who they defined as family. For example, some children describe friends as being like sisters and brothers. This and other research, in particular Selwyn and Lewis (2023), highlights the varied experiences of children in varied foster care arrangements and how important it is to understand and respect each individual story rather than making assumptions.

Regarding foster carers, there is also broad ranging research regarding their experiences of recruitment, retention, training, support and complaints, what they expect from social workers, managing contact arrangements and their views on being a foster carer. A very good overview of some of the key issues is provided by Engelhardt and Royse (2023).

Characteristics of residential childcare

Background

Like foster care, residential care for children has a long history: nurseries, residential schools, orphanages and other institutions go back to the middle ages and even earlier. In Britain in the nineteenth and early twentieth centuries, most children looked after by the Poor Law Boards and by charities were in residential institutions (for further detail regarding the history of residential child care, see Parker, 1990 and Higginbotham, 2017). Even though foster placements became the placement of choice from the late 1940s and early 1950s onwards, the use of residential care remained very significant. In the 1980s, residential care as a placement option decreased. It is important to say that although residential care is often in the media for all the wrong reasons (historic institutional child abuse and neglect, queries about its purpose, cost, and effectiveness), it does remain a positive choice for a small number of young people, often because their behaviour or their circumstances mean that foster care placements are unsuitable or have been unsuccessful.

Types, numbers and regulation of residential care facilities

The different types of residential child care include children's homes, residential schools, residential family centres (for assessments), short-break residential care and secure accommodation. Some children's homes are still provided by local authorities, although numbers are increasingly run by private agencies, including private equity companies. As with foster care, there are national standards against which children's homes are inspected. Some homes employ fully qualified social workers whilst others use social care workers who may have other kinds of qualifications. Like social workers, social care workers are registered and professionally regulated; there are professional standards which workers must reflect and adhere to in their daily practice.

There are over 2,880 residential children's homes of all types in England, providing a total of 10,818 places and over 3,812 social care providers according to Ofsted's most recent report regarding children's social care data in England (Ofsted, 2023). Private companies in England run 80% of residential child care provision. These all have to be registered and inspected. Whilst other jurisdictions are smaller (and therefore the total numbers are smaller), all share in common this complex mix of type and provider of residential child care. Another aspect shared in common is that there has been an expansion in the number of residential child care homes (and total number of available places) reflecting an overall growth in demand. Minimum standards for children's homes are in place in all jurisdictions and social care workers in residential child care are registered and therefore required to practice in line with professional standards.

What sort of children and young people are in residential care?

The most obvious thing to say about children in group care, as compared to children in care in general, is that they are older. This is in part because residential care is often used as an option when other options have been tried and failed or are no longer available. It also because policy and practice reflects the view that use of residential child care should be limited and only when clearly appropriate; and also that, as outlined in the Guidelines for the Alternative Care of Children (United Nations, 2010), it should not normally be used for the placement of younger children. Residential child care represents the first placement for only approximately one quarter of children and young people. The majority of children and young people living in residential care have significant mental health issues (Bronsard et al., 2016) and a number have significant emotional, behavioural and social difficulties which manifest through disruptive and disrupting behaviour (Campos et al., 2019). There is some evidence that placing young people with complex needs together in the same residential children's home can be problematic (Mazzone et al., 2018).

Working in residential care

Tasks undertaken and skills needed in residential care

The tasks involved in residential work with children and young people are of course centred in establishing and maintaining a reliable daily routine and providing for the physical and emotional care for children and young people. Tasks may also include:

- assessment;
- therapeutic work;
- working with group dynamics;
- management of challenging behaviour;
- working to prepare young people for return home;
- working with families;
- preparation for foster care;
- preparation for independence.

It is clear that, given the needs of the children and young people in residential child care and the multiplicity of tasks undertaken, working in this area requires a highly developed skills base. The knowledge, skills and values required are outlined in documents such as the practice guidance for residential child care workers produced by Social Care Wales (2017).

In summary, residential workers need to have:

- *knowledge and understanding* of the impact of abuse and neglect on the wellbeing of children and young people, trauma-informed approaches, attachment, family functioning and dynamics as well as team work, organisational cultures and dynamics, and social, political and economic factors that influence residential child care provision;
- *skills* in listening, observing, communicating, intervening and assessment, and the ability to understand emotional reactions and feelings in young people as well as in themselves;
- *personal qualities* and *values* consistent with the aims and philosophy of the establishment: these include being warm, friendly, empathic, reliable, honest, genuine, clear, fair, assertive, consistent and demonstrating a concern for equality and social justice.

Some of this can be acquired in practice, particularly where staff work in settings where there is already good practice and support for learning and development. Some of it can best be learned through formal education and a structure of qualifications. More recently there has been an increased emphasis on professionalisation of the residential care workforce, and more staff hold relevant qualifications. That said, there is a fair amount of workforce turnover and difficulties retaining a qualified staff group. This contrasts with the situation in some European countries, where residential care is regarded as a relatively high-status profession, and where residential workers may be expected as a matter of course to have qualifications at degree level or beyond in social work, psychology, teaching or 'social pedagogy' (see Chapter 11).

Success and failure in residential care

It is sometimes suggested that residential care has no place in modern child care. People argue that all children should be in families, that the risks of abuse are too great, or that residential care is not cost-effective. However, not all children want to be in families, and adolescents who have poor relationships with their parents often prefer group living, at least for a time. While there are accounts from people who lived in residential child care of experiences of abuse, neglect and harm (see later in this chapter), there are also accounts from people who thrived in residential care (see Smith, 2022). It is important, if only out of respect for all those children and young people who have had good experiences, to remember that children's homes can be a place for good, purposeful, professional care with proper standards and safeguards.

What makes for success in residential care can be evaluated in several ways (Whittaker et al., 2022). First, as noted above, the views and experiences of children and young people who live in residential child care are vital. Ensuring that children and young people have access to information and services relating to complaints, advocacy and representation helps contribute to successful settings. Ensuring that children and young people are actively engaged in decisions regarding the setting they are in is also important. This includes freedom to exercise choice and agency over what the meals are, who helps cook them, what social activities are undertaken, and how rooms are furnished. All of this is premised on positive, reciprocal, respectful and meaningful relationships between young people and staff based on principles of empowerment, and from which positive outcomes on individuals' self-esteem, wellbeing and confidence can be seen.

Second, success can be evaluated in terms of the organisational setting and the staff team. Children's homes work best if they have a clear vision, mission statement, aims and objectives, articulated in strong, clear leadership and implemented by a unified team of motivated, skilled workers who share common values and approaches (Smith et al., 2013). Success can also be thought of in terms of the effectiveness of particular therapeutic approaches adopted by residential care settings and how these impact on young people's health, education, social, emotional and material outcomes. There is a growing body of research focused on therapeutic approaches (Whittaker et al., 2022). In one example, in Northern Ireland, each of the five Trust areas adopted a different therapeutic model (SCIE, 2012) to underpin the delivery of residential child care. More recently, one therapeutic approach has been developed. Known as the Northern Ireland Framework for Integrated Therapeutic Care (NIFITC), (Teggart et al., 2022) this will underpin all service delivery for children in care. Other writers have highlighted how the structures, processes and practices associated with residential child care could be realigned through the introduction of new frameworks and models so that all settings are therapeutically aligned and delivered through attachment and trauma informed approaches (Barton et al., 2011) and social pedagogical approaches (Berridge et al., 2011), for example. Of course, the approach or model adopted by each residential care unit has implications for the roles of staff and relationships between staff and young people, as explored further below.

Roles and relationships in residential care

As indicated above, residential workers usually operate as members of a team and look after children in shifts, and so communication is critically important. Unlike foster carers who live together as members of a family, opportunities for residential workers to exchange information and ideas often take place in staff meetings or in the office. It can be a challenge to find space for these discussions to take place.

One of the other challenges for staff is to ensure that each child or young person has the chance to develop one or two close relationships, and that there is at least someone in the home who has something comparable to the knowledge of the child and their situation that a parent might have. 'Key worker' systems are often used as one way to achieve this; but of course the key worker is not always there when a child needs attention, so it is important that the whole team has a shared understanding of each child or young person and their circumstances and needs.

Another challenge for residential care workers is ensuring effective partnership relationships with all other involved professionals. There is always potential for confusion, overlap or misunderstanding, and so regular, consistent and open communication is vitally important. The relationship between the field social worker for the child and their family and the residential team, especially the keyworker, is an essential foundation for good care and planning. This can only be based on mutual respect and understanding of each other's roles. Some writers have proposed new frameworks that highlight and reinforce the importance of relationships at all levels and within the structures, systems and processes of residential child care (Anglin, 2014; Marshall, 2022; Whittaker et al., 2022).

Children's views of residential care

In a government commissioned report on residential care by Hart et al. (2015), research regarding children's perspectives was reviewed and organised under the themes of their views about: relationships with staff; institution or home; rules and control; relationships with family; the voice of parents; relationships with peers; being involved; programmes and interventions; and moving on. They found that 'the biggest single variable that determines satisfaction with placement is the child's relationship with staff' (Hart et al., 2015, p. 81). They also found that children valued 'the feel of the home', highlighting negative views about institutional features such as the locked kitchen, the locked office, staff spending time in the office, and the risk adverse attitude towards children's engagement in activities and hobbies. This corresponds with other research in the area (Emond et al., 2014; Brown et al., 2018; Marshall, 2022). Children also felt more settled in residential child care where their relationships with their parents, siblings and friends were valued and where contact was facilitated. Lastly, things worked better where children were actively and fully involved in decision making. Other more recent research (Marshall, 2022; Graham et al., 2023) confirms these findings indicating that above all, high-quality, meaningful and positive relationships are central.

The relationship between residential and foster care

What determines which children go into foster care and which children go into residential care? Age is one factor: young children will normally be fostered unless they are thought to need specialist therapeutic residential care (the Children's House run by Barnardo's in Northern Ireland is one example). Another factor is that a shortage of short-term foster placements may result in a residential placement being sought. In other situations, it might be a case of 'fit' – some residential children's homes may not be suitable because of aims and objectives, and some young people may decide that a particular setting is not one they wish to live in.

A recent review of research comparing residential and foster care (Li et al., 2019) against three outcomes (internalising behaviours, externalising behaviours and perception of care) has noted that on all outcomes, children and young people in foster care had consistently better experiences and fewer problems compared with children in residential care. Of course, this does not mean that every child will do better in foster care. A study by James et al. (2022) that compared residential child care across five countries noted similar trends, namely increased demand, increased private provision and professionalisation of the workforce. It also noted nuanced differences in the way the care is delivered in different settings and different countries, reflecting different cultural, social, political and economic norms.

Supporting children and young people in residential and foster care

Roles in relation to placements

Field social workers have to work together with all those involved in providing a home for children and young people, whether this is in residential care or foster care. The field social worker normally has the lead responsibility for ensuring that the agreed plan is implemented in line with statutory regulations, and that identified tasks are allocated, followed through, and reviewed. As part of the overall plan, tasks are also allocated to and undertaken by residential workers, by foster carers, or by parents. These could include providing transport for times spent with family and friends, transport to and from school, liaison with medical, educational and therapeutic professionals (Cosis Brown, 2014).

What is important is that everyone understands who is doing what. This is particularly important regarding education, for example, where the statutory guidance in England, Wales and Northern Ireland, regarding the education of children in care, requires that every child has a personal education plan (PEP). There has been confusion between social workers and teachers regarding who takes the lead role, who completes the paperwork and who oversees the implementation of the plan. In England, Scotland and Wales, the role of the Virtual School Head, who has a statutory duty to improve the educational experiences of and outcomes for children in care, is designed to address this and other educational issues for children in care (Sebba and Berridge, 2019). In Northern Ireland, the Education Authority has a Looked After Children Champion, who oversees strategic and policy initiatives regarding the educational experiences and outcomes of children in care.

At the centre is the child or young person, but what does this mean in practice? Social workers need to be aware that all children, regardless of age and other characteristics have a right to express their views and for these to be taken seriously. The UNCRC makes clear that it is not possible to determine what is in the best interests of a child or young person without them expressing their views and having these considered. Social workers therefore need highly developed communication skills which include:

a sharing accessible information about what's going on and why in a clear, consistent way;
b listening to the verbal and non-verbal messages expressed by a child or young person;
c ensuring that children's views and experiences are at the centre of all decision making;
d making sure that views and experiences are actively considered and that a record is kept as to the ways in which a child/young person's views were

considered, what impact they had on decision making, and if they had little impact the reasons why;

e following up with children and young people regarding meeting outcomes and being accountable to them.

Supervising placements and inspecting placement resources

Regular visiting to children and young people in foster care and residential care is part of the process by which social workers ensure that they are being properly looked after (Cosis Brown, 2014). The minimum frequency of visits is set out in statutory guidance (e.g. in England it is the Care Planning, Placement and Case Review (England) Regulations, HM Government, 2010). These guidelines state that a child in care must be visited within one week of the start of a new placement, then at intervals of not more than six weeks part during the first year of placement and thereafter at intervals of not more than six weeks. It also provides for more frequent visits as necessary/appropriate. The purpose of visits is to ensure that a good standard of care is being offered, to gain information on daily routines, to observe the relationship between carers and the young person and to maintain a good relationship with the child or young person. Given that part of the purpose of the 'statutory visits' is to ensure standards of care, social workers should spend some individual time with the child, so that there is a 'safe space' for them to talk about anything that is worrying them. Many social workers have noted that the car is a safe space for talking, and that sometimes it is here that really important conversations can take place.

Reviews conducted about and with children and young people are also another part of the process by which social workers, professionals, parents, carers and the child agree the plan for the child and their respective roles and responsibilities and tasks to be carried out. Statutory guidelines outline the frequency at which these meetings take place, but it is important to note that these are *minimum* standards; reviews should take place more often if needed. It is likely that a family placement worker will also be in regular contact with the foster carers, and from time to time there will also be a review of their terms of approval as carers, quite separate from the child's review.

Although placement standards are independently monitored (by Ofsted in England, the Care Inspectorate in Wales and Scotland, and the Regulation and Quality Improvement Authority in Northern Ireland), the social worker still has a professional responsibility to satisfy themselves that the child's welfare is being safeguarded and to take appropriate action if not. (They also have a responsibility to take appropriate action if they have concerns about the welfare of other children and young people in the same home or establishment.)

Identifying and supporting educational, health and identity needs

In Chapter 2, we outlined the needs of children in care. Their health, education and identity needs are crucial to their immediate and longer-term health and wellbeing. The role of the social worker whether children are in foster care or residential care is to: form close working relationships with education and health providers; ensure that every child's needs are clearly and accurately identified; ensure that relevant information is exchanged between professionals (e.g. a child's health needs may impact on educational attainment and achievement and it is essential that education providers know the nuanced and personal details of each child in care); ensure that clear plans are developed (personal education plans) and that people's responsibility's for delivering on the plans are clearly identified; and to review progress on plans in a timely and regular manner ensuring that children's own perspectives on their progress and ongoing needs are at the forefront.

Additional work regarding identity needs may include facilitating virtual or face-to-face contact with significant people in a child's life (so long as that contact is deemed in the best interests of the child) and to develop a digital and/or hard copy life story book, so that each child has a record of who they are, where they come from, who is in their family, where their family lives, why they came into care, who they have lived with whilst being in care, and what memorable events have taken place (such as birthdays, holidays, school events, school reports) and so on. The more information a child has that is held in one place, the better sense of their own identity a child is likely to develop. For many children in care, they have been in contact with many professionals, social workers and carers. Each of these adults holds memories about the child, what has happened, when and why. It should not be left to a child in care (or indeed a former child in care) to go round finding and collecting people's memories of them and piecing together their own fragmented past, but it should be the responsibility of the social worker to ensure that there is a living, rolling comprehensive record that can be added to by adults and the child alike, so that everything is held in one place and accessible (a bit like the old fashioned family photo album, for example).

Advocates and independent visitors

In light of recent institutional abuse inquiries (see section below), it is recognised that if children and young people are to be effectively protected from harm, and their wishes and feelings properly taken into account, it is not enough to rely either on children and young people to speak up for themselves or on the skills and commitment of those looking after them. The combination of the power imbalance between adults and children, and the particular vulnerability of children and young people in care, means that some form of outside support is necessary. The system in England and Wales distinguishes between *independent visitors* appointed to befriend a child who has little or no support from their own family (there is a duty to appoint if the child is willing and would benefit), and *advocates* whose job is to speak for the child or young person and to support them to express their views and experiences. Advocates are appointed by the local authority or a care provider, or by an organisation funded for this purpose. A variety of advocacy groups exist. Specific to Wales is the right to an 'active offer' of advocacy for looked after children and young people (and other children receiving statutory services) (Welsh Government, 2022).

In addition, children and young people (including those in care) are represented by and have access to the Office of the Children's Commissioner. There are Children's Commissioners in all four jurisdictions of the UK. Their job is to (a) promote awareness and understanding of children's rights and the role of the commissioner, (b) monitor and review policy and practice and (c) advise the government and communicate with children and young people. The Children's Commissioners have been involved in campaigns and work to change policy and practice regarding children and young people in care.

Abuse in care and how it can be prevented

Abuse of children in residential care has been the subject of a series of major scandals in recent years, among the most notable being:

- The Waterhouse Tribunal in Wales (https://www.iicsa.org.uk/key-documents/14231/download/accountability-reparations-report-19-sep-2019.pdf) which focused on the operation of a conspiracy to abuse children for the sexual gratification of powerful adults (some of them working as part of a network) which went undetected or unchallenged for many years.
- The Historical Institutional Abuse Inquiry in Northern Ireland (https://www.hiainquiry.org) which covered abuse of children under 18 who lived in children's homes, borstals, training schools, juvenile justice centres, hospitals, and orphanages between 1922 and 1995 in Northern Ireland.
- The Scottish Child Abuse Inquiry (https://www.childabuseinquiry.scot) which at the time of writing remains ongoing and was set up in 2015 to focus on the abuses of children in care.
- The Independent Inquiry into Child Sexual Abuse in England (https://www.iicsa.org.uk/index.html) which published its final report in 2022.

The events covered by these reports are, in the main, historical and the abuse they report appears to have been endemic. That said, it is important to bear in mind that not all children and young people living in residential care have been abused. To assume such makes it hard for those who have had good experiences in residential care to tell their stories. It is also fair to say that since then the system has changed considerably. Children's homes are now subject to much closer outside scrutiny and staff are better trained and supervised (as well as being subject to criminal convictions checks). There are also clearer definitions of the purposes of residential care, both in particular establishments and in individual cases; and the general planning of residential provision is integrated into overall children's services planning. However, as we know, this does not mean that children are no longer abused.

In general the issues of abuse in foster care have received much less attention than have the same issues in residential care, although various Inquiries as part of their remit have considered the abuse of children in foster care. Reports contain some disturbing accounts of abuse by adults who lived in foster care as children. It is believed that much abuse in foster care goes undetected, and that the incidence of abuse in foster care is higher than in ordinary family homes (Landers et al., 2021).

Ofsted in England publish figures regarding the total number of complaints made against foster carers, the type of abuse reported and the outcome of the investigations. In the most recent bulletin, Ofsted (2023) note that there were 3,010 complaints, most of which concerned physical abuse, and that in 52%, the investigation confirmed that no further action needed to be taken and 18% resulted in continued monitoring. What happened to the remaining 30% is not reported. There is also research that explores the impact on foster carers of unproven allegations. Plumridge and Sebba (2016) note the lack of support that carers were given following the allegation, and the lack of follow up training following the allegations. Over 80% of carers continued to foster in these cases.

There are several issues highlighted in these statistics. First is the vulnerability of children and young people in foster care and the critical role played by the social worker in forging a trusting relationship with a child or young person so that they feel able to tell someone about any abuse they are experiencing. Second, is the fact that many children and young people do alert someone, as indicated by the number of complaints. Rather than leading to complacency, this should serve as a reminder to social workers that children and young people need accessible information and easy access to robust complaints systems and rights to redress, representation and advocacy. Third, the figures highlight the vulnerability of carers who care for children and young people with difficult experiences and significant social, emotional and behavioural issues. This is why carers should be supported by the agencies, trusts and local authorities that they work for through provision of finances and access to training, support, peer support and respite. One of the issues touched upon is the difficult behaviour of some children in foster care – usually a direct manifestation of their adverse childhood experiences and wider social structural disadvantages. This is considered in further detail below.

Support with difficult behaviour

A number of recent studies report the challenging issues that some children and young people in residential and foster care may be experiencing, and the impact these can have on them and their carers in the short and long term. Often categorised as internalising and externalising behaviours, examples of the former include: depression, anxiety, social withdrawal, self-harm and eating disorders, selective mutism and suicidal thoughts. Examples of externalising behaviours include verbal and physical aggression (biting, kicking, hitting), disruptive and defiant behaviour, bullying and stealing.

Managing these emotional or behavioural difficulties can be a real challenge for any placement. There is sometimes little congruence between social workers' and foster carers' understanding of the reasons for children's difficult behaviour, still less about appropriate strategies for managing it. With the right type of specialist training and ongoing support (including access to therapeutic services), carers can be helped to understand that these behaviours are often adaptive strategies from their early years which may be long-standing and resistant to change, rather than a product of poor parenting by the foster carers or residential staff. There is a need for all carers to have a realistic understanding of the prospects for change, and access to specialist therapeutic services where necessary to understand and manage complex difficulties. The development of particular innovative and creative approaches can be seen to help, for example 'team parenting for children in foster care' (Caw and Sebba, 2014) which highlights an integrated approach to the delivery of therapeutic care. Therapeutic work in care is considered next.

Therapeutic work in care

Many children in the care system have acute problems with their social, emotional and psychological well-being, with their behaviour, identity and relationships with other people. Many have been abused or neglected and may need help in dealing with the consequences of that. For many children and young people a secure, stable placement with good care provided with warmth and affection will be sufficient for the process of healing and growth to take place, or at least to begin. For some, however, more is needed, including in some cases specialised therapy.

The extent to which therapy can be made available as part of a care placement is highly varied and variable, and as noted earlier often relies on specialist services provided by the agency. In other cases, additional therapeutic input – individual psychotherapy, counselling, life story work, group work, play therapy – may need to be arranged either in the home or elsewhere, often at an outpatient clinic and through the Child and Adolescent Mental Health Service, where that is available. It is critically important not to neglect the needs of some children and young people for therapy. It is expensive, and difficult to manage competing priorities with a limited budget – especially if the placement itself is already costing a lot. However, access to therapeutic services can be a vital aspect of caring for children and young people in care. More research to explore children and young people's own experiences and views of the services they receive and what helps best would be highly beneficial to social workers, given the dearth that currently exists.

Summary and conclusion

We hope this brief review of residential and foster care has given a helpful picture of the different types of placement and some of the ways in which they can be used for the benefit of children and young people. The most important points to take away are:

- Both types of placement have their strengths, and in the end it is a matter of asking 'what is going to be the most helpful placement for *this* child or young person?'
- The success of a placement depends to a large extent on the atmosphere of the household or culture of the establishment, the commitment of carers to working directly with children and young people and access to the relevant wider support systems be they financial, practical, material and/or therapeutic.
- All placements must be open to the outside world, to advice, supervision and scrutiny, in order to safeguard and promote the welfare of children and young people.

The focus of this chapter has been on all types of placement for different purposes, short-, medium- and long-term. In the next chapter, we will look in more depth at what is involved in achieving permanence for children and young people.

GUIDE TO FURTHER READING

On foster care, good general books include Cosis Brown (2014) and Goodyer (2011). Bond (2019), which although written for foster carers and parenting, is useful for social workers working with foster carers. Schofield and Beek (2014) focus on attachment and foster care and Alper and Howe (2016) provide theoretical and practical insights regarding the assessment of potential foster carers. McCormick (2018) is an essential read regarding sexuality and foster care.

There are some useful books about foster care written for children – see, for example, Denton (2019), and Marlow and Garland (2022).

On residential care, Frost et al. (2020), Smith (2009) and Smith et al. (2013) are excellent start points. Del Valle et al. (2014), Barton et al. (2011) and Whittaker et al. (2022) consider international perspectives. Jackson (2023) provides practical insights for new employees in residential child care homes. Margaret McGuckin (2023) outlines her lived experience in residential child care and her fight for justice. Daly (2014) and Rus et al. (2017) focus more broadly on institutional abuse, current practice and redressing abuse experienced.

CoramBAAF (https://corambaaf.org.uk) and The Fostering Network (https://www.thefosteringnetwork.org.uk) both provide a wide range of valuable material, and their websites are also worth consulting. Other useful websites are Barnardo's (https://www.barnardos.org.uk/foster) and the Social Workers Toolbox (https://www.socialworkerstoolbox.com/category/adoption/fosterin).

References

Alper, J. and Howe, D. (2016) *Assessing adoptive and foster parents: Improving analysis and understanding of parenting capacity.* London: Jessica Kingsley Publishers.

Anglin, J. (2014) *Pain, normality, and the struggle for congruence: Reinterpreting residential care for children and youth.* Abingdon, Oxfordshire: Routledge.

Barton, S., Gonzalez, R. and Tomlinson, P. (2011) *Therapeutic residential care for children and young people. An attachment and trauma informed model for practice.* London: Jessica Kingsley Publishers.

Berridge, D., Biehal, N., Lutman, E. and Palomares, M. (2011) *Raising the bar? Evaluation of the social pedagogy pilot programme in residential children's homes.* London: Department for Education.

Bond, H. (2019) *The foster carer's handbook on parenting teenagers.* London: CoramBAAF.

Brady, B., Dolan, P. and McGregor, C. (2019) *Mentoring for young people in care and leaving care: Theory, policy and practice.* Abingdon, Oxfordshire: Routledge.

Brady, E. and Gilligan, R. (2019) 'Exploring diversity in the educational pathways of care-experienced adults: Findings from a life course study of education and care', *Children and Youth Services Review*, *104*, 104379.

Bronsard, G., Alessandrini, M., Fond, G., Loundou, A., Auquier, P., Tordjman, S. and Boyer, L. (2016) 'The prevalence of mental disorders among children and adolescents in the child welfare system: A systematic review and meta-analysis', *Medicine 95*(7), e2622

Brown, T., Winter, K. and Carr, N. (2018) 'Residential child care workers: Relationship based practice in a culture of fear', *Child and Family Social Work*, *23*(4), 657–665.

Campos, J., Barbosa-Ducharne, M., Dias, P., Rodrigues, S., Martins, A.C. and Leal, M. (2019) 'Emotional and behavioral problems and psychosocial skills in adolescents in residential care', *Child and Adolescent Social Work Journal*, *36*, 237–246.

Caw, L. and Sebba, J. (2014) *Team parenting for children in foster care: A model for integrated therapeutic care.* London: Jessica Kingsley Publishers.

Cosis Brown, H. (2014) *Social work and foster care.* London: Sage (Learning Matters).

Daly, K. (2014) *Redressing institutional abuse of children.* London: Palgrave Macmillan.

Del Valle, J.F., Sainero, A. and Bravo, A. (2014) Needs and characteristics of high-resource using children and youth: Spain. In Whittaker, J.W., del Valle, J.F. and Holmes, L. (eds.) *Therapeutic residential care with children and youth: Developing evidence-based international practice* (pp. 49–62). London and Philadelphia, PA: Jessica Kingsley Publishers.

Denton, J.A.M. (2019) *Foster care and me.* Tolworth: Surbiton: Grosvenor House Publishing.

Elvin, A. and Barrow, M. (eds.) (2017) *Welcome to fostering. A guide to becoming and being a foster carer.* London: Jessica Kingsley Publishers.

Emond, R., McIntosh, I. and Punch, S. (2014) 'Food and feelings in residential child-care', *British Journal of Social Work, 44*(7), 1840–1856.

Engelhardt, E. and Royse, D. (2023) 'Information needs of current and prospective foster caregivers: A content analysis of Reddit posts', *Journal of Public Child Welfare, 17*(2), 356–374.

Firmin, C. and Lloyd, J. (2023) *Contextual safeguarding. The next chapter.* Bristol: Policy Press.

Frost, N., Mills, S. and Stein, M. (2020) *Understanding residential child care.* London: Routledge.

Graham, A., Canosa, A., Wall, J., & Thomas, P. (2023). Child-safe organizations and the ethics of empowered inclusion. *Children & Society*, n/a. doi:10.1111/chso.12732.

Goodyer, A. (2011) *Child-centred foster care: A rights-based model for practice.* London: Jessica Kingsley Publishers.

Guishard-Pine, J., Coleman-Oluwabusola, G. and McCall, S. (2016) *Supporting the mental health of children in care: Evidence-based practice.* London: Jessica Kingsley Publishers.

Hallet, S. (2017) *Making sense of child sexual exploitation: Exchange, abuse, and young people.* Bristol: Policy Press.

Hart, D., La Valle, I. and Holmes, L. (2015) *The place of residential care in the English child welfare system.* London: Department for Education.

Hayden, C. (1999) *State child care: Looking after children?* London: Jessica Kingsley Publishers.

Higginbotham, P. (2017) *Children's homes: A history of institutional care for Britain's young.* Oxford: Casemate Publishers.

HM Government. (2010) *The care planning, placement, and case review (England) regulations.* London: HM Government. Available here https://www.legislation.gov.uk/uksi/2010/959/contents/made (accessed 27.01.24).

Ie, J., Ursin, M. and Vicente-Marino, M. (2022) 'Foster children's views of family: A systematic review and qualitative synthesis', *Children and Youth Services Review, 132*, 106337.

Jackson, A. (2023) *Dilemmas and decision making in residential childcare.* St Albans, Herts: Critical Publishing.

James, S., Wilczek, L. and Kilian, J. (2022) 'A comparative analysis of residential care: A five-country multiple case-design study', *Child Youth Care Forum*, *51*, 1031–1062. https://doi.org/10.1007/s10566-021-09666-6.

Landers, A.L., Danes, S.M., Campbell, A.R. and Hawk, S.W. (2021) 'Abuse after abuse: The recurrent maltreatment of American Indian children in foster care and adoption', *Child Abuse and Neglect*, *111*, 104805.

Li, D., Chng, G.S. and Chu, C.M. (2019) 'Comparing long-term placement outcomes of residential and family foster care: A meta-analysis', *Trauma, Violence, & Abuse*, *20*(5), 653–664.

MacAlister, J. (2022) *The independent review of children's social care*. London: Department for Education.

Marlow, H. and Garland, S. (2022) *Room in the nest*. Milton Keynes: Holly Marlow.

Marshall, G. (2022) *Recognition and residential childcare: A small scale study of the applicability of Honneth's conceptual framework*. Belfast: Queen's University Belfast.

Mazzone, A., Nocentini, A. and Menesini, E. (2018) 'Bullying and peer violence among children and adolescents in residential care settings: A review of the literature', *Aggression and Violent Behavior*, *38*, 101–112.

McCormick, A. (2018) *LGBTQ youth in foster care: Empowering approaches for an inclusive system of care*. London: Routledge.

McGuckin, M. (2023) *'I did it for you'. One woman's journey to become a voice for the voiceless in the Northern Ireland residential care system*. Ireland: BookHub Publishing.

O'Neill, T. (2020) *All my brother's secrets: A powerful true story of love, loss, and brutality*. Bishopsbriggs, Glasgow: HarperElement.

Ofsted. (2023) *Children's social care data*. Available https://www.gov.uk/government/statistics/childrens-social-care-data-in-england-2023 [last accessed 02.04.24].

Ott, E., Buehler, E., Suh, E., Pinto, V., Sanders-Ellis, D. and Browning-Lee, H. (2021) *Independent evaluation of the Mockingbird Programme in ten local authorities*. Wales: What Works for Children's Social Care.

Parker, R. (1990) *Away from home: A history of child care*. Ilford: Barnardo's.

Plumridge, G. and Sebba, J. (2016) *The impact of unproven allegations on foster carers*. Oxford: Oxford University, Rees Centre.

Rus, A.V., Parris, S. and Stativa, E. (2017) *Child maltreatment in residential care: History, research, and current practice*. New York: Springer.

Schofield, G. and Beek, M. (2014) *The secure base model: Promoting attachment and resilience in foster care and adoption*. London: BAAF.

Sebba, J. and Berridge, D. (2019) 'The role of the virtual school in supporting improved educational outcomes for children in care', *Oxford Review of Education*, *45*(4), 538–555.

Selwyn, J. and Lewis, S. (2023) 'Keeping in touch: Looked after children and young people's views on their contact arrangements', *Adoption and Fostering*, *47*(2), 120–137.

Smith, M. (2009) *Rethinking residential child care: Positive perspectives*. Bristol: Policy Press.

Smith, M. (2022) 'Beyond a single story: Peripheral histories of boys brought up in a residential school,' *Ethics and Social Welfare*, *16*(3), 290–305.

Smith, M., Fulcher, L. and Doran, P. (2013) *Residential child care in practice: Making a difference.* Bristol: Policy Press.

Social Care Institute for Excellence (SCIE). (2012) *Therapeutic approaches to social work in residential child care settings.* Egham: SCIE.

Social Care Wales. (2017) *The residential child care worker. Practice guidance for residential child care workers registered with Social Care Wales.* Cardiff: Social Care Wales.

Teggart, T., Mooney, S., Blair, C. and Leonard, R. (2022) *Connecting care: An overview of the Northern Ireland framework for integrated therapeutic care for care experienced children and young people.* Belfast: Department of Health.

The Fostering Network. (2021) *State of the Nation's foster care 2021 report.* London: The Fostering Network.

United Nations. (2010) *Guidelines for the alternative care of children. A/RES/64/142 (Sixty-fourth session).* Geneva: United Nations. Available here https://www.refworld.org/docid/4c3acd162.html (accessed 27.01.24).

Vanderwill, L.A., Salazar, A.M., Jenkins, G., Larwelle, J., McMahon, A.K., Day, A. and Haggerty, K. (2021) 'Systematic literature review of foster and adoptive caregiver factors for increasing placement stability and permanency', *Journal of Public Child Welfare*, *15*(4), 487–527.

Whittaker, J.K., Holmes, L., del Valle, J.C.F. and James, S. (2022) *Revitalizing residential care for children and youth: Cross-national trends and challenges.* Oxford: Oxford University Press.

9

ADOPTION AND WORKING FOR PERMANENCE

CONTENTS OF CHAPTER

- Introduction
- What is 'permanence'?
- The rights of parents, children and permanence
- Ways of achieving permanence
- Adoption and its place in child care
- Good practice in adoption and post-adoption services
- Summary and conclusion
- Guide to further reading

Introduction

We often hear how important it is that all children and young people have the opportunity to experience stability and security as they grow up. Stability means constancy of positive and predictable relationships, routines and location without being subject to unexpected change. This creates a sense of security. Both stability and security are important in the development of a secure identity and a sense of belonging. Most children and young people who come into the care system have experienced disrupted stability and security. Some return home quite soon, while others remain in the care system for years. This group of children require a permanent home as soon as possible, so that they too have the opportunity to experience stability and security. There are various ways of achieving permanence. This chapter considers what is meant by permanence, and how it is related to concepts of attachment, parenting and the rights of parents and children. Different ways of achieving permanence are explored and the advantages and disadvantages of each outlined.

DOI: 10.4324/9781003503194-9

> **Exercise 9.1 Annie in long-term care**
>
> Annie has been with Mr and Mrs Farmer for six months, and appears to be happy there, although there are still tensions in her relationship with the Farmers' own children.
>
> Over a recent bank holiday weekend Annie's mother became severely depressed and took a fatal overdose. It has been agreed that she and Sarah now need permanent placements. Their aunt has offered to continue to foster Sarah with a view to possible adoption, but is unwilling to take on both girls. Annie's father has asked to re-establish contact. He has a new wife and twin babies, and is not offering to care for Annie. Mr and Mrs Farmer would like to keep Annie on a permanent basis, if approved to do so.
>
> *What are Annie's needs, in the short and long term?*
>
> *Who is most likely to be able to provide what she needs?*
>
> *What legal arrangements are most likely to provide what she needs?*
>
> *What about Sarah?*
>
> *How should decisions about Annie's future care be made?*

In particular, we consider the place of adoption in planning for children, and social work practice with children and families for whom adoption is the preferred route to permanence.

What is 'permanence'?

'Permanence' in practice means making a long-term plan for how a child will be cared for until they reach adulthood. The arrangement should be one in which, as far as possible, the core caring relationships will remain unchanged throughout childhood. The aim is that these relationships will provide security, stability, continuity, commitment, a sense of belonging and a positive sense of identity to help ensure positive life chances and outcomes. Historically, the word 'permanence' has been associated with adoption. However, the concept of 'permanence' is broader than that. For example, Sinclair et al. (2005) outlined four differing meanings of permanence. Objective permanence refers to the legal status which confers a sense of permanence in that carers take on all or shared parental responsibility. Subjective permanence refers to the sense of belonging that children feel and perceive in their placement. A sense of belonging can be strengthened by enacted permanence which refers to a family carrying out their activities, routines and norms as if the child is part of the carers family, and uncontested permanence is when the child feels no sense of divided loyalty between birth family and placement – everyone involved accepts the arrangement.

With Sinclair's work in mind, it is clear that children may experience all, none or some of these dimensions of permanence and that their experiences could change over time. It is also clear that objective permanence is most likely to create the conditions in which the other dimensions of permanence can be experienced. Another way in which the concept of permanence is broader than adoption is noted by the range of options to achieve permanence, including returning to and living back at home with immediate family, long-term fostering (with relatives or non-relatives), residential care and adoption. These outcomes can be achieved using a number of legal pathways, including care orders, adoption orders, special guardianship orders (England, Wales and Northern Ireland) and child arrangement orders (England only). In Scotland, permanence can be also achieved via a compulsory supervision order under the Children's Hearings (Scotland) Act 2011, or by a permanence order under the Adoption and Children (Scotland) Act 2007.

Birth parents and psychological parents

While the plans will differ depending on their own individual circumstances, the shared aim for all children and young people is that they have the opportunity to experience a positive family life, with stability, security, safe and supportive relationships throughout childhood and into adulthood. Within this, the development of consistent, meaningful, positive relationships with a significant adult is central. This person could be a natural parent, a relative or a foster or adoptive parent. Non-birth parents are sometimes referred to 'psychological parent(s)' who, in the same way as birth parents, have established emotional ties with a child and an ongoing, positive relationship in which the child or young person feels safe, cared for and a sense of belonging. This may be communicated in words and through behaviour, and will often require sensitive listening.

Attachment theory and permanence

In thinking about what permanence means in practice and how to achieve it, it is helpful to return to attachment theory (Bowlby, 2012; Howe, 2011; Schofield and Beek, 2006). For some children who do not have secure attachments, a primary objective will be to give them the opportunity to develop these. For others who have strong attachments but who cannot continue to live with the same people, the aim will be to build on these and support the child to develop new relationships. Attachment here refers to the proximity-seeking behaviours of a child (seeking attention from their main carer to get a need met), the adult carer's responsiveness to the proximity-seeking behaviour and the impacts of patterns of responsiveness or non-responsiveness over time.

There are four main types of attachment – secure, avoidant, ambivalent and disorganised. Schofield (2003, p. 8) describes their importance as follows:

> Those [children and young people] who have experienced consistent patterns of rejection may have learned to deactivate their proximity-seeking attachment behaviours and demonstrate an avoidant attachment pattern. Those who had insensitive, unpredictable care may have learned to hyperactivate their attachment behaviours and demonstrate an ambivalent/resistant attachment pattern. Many maltreated children who have experienced particular kinds of frightening and unpredictable environments will have developed representations of caregivers as dangerous or neglectful and will have found it impossible to organise a strategy for coping. They may demonstrate a disorganised attachment pattern'.

It follows that these different patterns have consequences for: the kind of placement that will meet the needs of the child; the kind of preparatory work that will have to be done; and the support that carers will need in placement. These consequences apply equally whether a child is going to live in a foster home, residential home, or be adopted, or return to their family of origin. A particular concern is for children and young people who have had inconsistent, neglectful and abusive care, compounded by several placement moves and carers who are not able to cope with the complex needs of these children. The worry is that the child or young person experiences deeper mistrust and it becomes very challenging indeed to create a permanent home for the child.

That said, children and young people are not objects to whom things are done, they are active in their creation of meaning, and in devising their own strategies for dealing with events and experiences. Children often show remarkable adaptability, flexibility and ability to form new, positive relationships and to develop secure attachments with multiple significant adults. Hence, it is important to acknowledge that the impact of poor attachment experiences is not necessarily enduring but can change with time and the right relationships. As social workers, we must avoid pigeonholing children and young people because that negates one of the central tenets of social work – the capacity of individuals to change in the right environment, with the right supports, right relationships and right opportunities. Good practice works with the grain of the child's own coping strategies, seeking to modify them when this is necessary and appropriate; it does not impose solutions on the child.

The rights of parents, children and permanence

Achieving permanence for children involves careful attention to the rights of all involved. As noted in earlier chapters, the Human Rights Act 1998, the UNCRC and childcare legislation makes clear that the best place for children to grow up is usually within their families unless this is not in their best interests due to harm, abuse, neglect and/or exploitation. Decisions made for children to be cared for away from home should be based on a consideration of the rights of parents. For example, the UNCRC makes clear that in their role as having primary responsibility for the upbringing of their child (Articles 5, 18 and 27), parents should have had access to a range of supports (Articles 18 and 27). Furthermore, under the Human Rights Act 1998 parents have a right to private and family life and to a fair trial (Articles 6 and 8). The right to a fair trial includes consideration of the information parents have received about any concerns noted by social services, the opportunities they have had to address concerns and the processes, practices through which they have been consulted and involved in all decision making. Clearly parents' rights are not upheld if they are not informed about concerns, if they are not involved and consulted about decisions being made and if they are not given access to timely and appropriate supports.

Decisions about permanence also need to reflect the rights of children. Children have a right to life, survival and development (Article 6), and in cases of child abuse, neglect, harm and exploitation, this right is interfered with, and the state has an obligation to protected them (Articles 19, 32, 33, 34, 35, 36). Decisions regarding alternative care need to be based on what is in their best interests (Articles 3, 9), and to ensure that their rights to family and privacy have not been unduly interfered with (Article 16) and to consider the range of placements available (Articles 20, 21) for as long as is needed. In making alternative arrangements, consideration should also be given to a child's right to health (Articles 24, 25), education (Articles 28, 29), leisure and play (Article 31); to involvement in decision making (Articles 2, 3, 5, 12, 13); and to their own identity (Articles 7, 8, 30). Special attention should be paid to the rights of children with disabilities (Article 23) and to the rights of refugee and asylum-seeking children and young people (Article 22).

Issues of concern that have been highlighted in social work practice regarding their rights and permanence planning concern include whether and how far all parents have had access to relevant, timely and appropriate family support services (Dolan et al., 2020; Winter et al., 2022) and whether children and young people in care have had opportunities to participate in all decisions made about them, and their rights to identity and to the preservation of that identity (name, nationality, right to know parents/be cared for by them) respected and upheld. These issues will be further considered throughout this chapter.

Ways of achieving permanence

As noted above, the ways of achieving permanence are varied. Government guidelines in the UK note that permanence options can include the following:

- Returning home to birth parents
- Living with wider family or friends in a kinship arrangement
- Living with long-term non-relative foster carers
- Living with adoptive families
- Living in residential care
- Living in the current short-term placement which is made long-term.

(Department for Education, 2016, p. 1)

Returning home to birth parents

Most children and young people in care experience permanence with their own families by returning to live with them or living with them while an order is in place. If being returned home, this process is also known as re-habilitation or reunification. For a return home to be successful, the reasons for care entry need to have been sufficiently addressed. Parents may need to address addiction, mental health, or relational issues, change their style of parenting, or learn new skills. Changes in the family's physical or social circumstances may be needed – better housing, better integration into their local community or maybe a move to a new area. Support from relatives may need to be built into the placement plan. In some cases, action may be needed to ensure that members of the family or their social circle who have abused the child are no longer in a position to do so. The family (child and parents) may need therapeutic support together to learn new and better ways of living together. The young person may need their own support.

Success relies heavily on parental willingness and capacity to engage with professionals offering help. A review of research (Carlson et al., 2020) on interventions found that support which had a family focus was more likely to engage parents and so to result in successful reunification. Of course, any intervention to address underlying difficulties takes time and resources to work effectively. For very young children, in particular, there may be difficult decisions regarding their long-term care arrangements. Considerations revolve around how long a child should wait for the family's difficulties to be addressed versus their need for permanence as soon as possible. All these factors can make the planning of a return extremely difficult and stressful for everyone involved – the child, the parents and family, the temporary carers, and the social worker. It can sometimes be very difficult to decide whether or not it is realistic, and in the child's interests, to plan for return at all.

Despite this, the available research tells us that for most children and young people return home remains the best way of providing permanence, because it builds on existing relationships and networks and fits with the basic rights underpinning childcare legislation which are founded on the principle that children will normally be brought up within their birth families. That said, it is by no means always successful. Carlson et al. (2020) conducted a recent review of research studies focusing on reunification and found that between 47% and 63% of children in care who returned home re-entered the care system.

This level of failure raises the question whether better assessments, based on clear predictive factors, could possibly result in better planning. There is evidence that certain factors are especially likely to be predictors of stability on return home (Carlson et al., 2020; Martín et al., 2020; Vanderwill et al., 2021). These include: the child's age (younger age is associated with more success); length of time in care; number of times in care (less time in care and fewer times in care); notable improvements in parents managing and addressing their difficulties; preparation time prior to the return home; and the provision of ongoing support from social services. Other notable factors that have an impact include social structural factors – housing, employment, and access to material, practical, social, and financial resources, and sources of support. These factors must be considered alongside more personal issues affecting children and families. Better planning could also be assisted by making available more research on children's and young people's experiences of reunification, which is notable by its absence.

Permanence with substitute families

For some children and young people, the route to permanence will be with a new family. This could be with the extended birth family, with family friends, with non-relative foster carers or with adoptive parents. A permanent substitute family will be the preferred option for any child whose parents are unlikely ever to provide good enough care, or at least not within a timescale that is realistic for the child.

As we have seen, 'family' and 'permanence' in this context may mean different things. It certainly does not necessarily mean a married couple with children of their own – although in many cases, it will. Anyone regardless of age, marital or partnership status, sexuality, ethnicity, (dis)ability, religion, or employment and housing status can in principle provide a good permanent home. What is important is to ensure that the family is right for this particular child – that they will be able to meet the child's identified needs including the need to form secure attachments, support the child to recover from any harm and trauma they may have experienced, and provide opportunities for personal growth and fulfilment.

The task of identifying a family who will be right for a particular child is not a straightforward one. Although there is considerable research evidence as to which kinds of placements are successful, it is not always clear and unambiguous as each child and family is unique (Sariaslan et al., 2022; Paine et al., 2021). That said, there is now considerable evidence that the older a child is placed within an adoptive placement, for example, the greater the likelihood of the placement failing to provide a long-term home. The reason for this is not age per se, but rather the fact that the older the child at adoption, the more adversity they may have been exposed to prior to their placement which will manifest in social, emotional and behavioural issues in the adoptive placement (Hjern et al., 2020; Raynor, 2021). Other evidence is less clear and sometimes we simply do not know why things do not work as intended (Paine et al., 2021).

In Chapter 2, we highlighted the needs of children and factors leading to coming into care. These factors (described as child, carer and context factors) are also relevant regarding adoptive placements. With regard to child factors, exposure to pre-placement harm, abuse, adversity and trauma, personality, coping mechanisms, age, disability, gender and cultural, religious, background, can all have an impact. In relation to carer factors, a synthesis of existing research (Palacios et al., 2019) highlights that stability of personal partner relationships and age of carers are important, as are their expectations and parenting abilities. A further important factor concerns the suitability of the placement in terms of match according to culture, religion, ethnicity and language for example. Knowing the child prior to placement and a willingness to seek help when needed are associated with stability. Pre-placement preparation including visits, provision and exchange of full information, and opportunities to seek advice are all connected with a greater likelihood of success. Access to ongoing therapeutic, practical, and financial help is also important (Brown and Campbell, 2007). Finally, social structural and contextual factors such as marginalisation, discrimination and social class are relevant.

Schofield's longitudinal study Growing Up in Foster Care (which ran between 1997 and 2006) documents many different aspects of children's pathways through foster care into adulthood. Schofield and Ward (2011) have identified seven distinct 'pathways', which she labelled 'close and special', 'testing out', 'distant and self-reliant', 'anxious and fearful', 'breakdown and rebuilding', 'rescue, relief and recovery', and 'hurt, angry and disappointed'. Without further elaboration, these words in themselves give a flavour of the diverse and intense emotions that can be involved in permanent placements – whether or not they are 'successful'. Among Schofield's findings was that even young people whose placements had 'broken down' might still regard the foster parents as their 'real parents'. Other very informative reading on pathways and outcomes has been undertaken by Iwaniec (2006), Ward et al. (2006), Fernández (2012), and McSherry et al. (2013).

Concurrent planning

A key theme underpinning childcare legislation is that children are best brought up within their immediate families and that, according to the same legislation (and reflected in the UNCRC), the state must provide assistance and support to parents to help them care for their children. When children can longer live at home, social workers are obliged to see and test if there is any possibility of children returning home to their immediate family. This means the immediate family being expected to address the problems that led to their children being removed.

As outlined at the start of this chapter, social workers have to straddle the balance between, on the one hand, giving the immediate family long enough to show that they can address their problems and, on the other hand, making timely decisions for children so that their long-term care can be sorted as soon as possible – outside the birth family if necessary. One can feel torn between the wish to ensure that a child's future is secured without undue delay, and reluctance to miss an opportunity to rebuild the family. Delay may make it harder to place the child successfully in a new family, but definitive action may be hard to justify until the parents have been given a chance to tackle their problems. **Consider Exercise 9.2 and then use it to reflect on the issues in the rest of the chapter.**

At a legal level, social workers are charged with putting the child's interests first, but this does not necessarily help, precisely because it is not always clear and certain what *is* in the child's best interests. At a practical level, to help address these difficulties 'concurrent planning' is sometimes used (Kendrick, 2009, 2010). First developed in Seattle, United States, in 1981, the aim is to distinguish families where the chances of children's successful return are extremely unlikely from those where there is some hope and evidence that progress can be made and sustained by the parents (Pecora et al., 2018).

Exercise 9.2 A planning dilemma

Jenny is aged two and has been admitted to care as result of neglect. Lorna, her mother, is a single parent with no other children. She has moderate learning difficulties and attends a special school. It is clear that Lorna has a limited understanding of the needs of a young child, but she is very fond of Jenny and was upset to find that she had not been meeting her needs.

An initial assessment at a family centre suggests that over time Lorna could be helped to give good care to her daughter. The recommended programme is expected to take 12 months. There is of course no guarantee of success.

How would you make a plan for Jenny, bearing in mind her need for permanence?

On the basis of this 'differential diagnosis', immediate permanent placements are sought for those who are very unlikely ever to return home. For children where there is enough evidence that things could change and reunification could take place, they are placed with carers who are approved as both foster carers and adoptive carers. They are known as dually approved carers. In the event that things work out well, the child will return to the birth family and in the event it does not work out well the carers will go on to adopt the child (as you will have noticed in the case study of 'Jenny' in Exercise 9.2).

The aim of concurrent planning, as outlined by Ward et al. (2006), is to reduce the number of moves a child might experience until a final decision regarding their long-term care is reached, and to reduce delay in decision making. The success of the model depends on having a pool of prospective families who are willing to care for young children with the hope of adoption but who are also willing to support the child's birth family knowing that if they succeed the child may return home. The personal accounts of carers show that this can be challenging, because a relationship with a child is formed with the hope of adopting the child whilst also accepting that the relationship will end if the child returns home. This can be experienced as both painful and stressful.

As outlined by Hill et al. (2020), these types of placements are different from concurrent placements. In England, the Children and Families Act 2014 imposes a duty to consider fostering for adoption in all cases where the care plan indicates potential adoption. Fostering for adoption carers are primarily approved as adopters and temporary approval is granted for them to be the interim foster carer of the specific child – again, this is to reduce the number of moves and ensure timely decision making. Carers are made aware of the court process and the fact that decisions and outcomes cannot be guaranteed (although this option is usually chosen in cases where it is very unlikely that the child will be returned home).

Another type of arrangement is known as 'parallel or twin track' planning. The child involved is placed in temporary foster care whilst the plan to return the child home is pursued. At the same time, an alternative permanence plan is put in place, normally with different carers (adopters or long-term foster carers).

Long-term foster care or adoption?

Social workers may be faced with the question 'what is better for this child, long-term foster care or adoption?' There are a number of factors to be considered here, including the age, background circumstances and needs of the child, the type of long-term foster care placement being considered, and the wishes and feelings of the child. If legal permanence is a priority concern, then adoption may be favoured – because it severs birth parents' parental responsibility and transfers this to adoptive carers. This compares with other legal options including residence orders, special guardianship orders and care orders, where parental responsibility continues to be shared between birth parents and the new carers or the local authority. However, legal permanence is not the only consideration. Children and young people may achieve emotional/relational permanence in long-term fostering arrangements, especially if the child is clear that they do not want to be adopted, is closely attached to their current foster carers, has a high level of continuous birth family involvement, or is older.

Some argue that the advantages of adoption are connected in part with the nature of the commitment made, which means that the adoptive parents are less likely to give up when things go wrong, and that the child may therefore feel more secure. Others point out that this deep commitment to the child can also be offered in foster placements, especially kinship placements. It is argued that if long-term foster carers are given delegated authority (which can be done through a variety of legal arrangements), they can operate as any other family and the child can feel a firm sense of belonging. In recent years more children have come to be cared for in such arrangements. These placements can still break down; however, Konijn et al. (2019) found that a number of factors may create instability, including aggressive behaviour from the child or inappropriate expectations on the part of foster carers.

Adoption and its place in child care

Background – adoption in contemporary society

Legal adoption, which transfers the status of parent to someone new, is not universal (Smolin, 2022). In England, it has only existed in its modern form since 1926, and in some countries or cultures it is still not recognised. Its emergence reflects wider social, economic, religious and political influences. Variations in the law, policy and practice of adoption in different countries are therefore evident Pösö et al. (2021).

In the UK, it was introduced following the First World War, partly in response to the needs of families affected by the death or disappearance of parents and by children being conceived outside marriage. At the time it was not socially acceptable to have children outside of marriage, hence adoption was used primarily to provide new homes for babies whose mothers were unable to keep them, and babies for couples who were unable to conceive. As recently as the 1960s, unmarried mothers frequently felt coerced by professionals, by families and by societal pressures to give up their children for adoption. 'Forced adoptions' were often connected with mother and baby homes run by churches and charities. Adoption took place under a veil of secrecy, and children often had no idea of their adopted status until they reached adulthood, or even later. In England and Wales, the Joint Committee on Human Rights in 2022 conducted an inquiry into the experiences of unmarried women whose babies were removed from them and adopted between the period of the Adoption of Children Act 1949 and the Adoption Act 1976. It concluded that many women had their rights seriously violated, and called on the government to issue an apology (Joint Committee on Human Rights, 1922).

It is notable that social practices did change radically with the social changes in the late 1960s and 1970s. The lessening of stigma attaching to being an 'unmarried mother' and greater availability of contraception meant far fewer babies needing new families. At the same time, the increased prevalence of divorce led to a demand for adoption by stepfathers, as a way of establishing relationships in reconstituted families. There was also a change in the theory and practice of adoption. It came to be recognised that the practice of not informing children that they were adopted had the potential to cause huge difficulties for them as they grew up. It became standard practice that social workers encouraged adopters to explain the situation honestly to the child involved. This move was further strengthened by the Children Act 1975 which gave adopted people the right to have access to their original birth records once they reached adulthood.

Since the 1980s, there have been further changes to adoption practices and processes, as will be further explored below. There have also been changes regarding the profile and characteristics of children adopted, and the profile of people choosing to adopt. The biggest change has been in the increasing proportion of children being adopted from the care system, in particular older children and disabled children. The children for whom adoptive placements are now sought are less often new born babies; they tend to be older, known to social services for some time, have had difficult experiences and a range of individual needs. Lastly, the characteristics of people seeking to adopt have also changed. The diverse nature of children needing adoption from care has meant that a much wider range of people have tended to come forward or to be recruited as adopters. Many of the more traditional adopters, typified by the infertile couple wanting a healthy baby, have been diverted into intercountry adoption, increasingly sophisticated infertility treatment, or surrogacy. That said, it does remain a controversial area of practice (Pösö et al., 2021).

Hence, in the present day, the main types of adoption are stepparent adoptions and the adoption of children from care. In the case of step-parent adoptions, it is surprisingly difficult to find out information on the number of successful stepparent adoptions in any one year in the courts across the UK. The application process usually begins as a decision by a family to make an application and this then becomes the province of social workers when the court appoints a social work agency to inquire and report on the welfare of the child(ren). In stepparent adoptions, sometimes the court will also appoint an independent person to represent the wishes and feelings of children. In Northern Ireland, this person is known as a Children's Court Guardian, in England and Wales, they are known as a Family Court Adviser, and in Scotland, a child welfare reporter could be appointed, or a curator ad litem to independently in represent the child in litigation and/or adoption cases. Stepparent adoptions are not a central focus of this book, whereas adoption from care on the other hand is, as we have already seen. However, in looking at some of the practice issues, it may be helpful to put it in the context of adoption work more generally. This part of the chapter will be based on key features of the law and practice of adoption across the UK, in England, Scotland, Wales and Northern 'Ireland'. Much of the content will also be applicable to work in other countries.

Adoption services and the legal obligations to provide them

As noted above, the precise arrangements for adoption services vary between countries, even within the UK. Since the first adoption law (in 1926 in England and Wales, 1929 in Northern Ireland and 1930 in Scotland), there have been changes in each jurisdiction.

In England and Wales, the core legislation now is the Adoption and Children Act 2002, as amended by the Children and Families Act 2014. A key feature is the duty on Local Authorities to consider 'fostering for adoption' placements for those children for whom adoption is the care plan. This is one of several changes designed to reduce the number of moves experienced by children in care and to speed up the adoption process. Other additions to the Regulations include the Adoption Information and Intermediary Services Regulations 2005, which place a duty on adoption agencies to provide an information and intermediary service for anyone adopted before 2005 to assist adopted people to access information about their adoption and to facilitate contact. These regulations are supported by additional regulations regarding the purpose, management and governance of adoption agencies including the type of information to be held by adoption agencies. More recently, in addition to the publication of National Minimum Standards on Adoption (2011), there have been publications exploring delays in adoption cases, regionalising the service and new Statutory Guidance on Adoption (Department for Education, 2013).

The statutory guidance on adoption contains a chapter on contact between children adopted and their birth families. It points to changes made by the Adoption and Children Act 2002 which imposes a duty on the court, when making an adoption order, to consider the existing and proposed arrangements for contact with the child, and to seek the views of the parties to the proceedings on those arrangements. The court can make a contact order. That said, there is no presumption that contact should always happen. Each case must be determined individually, and decisions made in the best interests of the child not just in the short term but also long term too.

In a further development in Wales, and since 2014, all adoption services have been brought under the umbrella of a national adoption service with an aim to improve quality and experiences for all parties. The first decade of operation has shown real improvements in aspects such as life story work and pace of adoption assessments, and attention being given to birth parent experiences and sibling contact, as noted in reports by the National Adoption Service for Wales.

In Scotland, the current law is the Adoption and Children (Scotland) Act 2007, updated by the Children and Young People (Scotland) Act (2014) which made Scotland's Adoption Register law. Following this in 2016 Scotland's Adoption Register Regulations came into force. The purpose, management and governance of adoption agencies is set out in the Adoption Agencies (Scotland) Regulations 2009.

In Northern Ireland, adoption is governed by the Adoption and Children Act (Northern Ireland) 2022. Still being implemented at the time of writing, the new legislation emphasises both the rights of the child and the welfare paramountcy concept in adoption cases, addresses delay in adoption and introduces a new permanence option (special guardianship orders).

What all this legislation has in common is the provision for various routes to permanence including guardianship as well as specifying the circumstances in which placement for adoption and adoption orders are to be made and setting out the duties and powers of adoption agencies and services. Adoption agencies can be local authorities, Health and Social Care Trusts or adoption societies. Local authorities or Health and Social Care Trusts have a duty to plan the provision of adoption services in their area, either by themselves directly or by voluntary societies. In Scotland, for example, voluntary agencies include Barnardo's, Scottish Adoption, St Andrews Children's Society and St Margaret's Children and Family Care Society. All services must provide support for children for whom adoption is planned, as well as support for parents and prospective adopters. The services required may include provision of information, advice and counselling, practical services including accommodation, assessment of children and adopters, and placement. Decisions about the approval of adopters and the placement of children for adoption have to be considered by an independent adoption panel, and as noted, various regulations specify how this is to work.

Good practice in adoption and post-adoption services

Good practice starts, as always, with assessment (Dibben, 2020; Dibben et al., 2021). Given that adoption involves finding 'a family for life' for a child, the critical role played by assessment cannot be underestimated.

Assessment in adoption work relates to the child, the birth parents and the prospective adopters (the 'adoption triangle'). Good assessment depends on: (a) detailed knowledge of the child, their individual circumstances, their family relationships (including siblings) and their needs now and into the future; (b) clear understanding of the birth parents' needs and circumstances, and their perception of adoption with all its implications; and (c) deep insight into the lives, motivations, strengths and family relationships of the prospective adopters.

Assessment of the child must focus in particular on any physical, emotional, psychological and emotional need that requires ongoing intervention and support, as well as on relational needs such as sibling and other family relationships that may demand post-adoption contact arrangements. Most importantly, children – including very young children – have their own views which must be ascertained and taken into account. Often children's views are not clearly expressed, and social workers should ensure that information is accessible and child friendly.

Assessment of parents should take account of their position of relative disadvantage, which will often feature poverty and social exclusion, or needs arising from substance misuse, domestic violence and mental health issues. These may affect their understanding of, access to, and participation in processes and procedures. As for adopters, it is crucial to clarify their expectations of the adoptive process, the child they wish to adopt and their future family lives. Coupled with assessment, it is important to ensure that all parties have the information they need – that parents have as much information as possible about the people who will be adopting their child, that adopters have as much information as possible about the child and family's history (including medical history), and that children have as much information as possible about the adopters, the process, and about themselves and their families.

Adoption is intended to be a lifelong commitment, and it can raise complex issues. Areas of particular complexity can relate to contested adoption hearings, post adoption contact arrangements and post adoption support services. With regard to contested adoptions, courts do have the power to order an adoption without agreement, even in the face of parental opposition, if the child's welfare requires it. In general, we know that children are more likely to make successful transitions if they feel that they have 'permission' from those to whom they are attached; but some parents, even when they can see that it is right for a child to be adopted, cannot bring themselves to give their formal consent.

Contested adoptions can be extremely stressful processes for everyone concerned, and an increasing number of adoptions in the UK are contested. Courts in England and Wales are now able to deal with the issue of consent before placement in making a *placement order*, which reduces the problem of a child spending considerable time with adopters in a state of uncertainty as to whether the adoption would eventually be allowed to go ahead, or of parents feeling that the agency has pre-empted the court's decision by allowing the child to establish a bond with the prospective adopters before the issue of consent has been tested. Previously this was dealt with by a step known as 'freeing for adoption'. (Placement orders also apply in Northern Ireland since 2022; in Scotland the equivalent provision is a permanence order.)

Post adoption contact arrangements between children and various birth family members are now a core consideration when making an adoption order (Smith and Logan, 2004; MacDonald, 2016). The term 'open adoption' has been used to indicate adoptions that are openly acknowledged and not kept secret but may also refer to a greater or lesser degree of contact between the birth family and the adoptive family. This 'openness' may be thought of as a continuum. At a minimum, 'openness' may imply merely that the child is actively aware of the existence and whereabouts of the birth parents or other family members. Greater 'openness' may include the regular exchange of letters or emails, photographs or news, or even some face-to-face contact. The aim is to build a relaxed and friendly relationship between the birth parent(s) and the new family from the start, in which continuing social relationships are possible (see Box 9.1). Advocates of this approach to adoption argue that it produces a situation that is healthier for all, especially the child, and in which the rights of birth parents are better respected.

It is widely acknowledged that experiences of post adoption contact are varied and that nuanced policy and practice is required in which the views of all are recognised, acknowledged and weighed up in decision making and planning (MacDonald, 2016). A recent report from the Nuffield Family Justice Observatory (2021) highlights the benefits of post-adoption contact, the challenges and the methods used, and makes a series of recommendations for future practice. These include:

- There is a focus on the quality (rather than quantity) of contact.
- The views of children and young people are sought, and actively taken into account in decision making.
- The importance of wider family ties for children with their siblings, grandparents, aunts and uncles is recognised.
- There is clarity about the purpose of contact.
- Contact plans are specific to the individual child, their unique family and adoptive family circumstances and regularly reviewed.
- There is ongoing professional support for the child, birth parents and adoptive parents.

As a child gets older, the question of why they were 'given up' for adoption becomes salient, and an honest but helpful answer to this must be prepared

Box 9.1 Telling children about their past

Part of positive identity formation is knowing the small (and to others) insignificant aspects of one's own family history.

For children who live in their family homes throughout their childhood and into adulthood, their personal narrative is built up through parents and siblings recounting memories, events and major milestones (I remember when you used to sleep with a teddy called Kevin or when you were a child you did not like going on car drives unless you could listen to your favourite songs) and so on.

For children who live in care, this narrative is often missing. When children become adopted, the fact that the narrative is missing comes to the fore. Generally, as the child settles and develops, they begin to ask more about the detail of their background. Adoptive carers need to be in a position where they can outline the reasons leading to the child's adoption and they need to make available as much information about the birth family as they can.

Adoptive carers will be worried about how much to say, when to say it, how to say it, what the impact on the child might be; and what the impact on their own relationship with the child might be. Adoptive carers need to find a balance between not saying anything to saying too much and they need to go at the child's pace and not their own pace. The value of a 'life story book' is that it is a written and photographic record of the child's birth family background and it can be returned to (or left) at the child's pace. The story can have further detail added as the child's own understanding develops.

in advance – with the help of the parent(s) if this is possible. A life story book or similar record can be invaluable, whether this is produced digitally or on paper – see Box 9.2. Actual physical photographs and letters are still full of meaning in a digital age. Accounts by adults who have been adopted illustrate the range of experience (Harris, 2012). Having said this, common themes that underpin varied accounts relate to identity, belonging and acceptance (Harris, 2012; Brodzinsky, 1993).

Post-adoption support is a legal requirement. This can include information, advice and practical support and should be carefully planned and agreed – for the child, the adoptive parents and the birth family. Several organisations working in the post-adoption field who have experience in working with families and promoting better services, are valuable sources of information and advice. Social workers should inform adoptive parents of the availability of support groups. Groups include Adoption UK which is a self-help group offering a source of valuable support from others who have had the experience

Box 9.2 Contact after adoption

Research indicates the complexities of face-to face contact in adoption. What helps to navigate the challenges involved include:

a the attitude of the birth-parents to the fact of the adoption and whether they can accept the new carers and the new care arrangements;
b the attitude, skills and confidence of the adoptive carers;
c the child's needs both in the short term and the long term; the availability of support for the adopted child, for the adoptive carers and for the birth parents;
d the assurance that children, birth parents and adoptive parents are the central people with whom social workers must consult and whose views must be taken into consideration;
e the acceptance that post adoption contact is not in the best interest of all children and that decisions and plans need to reflect the individual child and their unique situations.

Careful assessment is the key as is the recognition that relationships and needs are not static but change over time, therefore some degree of flexibility needs to be built in to allow for the changing interest of the child in birth family contact over time.

The ability of adoptive carers to have some form of relationship with the birth-parent may help in gaining further detailed information about a child's background that will not have been recorded in the case files.

of being adoptive parents themselves. Other organisations include Coram Adoption, Together for Adoption and PAC-UK, Family Action.

Support includes financial assistance. Where children are adopted from care, there is the possibility for a continuing monetary allowance to be paid, to cushion the blow to the child and family of losing the foster care allowance. This is especially important for disabled children, whose care can involve considerable extra expense. Since adoption allowances were first introduced, the number of disabled children adopted has increased substantially. Other supports include access to therapeutic services and to support groups where experiences with other adoptive carers can be shared. Given the complexities associated with adoption for the child, carers and parents in the short and long term, the importance of access to post-adoption support cannot be underestimated.

Intercountry adoption

Intercountry adoption is an area of practice that for a time was largely unregulated, leading to concern that children were being adopted without proper parental consent or by couples who did not have the right skills or attitude to make a success of it (Gibbons and Rotabi, 2016). There is still a wider political concern that attention should be given to improving conditions in their countries of origin, rather than taking children away to be brought up in a different culture. (This of course is not just an objection to intercountry adoption. It can be argued that much ordinary adoption practice amounts to removing children from poor families and handing them over to prosperous ones, and that it could be better instead to help the poor families to become more prosperous.)

As noted by Fong and McRoy (2016), the practice of inter-country adoption is now much better managed, at least in the UK. Adopters have to be assessed and approved by an adoption agency at home, and there has to be clear evidence that the child's interests have been properly considered in the host country. Romania, for example, has devoted considerable attention to improving practice in this area. The UK has now implemented the Hague Convention which regulates adoption between different countries. Partly as a result of these more effective controls, the incidence of inter-county adoption has fallen in recent years.

Policy and political issues in adoption

Adoption remains a politically charged aspect of childcare. There is a tension between parents' rights and adoption practices in which family relationships have been totally severed, names changed and therefore fundamental identity issues interfered with (Smolin, 2022). Reflections on these issues have recently been filtered through the accounts of unmarried mothers whose babies were forcibly removed from them and adopted in the 1940s, 1950s and 1960s, when being an unmarried mother was widely regarded as socially unacceptable. The personal toll for parents and children (now adults) is well documented (Sixsmith, 2013; Rotabi and Bromfield, 2017; Redmond, 2018; Joint Committee on Human Rights, 2022).

Furthermore, a return to a focus on the enduring nature of family and extended family has led to a renewed emphasis in court proceedings on demonstrating the absence of any suitable family option before granting adoption orders, as reflected in the declining trend in adoption orders since 2015. In addition, in this age of social media where the boundaries in and between families are far more porous, limits to the proposition that adoption can or should create 'pure' new family beginnings are more evident.

There have also been debates regarding the required characteristics of prospective adoptive carers with regard to their age, lifestyles and background characteristics (religion, ethnicity, and so on). Some have questioned the processes and procedures through which appropriate adoptive carers are assessed and approved, accusing social workers of being 'politically correct' and adding to unnecessary delays in decision making. There have been developments in law, policy, and practice to promote effective and timely decision making, but care still has to be taken; if inappropriate carers have been approved, this can be catastrophic. In the case of the Laura Castle who in January 2021 murdered a baby boy, Leiland-James Corkill, placed with her and her husband for adoption (Box 9.3), the reporting revealed that critical information relevant to the suitability to adopt assessment of Laura and her husband, had not been shared by Laura and/or between agencies. This included Laura's own mental health issues (low mood, anxiety, and anger management), her physical health issues, alcohol abuse and financial worries.

Box 9.3 Flawed adoption assessment

Laura Castle, the mother identified as the suitable adopter for Leiland-James Corkill, would likely not have been approved as a suitable adoptive carer had the relevant and full information regarding her physical, mental, financial and alcohol related issues been made available.

The Child Safeguarding Practice Review (Pettitt, 2022) noted that the assessment and approval process had followed the relevant policy and procedures and included references, medical information, police checks and attendance by the couple at the required training and group sessions.

Reflecting back on the assessment, there were significant gaps in the health information provided by the couple which were then not picked up on by the GP. One learning point noted is that 'there is still a need for rigorous professional curiosity about the information shared from the assessing adoption social worker, the GP and the medical advisor' (para 4.7, pp. 4–5).

The review also noted that the family had loans and credit card debt without having the income to pay off these debts. Weaknesses in the design of the form meant that there was no requirement for the couple to indicate the total money owed and the family were in effect able 'to disguise what they owed and that they were only paying the minimum amount each month, leading to the debt increasing' (para 4.15, p. 7).

It also became apparent that the talking therapy being received by Laura, and her issues with alcohol consumption, were not reported fully in the assessment process. The review was also able to highlight Laura's own admission that she was not bonding with Leiland-James. This combined with Leiland-James's own needs (milk intolerance and developmental delay), Laura's own anxiety and her anger management issues, were warning signs not fully identified and/or acted upon.

A culmination of factors coalesced leading to a catastrophic incident on the morning of 6 January 2021, Leiland-James when was being given his breakfast. He was crying and spitting out his food. Laura admitted in court that she had 'lost her mind' and shook him to try and silence him, accidentally hitting his head off the arm of the sofa. In fact, the nature of his head injuries indicated significant force and intentionality. Other less recent bruises were found and were found to be indicative of cruelty.

In lessons for learning (a) rigorous checking of all information provided by self-report is required, (b) medical assessments need to be completed more thoroughly, (c) information sharing between agencies needs to be improved and (d) a more immediate and proactive response to 'cries for help' by adopters is needed.

In a final point, a birth child to Laura and her husband and living in the household, had seen events unfold in the five months after his placement and yet was almost like a 'silent witness'. The Review recommended that 'the voice of other children in the household is sought at regular points in the assessment and placement' (Pettitt 2022, p. 19).

Key messages from research for practice

A review of research on adoption suggests several priorities. First it is of crucial importance, as alluded to above, that social workers further develop their understanding of the social, cultural, political and historical aspects of adoption practice nationally and internationally. Acknowledging the impact of historically dominant discourses that have maligned unmarried mothers, and singled out parents from different minority ethnic backgrounds, is a critical aspect to developing cultural competence in practice (Harris, 2014). Contemporary research, and indeed (as noted), inquiries, have begun to highlight the legacy of illegal and/or dubious adoption practices that took place in the UK and Ireland in the 1950s and the 1960s and involved unmarried mothers forcibly giving up their children for adoption in a context in which illegitimacy was constructed as socially unacceptable. Further afield, research has revealed historical violations of human rights in the system of intercountry adoptions, for example the Sixties Scoop in Canada where 20,000 indigenous children were removed from their families and placed with predominantly white carers (Bomberry and Hubbard, 2023) and ongoing examples (Loibl, 2021), in which poor families have been offered payment to give up a child for adoption, and where other irregularities include fake documents, partial information; all of which constitute illegal adoption practices.

Second, it is also crucial that there is further research exploring the processes of adoption and the experiences of birth parents, adoptive parents, social workers and children adopted to inform the ongoing development of sensitive, culturally attuned practice in this highly emotionally charged area of work. With regard to birth parents, research has revealed that many experience lifelong grief and loss akin to bereavement, having been involved in the adoption of their child, and that it has been a struggle for them to access services. Alper (2019) notes these issues and highlights examples of trauma informed long-term counselling services.

In relation to adoptive parents, further research is needed that explores the information they receive prior to the adoption and their access to ongoing support services after the adoption is finalised. We know that formal support after adoption needs to be substantial and reliable. Social workers may not have the skills to give this advice, so that specialised help may be needed, for instance from mental health services. This support should be 'on call' at times when families need it, and it has two dimensions – support for the adopters and direct support for the child. We should not assume that supporting the adopters is sufficient to support the child.

Regarding social workers, there is some research which explores how they assess applications for adoption and the process of getting applications and placements approved. It is important that there is research that explores biases, assumptions and practices regarding the entire adoption process.

In relation to children, we know that they have varied experiences of adoption. Some adults who were adopted have had happy, secure childhoods with a sense of belonging and being loved. Others have had a more difficult experience. One theme emerging from adult accounts is the need for ongoing contact with/information regarding their birth family and the network from which they were removed (Neil et al., 2011). Adoption has historically been constructed as 'a fresh start' but it can never be a completely fresh start in the sense that there is always a connection (biological if nothing else) to another past, another family, another context, and another history (see recent research Rawcliffe et al., 2022). Further research that highlights how multiple aspects of identity are accommodated, valued and owned is important.

Third, further research on adoption processes and practices is needed; in a context where there are ongoing delays and a reduction in the total number of children being adopted and where digital technology is pervading all aspects of our daily lives. For example, recent research has highlighted that contact arrangements, where they do exist, and life story work, could be modernised by the use of digital technology (MacDonald et al., 2023; Barnett-Jones and Manning, 2021).

Summary and conclusion

We hope we have done two things in this chapter. We have learned about the idea of 'permanence' – the different meaning that have been given to it, its relationship to ideas of attachment and 'psychological parenting', and the different ways in which it can be achieved. We have also learned about the institution of adoption – not just as one of the ways in which children can achieve permanence but also as a mode of parenting that is both regulated and politically contested. We have seen that there is evidence that for many children, who are not going to return to their families of origin, adoption as the most secure and permanent option is clearly preferable to any other. We have also seen that for other children, long-term foster care or other routes to permanence can provide a satisfactory solution, if there is commitment and if families are given sufficient autonomy. However, as also noted, the best way to provide permanence for most children is to maintain and strengthen their relationships with their own families, and this should be the object of most work with children and young people, even when they are in care.

GUIDE TO FURTHER READING

Fahlberg (2012, second edition) is still essential reading on working with children through the journey to permanent placement. Rossini (2014) outlines the social history of adoption in England and Wales from 1850 to 1961. Deblasio (2021) outlines the perspectives of birth mothers forced to give up their children for adoption in the UK; Redmond (2018) explores similar issues in Ireland. As for good practice guides, Lord and Lucking (2006) is a guide for social workers involved in adoption cases in England, and McNeill and Jack (2016) for Scotland. Swift (2020) offers a very useful practical guide for adopters in Scotland, and Allen (2021) similarly offers practical advice for adopters in England. Statutory guidance on adoption varies across the four developed nations of the UK. In Wales, a really useful publication produced by the National Adoption Service (2017) outlines the legal framework for adoption. In England, Ofsted's website has useful links to adoption law, statutory guidance and regulations. In Scotland, adoption law, regulations and guidance can be found on the Scottish Government's website. In Northern Ireland, updated information following the recent introduction of new legislation is still being developed. Issues regarding identity are explored by Triseliotis (1973) and more recently by Feast and Philpot (2003).

References

Allen, L. (2021) *How to adopt a child: Your step-by-step guide to adopting and parenting*. London: Vermilion.
Alper, J. (ed.) (2019) *Supporting birth parents whose children have been adopted*. London: Jessica Kingsley Publishers.

Barnett-Jones, B. and Manning, C. (2021) *Modernising post-adoption contact: Findings from a recent consultation*. London: Nuffield Family Justice Observatory.

Bomberry, A. and Hubbard, J. (2023) *The sixties scoop and the stolen lives of indigenous children*. Toronto: James Lorimer & Company Ltd., Publishers.

Bowlby, J. (2012) *A secure base*. Abingdon, Oxfordshire: Routledge.

Brodzinsky, D.M. (1993) 'Long-term outcomes in adoption', *The Future of Children. Adoption*, *3*(1), 153–166.

Brown, J.D. and Campbell, M. (2007) 'Foster parent perceptions of placement success', *Children and Youth Services Review*, *29*(8), 1010–1020.

Carlson, L., Hutton, S., Priest, H. and Melia, Y. (2020) 'Reunification of looked-after children with their birth parents in the United Kingdom: A literature review and thematic synthesis', *Child and Family Social Work*, *25*(1), 192–205.

Deblasio, L. (2021) *Adoption and law: The unique personal experiences of birth mothers in adoption proceedings*. London: Routledge.

Department for Education (2013) *Statutory Guidance on Adoption For local authorities, voluntary adoption agencies and adoption support agencies*, London: Department for Education.

Department for Education (2016) *Knowledge and skills statement: achieving permanence*. Available https://assets.publishing.service.gov.uk/media/5a81a08c40f0b62302698529/Knowledge_and_skills_statement_for_achieving_permanence.pdf [last accessed 02.04.24].

Dibben, E. (2020) *Undertaking an adoption assessment: A guide* to *collecting and analysing information for the prospective adopters' report (PAR) England*. London: CoramBAAF.

Dibben, E., Runciman, H. and Duncan, R (2021) *Undertaking an adoption assessment* (Scotland). London: CoramBAAF.

Dolan, P., Žegarac, N. and Arsić, J. (2020) 'Family support as a right of the child', *Social Work and Social Sciences Review*, *21*(2), 8–26.

Fahlberg, V.I. (2012) *A child's journey through placement* (second edition). London: British Association for Adoption and Fostering (BAAF).

Feast, J. and Philpot, T. (2003) *Searching questions: Identity, origins, and adoption*. London: CoramBAAF.

Fernández, P. (2012) *Becoming dads: A gay couple's journey to adoption*. London: CoramBAAF.

Fong, R. and McRoy, R.G. (2016) *Transracial and intercountry adoptions. Cultural guidance for professionals*. New York: Columbia University Press.

Gibbons, J.L. and Rotabi, K.S. (2016) *Intercountry adoption: Policies, practices, and outcomes*. Burlington, VT: Ashgate.

Harris, P. (2012) *Chosen. Living with adoption*. London: CoramBAAF.

Harris, P. (2014) "I started to feel not ashamed of who I was': Transracially adopted adults and adoption support', *Adoption & Fostering*, *38*(4), 346–360.

Hill, L., Gilligan, R. and Connelly, G. (2020) 'How did kinship care emerge as a significant form of placement for children in care? A comparative study of the experience in Ireland and Scotland', *Children and Youth Services Review*, *117*, 104368.

Hjern, A., Palacios, J., Vinnerljung, B., Manhica, H. and Lindblad, F. (2020) 'Increased risk of suicidal behaviour in non-European international adoptees decreases with age. A Swedish national cohort study', *EClinicalMedicine*, *29*. Available here https://www.thelancet.com/journals/eclinm/article/PIIS2589-5370(20)30387-4/fulltext (accessed 27.01.24)

Howe, D. (2011) *Attachment Across the lifecourse: A brief introduction*. London: Bloomsbury Publishing PLC.

Iwaniec, D. (ed.) (2006) *The child's journey through care: Placement stability, care planning, and achieving permanency*. Chichester: John Wiley and Sons.

Joint Committee on Human Rights (1922) *The Violation of Family Life: Adoption of Children of Unmarried Women 1949–1976*. London: House of Commons & House of Lords. Available at https://committees.parliament.uk/publications/23076/documents/169043/default/ [accessed 1.5.24]

Kendrick, A. (2009) *Better futures? Experience and outcomes of children and young people in* residential care'. *Care matters: Transforming lives – improving outcomes*. Scotland: Strathclyde.

Kendrick, J. (2010). 'Concurrent planning (2): 'The rollercoaster of uncertainty'', *Adoption and Fostering*, *34*(2), 38–48.

Konijn, C., Admiraal, S., Baart, J., Van Rooij, F., Stams, G.J., Colonnesi, C., Lindauer, R. and Assink, M. (2019) 'Foster care placement instability: A meta-analytic review', *Children and Youth Services Review*, *96*, 483–499.

Loibl, E.C. (2021) 'The aftermath of transnational illegal adoptions: Redressing human rights violations in the intercountry adoption system with instruments of transitional justice', *Childhood*, *28*(4), 477–491.

Lord, J. and Lucking, M. (2006) *The adoption process in England. A guide for children's social workers*. London: CoramBAAF.

MacDonald, M. (2016) *Parenthood and open adoption: An interpretative phenomenological analysis*. New York: Springer.

MacDonald, M., Wright, A.C., Taylor-Beswick, A., Gillespie, K. and Collings, S. (2023) 'Digital relationality, rights, resilience: Conceptualising a digital social ecology for children's birth family relationships when in care or adopted', *The British Journal of Social Work*, *53*(1), 216–235.

Martín, E., González-García, C., del Valle, J.F. and Bravo, A. (2020) 'Detection of behavioral and emotional disorders in residential child care: Using a multi-informant approach', *Children and Youth Services Review*, *108*, 104588.

McNeill, P.G.B. and Jack, M.A.F. (2016) *Adoption of children in Scotland*. Edinburgh: W. Green and Sons Publishers.

McSherry, D., Malet, M.F. and Weatherall, K. (2013) *Comparing long-term placements for young children in care: The care pathways and outcomes study-Northern Ireland*. London: British Association for Adoption and Fostering.

National Adoption Service (2017) *The legal framework for adoption: The Prospective Adoptive Parent's Guide*. Cardiff: National Adoption Service/ Gwasanaeth Mabwysiadu Cenedlaethol

Neil, E., Cossar, J., Lorgelly, P., Young, J. and Jones, C. (2011) *Supporting direct contact after adoption*. London: BAAF.

Paine, A.L., Perra, O., Anthony, R. and Shelton, K.H. (2021) 'Charting the trajectories of adopted children's emotional and behavioral problems: The impact of early adversity and postadoptive parental warmth', *Development and psychopathology*, *33*(3), 922–936.

Palacios, J., Rolock, N., Selwyn, J. and Barbosa-Ducharne, M. (2019) 'Adoption breakdown: Concept, research, and implications', *Research on Social Work Practice*, *29*(2), 130–142.

Pecora, P.J., Whittaker, J.K., Barth, R.P., Borja, S. and Vesneski, W. (2018) *The child welfare challenge: Policy, practice, and research*. London: Routledge.

Pettitt, N. (2022) *Report of child safeguarding practice review (Leiland-James Michael Corkill)*. Carlisle: Cumbria Safeguarding Children Partnership.

Pösö, T., Skivenes, M. and Thoburn, J. (2021) *Adoption from care: International perspectives on children's rights, family preservation and State Intervention*. Bristol: Policy Press.

Rawcliffe, C., Neil, E., Hancock, M. and Elias, L. (2022) *Maintaining relationships with birth families after adoption: What are adopted adults' views?* Norwich: CRCF, University of East Anglia.

Raynor, L. (2021) *Adoption of non-white children: The experience of a British adoption project*. London: Routledge.

Redmond, P.J. (2018) *The adoption machine: The dark history of Ireland's mother and baby homes and the inside story of how Tuam 800 became a global scandal*. Newbridge: Merrion Press.

Rossini, G. (2014) *A history of adoption in England and Wales (1850–1961)*. Barnsley, South Yorkshire: Pen & Sword Books Ltd.

Rotabi, K. and Bromfield, N. (2017) *From intercountry adoption to global surrogacy*. London: Routledge.

Sariaslan, A., Kääriälä, A., Pitkänen, J., Remes, H., Aaltonen, M., Hiilamo, H., Martikainen, P. and Fazel, S. (2022) 'Long-term health and social outcomes in children and adolescents placed in out-of-home care', *JAMA Pediatrics*, *176*(1), e214324.

Schofield, G. (2003) *Part of the family: Pathways through foster care*. London: BAAF.

Schofield, G. and Beek, M. (2006) *Attachment handbook for foster care and adoption*. London: BAAF.

Schofield, G. and Ward, E. (2011) *Understanding and working with parents of children in long-term foster care*. London: Jessica Kingsley Publishers.

Sinclair, I., Baker, C., Wilson, K. and Gibbs, I. (2005) *Foster children: Where they go and how they get on*. London: Jessica Kingsley.

Sixsmith, M. (2013) *Philomena*. Stuttgart: Pan Macmillan.

Smith, C. and Logan, J. (2004) *After adoption. Direct contact and relationships*. London: Routledge.

Smolin, D. (2022) *The legal mandate for ending the modern era of intercountry adoption. Research Handbook on adoption*. Berkeley, CA: Bepress.

Swift, R. (2020) *Adopting a child in Scotland*. London: CoramBAAF.

Triseliotis, J.P. (1973) *In search of origins: The experiences of adopted people*. Abingdon: Routledge and Kegan Paul.

Vanderwill, L.A., Salazar, A.M., Jenkins, G., Larwelle, J., McMahon, A.K., Day, A. and Haggerty, K. (2021) 'Systematic literature review of foster and adoptive caregiver factors for increasing placement stability and permanency', *Journal of Public Child Welfare*, *15*(4), 487–527.

Ward, H., Munro, E. and Dearden, C. (2006) *Babies and young children in care: Life pathways, decision-making and practice*. London: Jessica Kingsley Publishers.

Winter, K., Connolly, P., Millen, S. and Sweet, D. (2022) 'The UNCRC and family support: A case study of the early intervention support service', *Child Care in Practice*, 1–15. DOI: 10.1080/13575279.2022.2088473

10

LEAVING CARE AND AFTERCARE

CONTENTS OF CHAPTER

- Introduction
- What do we mean by 'leaving care'?
- Young people leaving care in their teenage years
- What we can learn from research
- Pathways to success
- What helps in practice
- Summary and conclusion
- Guide to further reading

Introduction

This chapter looks at work with young people before and after they leave the care system. In considering this group, the central themes of this book are relevant:

- In relation to children's needs and 'best interests', we see how the needs of this group of young people must be broadly defined, and as far as possible self-defined.
- Children and young people's rights and a 'listening' approach are hugely important in this area of practice. Leaving care services cannot work effectively without respect for the autonomy of young people, and we will see that some of the most effective leaving care services are those that create opportunities for young people to work collectively to improve their situation.

DOI: 10.4324/9781003503194-10

Exercise 10.1 Annie prepares to leave care

Annie's placement with Mr and Mrs Farmer broke down after three years, without the planned adoption being completed. After a period in a children's home she was placed with a specialist adolescent foster carer, Liz Green. She is now 17 and recently finished school with two GCSEs (an E in English and a D in Art). She has expressed some interest in pursuing studies in childcare.

Liz Green is fond of Annie, but plans to give up fostering shortly and move to the West of Ireland to pursue her interests in painting and marine ecology. On two occasions recently, Annie has been brought home by the police after being found drunk in town with a group of older friends.

What are likely to be the key components of a leaving care plan for Annie?

What are the responsibilities of the local authority and others?

What would be the result of a SWOT analysis (strengths, weaknesses, opportunities, threats) of Annie's situation?

- Working with difference and oppression is a strong theme. We focus in this chapter on the needs of three particular groups of care leavers:
  - Black and ethnic minority care leavers
  - Young disabled care leavers
  - Refugees and asylum seekers leaving care
- In relation to issues of parenting and the state, we will need again to think about what 'corporate parenting' means, and also about what standards of care are being applied.

As with all our chapters, this one incorporates recent research, reflecting changes to the extent developing policy and practice in this area and in which the views of young people themselves, mediated through research, have had a major impact on how policy and practice have developed.

What do we mean by 'leaving care'?

'Leaving care' involves a transition and can refer to the transition from 'care' to returning home to the birth family; or into an adoptive placement; or it can mean moving on to some kind of 'independent' or semi-independent living. The transition almost always means both a change in living accommodation and a change in legal status, but not necessarily at the same time. Leaving care is usually a gradual process, but it can on occasion be a sudden event.

Policy and practice regarding children and young people leaving care, in particular those transitioning to semi-independence and/or independent living, has advanced significantly over the last 20 years nationally and internationally (OECD, 2022; Brady et al., 2019). Early research in the UK (Stein and Ellis, 1983; Stein and Carey, 1986) drew attention to the many difficulties faced by young people who were pushed out of the care system, often at a surprisingly young age, without the education, life skills or experience necessary for them to succeed. Since then more recent research studies have drawn further attention to the poor life chances of this group of young people, and to their relative neglect by those responsible for promoting their welfare (Mendes and Snow, 2016; Mann-Feder and Goyette, 2019; OECD, 2022). This has led to many projects aimed at improving services for care leavers, and a series of changes in legislation aimed at giving them stronger entitlement to support and assistance.

Most discussion of leaving care is centred, quite rightly, on the group of young people in their teenage years transitioning into semi-independent and/or independent living. In this chapter, we will look at what is involved in helping them, and also at some of the changes in social provision for young people in general that may have left this group in a more exposed position. Although the specific legal duties may only apply to young people after the age of 16, *all* children leaving the care system (regardless of age, background and circumstances) have a right to do so in a way that improves their chances of a healthy and happy life. This means ensuring that the arrangements for their care, by parents or whoever has parental responsibility, are satisfactory. It also means making appropriate arrangements for the continuation of relationships or interests which the child may have acquired while in care. Another important consideration is that the UN Guidelines for the Alternative Care of Children, which are intended to enhance the implementation of the UNCRC, also acknowledge the importance of transitional and after-care support. This chapter therefore also explores progress towards realising the rights of youth leaving residential, foster care. The picture is that all jurisdictions have some way to go to meet the standards enshrined in the Guidelines and that some young adults leaving care with complex needs are not sufficiently empowered and enabled to exercise their rights.

Young people leaving care in their teenage years

Historically, the main focus of leaving care policy and practice was on young people aged 16 and up to 21. More recently, this has been extended to age 25 in the UK. Many other European countries also have policies and practices that extend support to care leavers until at least their 25th birthday (OECD, 2022). One of the reasons for the introduction of extended support, as we will see later in the chapter, is the recognition that young people leaving care require ongoing support into their adulthood, and that in contemporary society many young adults remain dependent on their families for longer than was the case historically. It is by no means unusual for adults in their 20s to continue living with their parents and depend on them for housing and some financial support as they continue in education and training. For example, recent statistical analyses by the ONS (published on their website in 2023) reveals a 13.6% increase in the number of families in England and Wales with adult children living at home between the census of 2011 and the latest census of 2021.

In reflecting on what it is like to transition from care, we know that adolescence is a time of transitions in general. Adolescence is marked by significant changes in terms of physical, emotional and psychological development, identity formation, education, employment, access to activities such as car driving and voting, for example (Brady and Gilligan, 2020). Most young people contending with these multiple transitions have the continued support of their parents and relatives – not only financial support, but practical, social and emotional support – and have enough time and space for at least some of those transitions to be planned and take place gradually.

While for some care leavers, they have positive experiences transitioning into adulthood (Chase, 2013; Brady and Gilligan, 2020), it is also the case that for young people leaving the care system, their experience is often very different. At the age of 17–18 years, whether ready or not, they are expected to make the transition to semi-independent or independent living

Box 10.1 Focal theory of adolescence

Over 20 years ago, one of us (Coleman, 1974, 1978) put forward a model of adolescent development which has come to be known as the focal model. In essence, this argued that an issue or difficulty arising from a particular relationship pattern comes into focus at a particular stage and, in time, comes to be replaced with another focal issue.

The model is similar to a stage theory, in that it proposes a progression from one focal concern to another, but it does emphasise that no fixed sequence is envisaged. An important implication is that those young people who have to deal with more than one issue at a time might be considered to be more at risk than those for whom issues are well spaced out. A young person who has to cope with family breakdown, for example, as well as having to adjust to a change of school and to a new peer group, may be particularly vulnerable.

(Coleman and Roker 1998, p. 593)

(Stein, 2012; Mendes and Snow, 2016). There are a number of reasons why this is particularly challenging. The first is that they have to navigate multiple transitions over a compressed time period, rather than a graduated approach (Stein, 1997, 2012), and are expected to adapt to the demands of adulthood at a younger age and at a faster pace. As Coleman's (1974) 'focal point' research demonstrated, adolescents who are able to deal with transitions in succession do better than those who face them all at once (see Box 10.1), and experience less of the stress, and distress, sometimes associated with this transition period. Yet care leavers, whose backgrounds may be quite unsettled and whose educational accomplishments are generally poor, are expected to manage multiple transitions over a short period of time.

Second, a proportion of young people leaving care in their teenage years have particular needs and vulnerabilities because of their backgrounds and the circumstances that brought them into care in the first place. This may mean that they are exceptionally susceptible to risks such as homelessness and unemployment, drug and alcohol abuse, mental illness and sexual abuse and exploitation. Third, care leavers are particularly susceptible to challenging economic conditions – escalating housing, energy, and food costs, declining real pay – as well as extended periods in further education and training, mean that many young people have to delay becoming fully independent. These issues are further exacerbated for care leavers who are disabled and from minority ethnic backgrounds (Graham, 2007; Stein and Munro, 2008; Stein, 2012; Mendes and Snow, 2016; Mupaku et al., 2021).

All these factors have important implications with regard to providing services that are helpful, sensitive and accessible to young people. First, if we want to help young people to move on successfully from care, we have to consider three distinct areas of service provision: services that are provided for care leavers directly; services that are provided for all young people in the age group; and services that are provided for young people in care *before* they leave. Second, service providers must recognise that young people will have their own views about what services they need. Reflecting a rights-based approach, services must respond to young people's needs as they define them, and they must be provided in ways that promote young people's self-esteem, self-confidence and agency. As we know, services that are experienced as stigmatised or demeaning will do the opposite – and they will be rejected.

It is obvious from listening to the experiences and views of care leavers that there have been (and remain) significant challenges transitioning into independent adulthood (Duncalf, 2010; Kelly et al., 2016; Mupaku et al., 2021). The speed at which the transition is expected to happen, the life skills and social supports it is assumed are in place and the lack of attention given to the profound impact of stigma are just some of the issues.

Legal frameworks, policies and guidance

In response to the growing evidence regarding the concerns, there have been significant legal, policy and practice developments all designed to secure better life chances for this group of young people. Importantly, with regard to legal requirements, the UN Guidelines for the Alternative Care of Children (UN, 2010, p. 6) note in paragraph 28 that the 'Principles in the present Guidelines are also applicable, as appropriate to young persons already in alternative care and who need continuing care or support for a transitional period after reaching the age of majority under applicable law'. Furthermore, the duties of responsibilities of Local Authorities or Health and Social Care Trusts are outlined in legislation, regulations, guidance and standards. A recent publication that is very helpful (Munro et al., 2024) undertakes a comparative analysis of leaving care policy and practice across the four nations of the UK.

In England and Wales, the key legislation is the Children (Leaving Care) Act 2000. The Act defines which young people are entitled to services: 'eligible children' are young people aged 16 and 17 who have been looked after for a prescribed period; 'relevant children' are eligible children who leave care; 'former relevant children' are young people over the age of 18 who were previously eligible or relevant children. The new law also defines who should provide those services; the 'responsible local authority' is whichever local authority last looked after an eligible or relevant young person. The responsible local authority is under a duty:

- to assess and meet the care and support needs of eligible and relevant children and young people; and
- to assist former relevant children, in particular in respect of their employment, education and training.

The responsible local authority is also under a duty to keep in touch with all its care leavers who qualify for these new support arrangements. All eligible, relevant and former relevant children and young people must have a *pathway plan*. This replaces the previous care plan. It encompasses education, training, career plans and any support that may be needed. It is envisaged that pathway plans will be reviewed every six months, or more frequently as needed. All eligible, relevant and former relevant children and young people must also have a *personal adviser* who helps to draw up the pathway plan and to make sure that it develops with the young person's changing needs and is implemented. The personal adviser is also responsible for keeping in touch with the young person after leaving care and for ensuring that they receive the advice and support to which they are entitled.

The Children (Leaving Care) Act 2000 gives the responsible local authority other duties in relation to former relevant children: to assist care leavers in higher education; to assist with costs associated with employment, and with costs of education and training up to the end of an agreed programme, and to give the young person assistance in kind, or exceptionally in cash 'to the extent that his welfare requires it'. Local authorities have the power to give similar assistance to other care leavers who do not qualify as former relevant children. 'Eligible' and 'relevant' children are not eligible for income support, housing benefit or income-based job-seekers allowance. Instead of this, local authorities are under a statutory duty to support them. There are exceptions for cases such as lone parents, and for disabled children, who could claim benefits if they were living with their parents.

In England, the legislation has been updated by the Children and Young Persons Act 2008 which requires local authorities to provide financial assistance to young people in education (including a £2,000 bursary if entering higher education). It has been further updated by the Children and Families Act 2014 which introduced the 'Staying Put' policy. In Wales, this scheme is known as 'When I am Ready' (Welsh Government, 2016). More recently in England, legislation has been further updated by the Children and Social Work Act 2017, which introduced the corporate parenting principles and the requirement on local authorities to provide personal advisors to care leavers until they reach the age of 25.

In Wales, the care leavers legislation was incorporated into the Social Services and Well-being (Wales) Act 2014 and the Care Leavers (Wales) Regulations 2015. Much of the wording is the same as England. However, there are differences in rights and services which include exemption from paying council tax for all care leavers in Wales. There is also a St David's Fund that is meant to act like a 'bank of mum and dad' so that personal assistants and social workers can provide discretionary help with items like driving lessons, training courses, smart clothes for interviews, rent deposits, emergencies and so on. Wales also introduced the Basic Income Pilot for care leavers. This provides for care leavers turning 18 years between July 2022 and June 2023, the opportunity to receive £1,600 per month (before tax) for a period of two years with the aim of providing the support they need as they transition out of care. Evaluations of the scheme are ongoing.

Changes to the upper age limit at which care leavers can receive support have also been implemented in Scotland and Northern Ireland and acknowledges some of the societal expectations regarding an extended supported young adulthood that we saw earlier in the chapter. In a further development in England, new regulations regarding the provision of supported accommodation, known as The Supported Accommodation (England) Regulations (2023), are designed to address the significant concerns regarding the quality and nature of accommodation offered to care leavers. These regulations also apply to 16–17-year-olds placed in supported accommodation. In 2022, there was an outcry about the fact that there were no explicit *care* standards or duties, even though these are still young people in care.

In Scotland, new regulations made under the Regulation of Care (Scotland) Act 2001 and the Children (Scotland) Act 1995 came into force in 2004. The Support and Assistance of Young People Leaving Care (Scotland) Regulations 2004 were designed to establish a very similar system to that set up in England and Wales, although the terminology is different – 'currently looked after person', 'compulsory supported person' and 'discretionary supported person' rather than 'eligible children', 'relevant children' and 'former relevant children'. However, the definition of 'responsible authority' is the same, as is the requirement for a pathway plan.

More recently in Scotland, the Children and Young People (Scotland) Act 2014 outlines the Scottish legal framework and is supported by the Support and Assistance of Young People Leaving Care (Scotland) Regulations 2015 (SSI 2015/62) which extended the categories of aftercare support provided for by the 2014 Act. Under the Children and Young People (Scotland) Act 2014, Scotland's 'Staying Put' policy (which is called 'Continuing Care') was introduced. Furthermore, under this Act, when support under 'Continuing Care' for young people leaving care ends, they are entitled to aftercare which could extend up until the age of 26 years old.

In Northern Ireland, the Children (Leaving Care) Act (Northern Ireland) 2002 applies and is supported by the Children (Leaving Care) Regulations (Northern Ireland) 2005. It mirrors the provisions of England and Wales. Further guidance is contained in the Children Order (NI) 1995 Guidance and Regulations, Vol Eight, Leaving and After Care. In Northern Ireland, a scheme called 'Going the Extra Mile' is similar to 'Staying Put' (Foley et al., 2021, p. 27). Lastly, the standards for Leaving Care Services in Northern Ireland (2012) outline the minimum standards for leaving and aftercare services.

Overall, the legislation in all four jurisdictions of the UK in relation to young people leaving care includes the following duties to young people leaving care:

- Access to a social worker or personal adviser
- Assessment of need
- Meetings to plan their transition
- A pathway plan which should address all the core areas of young people's lives – personal support, accommodation, education and training, employment, family and social relationships, life skills
- Access to support including accommodation, financial assistance, access to financial help if in training and/or higher education, access to ongoing advice and support

To ensure that there is accessible information made available to care leavers about their rights, advocacy and support organisations have produced information and guidance. These include Coram Voice, the Care Leavers Association, the Children's Commissioner for England, Voice of Young People in Care (VOYPIC), Become, Who Cares (Scotland) and Voices From Care Cymru.

What can we learn from research

Stein and Ward (2021) reviewed leaving care research in terms of its key messages and relevance for practitioners. They remind us that a continuing focus on care leavers is required because, despite the legal and policy developments outlined above, their needs frequently remain unaddressed, their access to services is often limited and their long-term outcomes can be compromised. Munro (2019) reiterates this with regard to the fact that young people leaving care remain disempowered and this affects their access to their basic rights as outlined in the UN Guidelines on Alternative Care. These issues can be even further challenging for minoritised groups including those who identify as black and Asian, LGBTQIA+, disabled and asylum seeking/refugee children and young people (Thoburn et al., 2005; Mendes and Snow, 2016; McCormick, 2018). Later in the chapter we will consider these issues further.

Needs

As indicated above, the needs of young care leavers vary widely between individuals and groups. However, at a more general level, recent research studies have highlighted commonly shared needs that arise for many young people leaving care (Mendes and Snow, 2016; OECD, 2022). These include exposure to harm, abuse and neglect which can lead to unresolved trauma. Trauma can be compounded by multiple, often unplanned, placement moves leading to fragmented care histories and identities. Disruption and instability are reflected in education where rates of absence, exclusion and school moves are higher for care leavers compared with the child population whole.

Educational outcomes are clearly affected; in terms of qualifications, care leavers generally fall far behind their peers (McNamara et al., 2019). Especially when combined with factors such as disability and poor mental health, these difficulties continue into adulthood leading to poor employment prospects and low income, with a further impact on ability to access high quality accommodation and a lack of choice (OECD, 2022). Associated issues are homelessness, physical and mental health problems, lack of social activities, unhappiness, isolation, feelings of stigmatisation and labelling (see Box 10.2).

Because young people leaving care have often started with powerful disadvantages such as poverty, family disruption or abuse, they are likely to need more support than others in managing the transition to adult life. If they

Box 10.2 David's story

Despite facing a long prison sentence and an uncertain future, David (19) is surprisingly relaxed and willing to talk openly about his life in care. Yet the care path that led him to prison is one filled with abuse, rejection and violence. David's connection with the care system was cemented almost from birth. At the age of one month, he came to the local authority's attention when his father abused him. Although the subject of a care order, he was still returned to his parents, a white English mother and AfricanCaribbean father.

By the age of six months he had been taken into care following serious neglect by his mother. He and his sister were then adopted by a white couple living in an allwhite suburb where they had no contact with black people. David was subsequently physically abused by his adoptive parents which led to his return to the care system. While in a residential home, he was abused by a staff member. No support was forthcoming. Instead he was moved from one residential placement to another.

With each move, David became more rootless, disturbed and aggressive. Over time he became virtually unmanageable. His care records show clear signs of psychological trauma stemming from his early abusive experiences. Attempts to manage his challenging behaviour through placements in residential children's homes with education and sociotherapeutic units failed. Labelled as 'maladjusted', he was expelled from junior school. From this point on, he never gained a significant foothold in education.

David's identity was only addressed when he was 14 years old. That was when he requested to be sent to a blackrun residential project for young black people. Somehow, he managed to develop a significant relationship with a black couple who became his informal support and he responded to them positively.

But contact with his birth family was virtually non-existent. He was, in his view, well and truly institutionalised. When he left care, he was unable to cope. The only real family he had was his sister who had also been abused by the adoptive parents. She became an underage mother and had regular contact with the police. At the time of interview, David had limited contact with her.

No formal attempt was made to appropriately prepare David for leaving care. But he had had the benefit of living, albeit briefly, in a unit preparing young people for leaving care. Afterwards, he went to live with a family as a lodger, an arrangement that soon broke down. His next home was a selfcontained flat with a resident landlord, but he was unable to cope with independent living.

His survival in the community was short lived as he was arrested and detained in custody and is now serving a longterm prison sentence. He says that the only way he can live is in an institution. That is all he knows.

(from Ince, 1998, p. 38)

actually get less support, before leaving care and after, then it is not surprising that things go wrong. At the same time, it is important to remember that life is not inevitably bleak for care leavers. Many do well, and some do very well, whether because of their personal resilience or because they are given better support and opportunity (Stein, 2012).

Services

Stein (2006) suggests that there are three types of care leavers – those who 'moved on', 'survivors' and 'victims'. Those who 'moved on' usually left care later, with a transition that was well planned and well supported. Those described as 'survivors' experienced the transition as challenging (in terms of employment, accommodation and stable relationships) but seemed to be managing with access to practical and financial support. The third group of 'victims' were had experienced disruption throughout childhood which impacted on their educational, social, emotional and psychological wellbeing and also on their transition to independence, in particular employment and housing. In earlier work Stein (1997) reviewed the evidence in terms of preparation for moving on, accommodation, personal and financial support, and education, employment and training.

Despite the advances in policy since 2000, Stein's insights are still relevant. Häggman-Laitila et al. (2018) reviewed 30 studies of care leavers' experiences of transitioning into independence, using similar categories. With regard to *being prepared*, they found that most care leavers felt prepared for independent living in terms of attitude and outlook reporting feelings of hopefulness, resilience and inner confidence. However, whilst many had identifiable goals and aspirations, they were not always convinced they would achieve them. It appeared that individualised support that addressed those aspirations and pathways to success was most effective, and that a hindrance was the young person not being involved in shaping their transition process. In relation to access to services and support more generally, the systematic review identified money management, access to education, physical health services and supportive relationships as the top priorities for care leavers. As in many other studies, the importance of positive, affirming and enduring relationships came through strongly. However, the authors also note the importance of stable housing and employment, and that services and supports are often fragmented. The review pointed to the need for:

- *Individualised* support that involves the individual care leaver from the start and that builds on individual personal attributes to help care leavers identify their strengths and abilities;
- *Continuous* support that helps care leavers identify their goals, develop pathway plans for achieving their goals and that supports care leavers to review and reflect on their progress;

- *Holistic, integrated and coordinated* support so that needs (education, employment, accommodation and networks) can be addressed in a interprofessional way throughout all stages of the transition process and post transitions;
- *More understanding of the individual pathways* of care leavers that take account of intersectional issues such as age, gender, ethnicity, religion, language and sexuality;
- *More understanding of care leavers' experiences of individual services* such as supported accommodation, ongoing education and training.

As regards education, research into the views and experiences of care leavers (Gilligan, 2019; Gilligan and Brady, 2022; Harrison et al., 2023) suggests that early disengagement and disruption from education and the impact of low expectations can be reversed, particularly if young people have positive, supportive and enduring relationships with care providers, social workers and teachers. Targeted early intervention literacy and numeracy support may also show promise in terms of lifting attainment and achievement both in the short and the long term (Connolly et al., 2023).

Most local authorities and Trusts have leaving care teams. These teams can make a major contribution to improving services for young people, by promoting awareness of their needs, by acting as advocates, and by providing services directly, complementing the support provided by foster parents or residential workers – the 'prime carers'. The observations of Stein regarding this and other forms of personal support remain as true today as they did over 25 years ago – support should be *planned and negotiated* with young people, *proactive* rather than just responding to crises, *flexible* because of the variety of needs, and should address practical, financial and emotional needs.

Outcomes

As illustrated in the points below, there is a growing body of research, analysing data from the same groups of care leavers over some years, that illustrates that outcomes for care leavers remain poor. They are less likely than other young people to achieve well or continue in education (Mendes and Snow, 2016; Gilligan and Brady, 2022), to acquire higher-paying jobs (Zeira et al., 2023; Harrison et al., 2023) or to be living in stable, good-quality accommodation. And yet, as we noted earlier, some care leavers do well; and better understanding and appreciation of the factors contributing to success can help us to improve policy and practice in this area. One such factor is the value that young people obtain from enduring, supportive, positive relationships with people – whether family or friends, neighbours, volunteers, teachers, or indeed social workers – who believe in them and give them unconditional positive regard as illustrated in a systematic review of studies concerning care leavers' views and perspectives (Atkinson and Hyde, 2019).

Specific groups of care leavers

Much of the research regarding care leavers considers them as a whole group. We know rather less about the needs and experiences of specific groups, in particular minoritised groups such as black, Asian and mixed heritage care leavers; refugee and asylum-seeking care leavers; LGBTQIA+ care leavers; and disabled care leavers;. In the following sections, we focus on each of these groups in turn. Of course, some young people are members of more than one sub-group, and we also acknowledge the importance of 'intersectionality'.

Black, Asian and mixed heritage care leavers

We know that Black, mixed heritage and some Asian children are overrepresented in both children in need and children in care statistics. 'Black' here is defined as including Black African, Black Caribbean and any other 'Black' background; but there are important differences between these groups, as noted by Bywaters et al. (2020). For example, controlling for socio economic background, there are lower rates of being looked after for Black African children than for Black Caribbean children. In another example, within the category 'Asian', children identifying as Indian are less likely to have children's services involvement than children from Pakistani and Bangladeshi backgrounds – or than White British children).

In a report for 'What Works for Children's Social Care', Schoenwald et al. (2022) noted the paucity of research regarding outcomes for black children in care. Given this lack of research, what can we say about the pathways and experiences of young black care leavers? One exception is the work of Barn and Sidhu (2005). In a survey of 261 male and female, 16–21-year-old young people which included a significant number from minority ethnic groups (44%), through focus groups and interviews conducted in six local authorities in England, they note that Caribbean and mixed parentage young people in care achieved greater stability than white young people in care, if placed in matched placements, and that they were more likely to secure educational qualifications and go to college compared with their white peers – hence 'African and Asian groups emerged as two groups who experienced least instability in care and in education' (Barn and Sidhu, 2005, p. 80). This group of care leavers also reported that when in care, they were not always given appropriate cultural and/or racial support. On preparation for leaving care, no real differences between groups of young people in care were found. However, given the wider 'overt and covert racism' experienced by this group of care leavers, the need for an approach tailored to the specific racial, ethnic and cultural needs of Black, Asian and mixed parentage young people was recommended with attention to issues of race, ethnicity and self-conceptualisation.

Barn and Sidhu also note, by way of context to their own study, that

> nationally, people from many minority ethnic groups suffer very significant disadvantage in terms of both the educational qualifications they attain (Gillborn and Mirza, 2000) and higher rates of unemployment (see Barn, 2001). Moreover, when in employment, minority ethnic groups tend to get poorer jobs with lower pay (Ethnic Minority Employment Task Force, 2004).
>
> *(2005, p. 76)*

Ince's study (2004) of young black care leavers points to the strong link between the 'care careers' of black children and young people and their ability to cope with the experience of moving on from the system (Ince, 2004). Her research was based on talking to young people, and she analyses some of their individual 'career trajectories'. Ince claimed that for all the young people in her study prolonged exposure to a 'white Eurocentric model of care' adversely affected their self-perception and ability to cope after leaving care, while restricted contact with black family, friends and wider community made it harder for them to reintegrate with that community. In addition, some of the young people had experienced considerable movement and disruption, which led to a sense of rootlessness and instability that continued after leaving care – in some cases combined with feelings of rejection and powerlessness. Those young people who had experienced a stable foster placement, or who had remained in their family until their teenage years, were more optimistic about the future. Ince concludes by suggesting that preparation for young black people leaving care should attend not just to life skills, but also to the emotional and psychological impact of individual and institutional racism, reflecting rights and social justice. This, she argues, means building bridges to the black community and proactively recruiting black carers, volunteers, and 'social aunts and uncles'. Other supports should include:

- providing placements that reflect the needs of black children;
- representation of black people in agency decision making;
- attention to the educational needs of black children;
- advocates and independent visitors for young black people;
- enabling young people to test out living independently;
- work on identity and helping young people explore their racial origins;
- addressing racial harassment and abuse in care and education;
- not placing black children in mainly white areas.

Refugee and asylum-seeking care leavers

For asylum seeking, refugee and/or unaccompanied children and young people who are cared for by local authorities/health and social care trusts, they have particular physical, educational and linguistic needs as well as emotional, psychological and identity needs which require significant specialist support. There is limited research regarding refugee and asylum-seeking care leavers, but see Chase and Allsopp (2020), Devenney (2020). Bolaji (2022) notes:

> These young people are faced with additional uncertainties, risks and opportunities unlike those with a recognised status or their contemporaries living at home. Their pre-migratory, migratory and in-country trauma adds another layer to the challenges faced by those with no immigration issues. Also, they are transitioning into adulthood within a context of 'unrelenting and restrictive immigration policies, increasing interest in immigration and asylum' [reference in original].... Their journey to adulthood is more accelerated and compressed than their peers with no immigration issues.
>
> *(Bolaji, 2022, p. 34)*

In Bolaji's own research drawing on the accounts of refugee and asylum-seeking care leavers from Africa, she found that 'adapting to new systems and cultures could intensify their trauma', and that in addition 'refugee and asylum-seeking young people are likely to suffer from loneliness and social isolation in their host country' (2022, p. 110). She calls on professionals 'to pay more attention to the impact of pre-migratory, migratory and post-migratory experiences on these young people's transition into adulthood' (p. 112). Lastly, she notes that silence should not be mistaken for coping, and (like Kohli, 2011) that social workers need to understand what lies behind the silence. In another study by Ramsay (2020), it is noted that the leaving care pathways for this group of young people can be fraught with challenges as their legal status affects their access to benefits and services provided by social services, housing, education, and the health sector for example (Figure 10.1).

LGBTQIA+ care leavers

The acronym stands for 'Lesbian, gay, bisexual, transgender, queer (or questioning), intersex and asexual/aromantic/agender'. The + stands for all other identities not covered by the acronym. The acronym therefore refers to anyone who describes their sexuality and their gender identity in a variety of ways. Someone is described as *transgender* when their gender identity does

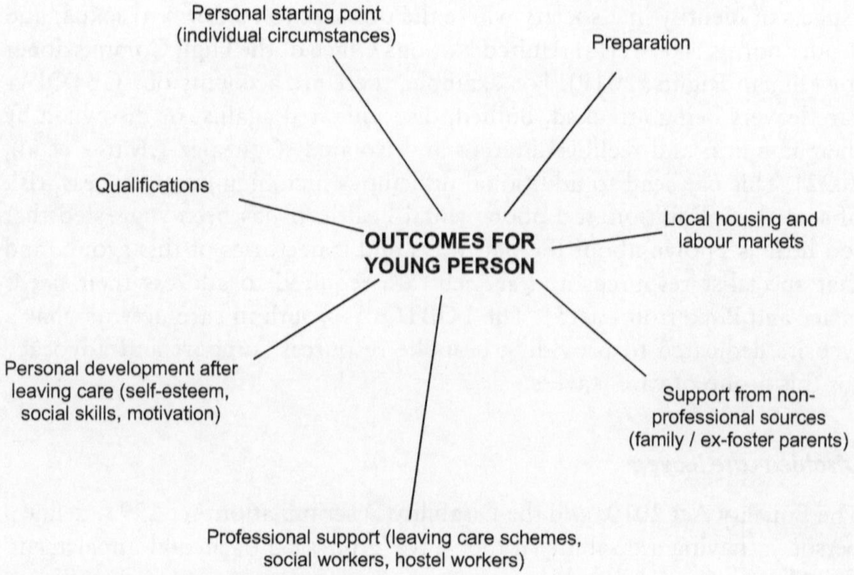

FIGURE 10.1 Factors influencing outcomes for care leavers.

Source: Biehal et al. (1995, p. 251).

not correspond with their biological sex at birth. The term *non-binary* is used when a child or young person does not identify as either 'boy' or 'girl'. A child or young person might, for example, identify as LGBTQIA+ because they are both gay (sexuality) and non-binary (gender identity).

Kaasbøll et al. (2022) undertook a scoping review as to what is known about the LGBTQIA+ perspective in child welfare services. Whilst this does not include children and young people leaving care, it does point to the challenges of understanding prevalence rates from the figures that exist (because of fear of reporting), the overrepresentation of LGBTQIA+ children in out of home care and the challenges they face at school, in the community and in accessing services. In a further scoping review by González Álvarez et al. (2022) which considered research regarding resilience in LGBTQIA+ young people in care, they found that the area was under researched and that studies focused primarily on adversities experienced. Further research is suggested as this will inform understanding as to the challenges faced and how these are overcome, adjusted to and/or coped with because, as González Álvarez et al. (2022, p. 2) point out, 'LGBTQIA+ persons are resilient, they can sustain, regain, and improve their physical and mental wellbeing when faced with adversities'.

It is well known that LGBTQIA+ care leavers too face a number of challenges, not least dealing with the prejudices, assumptions, biases, hostility and lack of understanding of others and having to navigate these aspects of identity in a society where the pressure to conform to sexual and gender norms is powerful (United Nations Office of the High Commissioner for Human Rights, 2019). For example, there are accounts of LGBTQIA+ care leavers being attacked, bullied, discriminated against or disowned by their families, and feeling different and isolated (González Álvarez et al., 2022). This can lead to additional difficulties including homelessness, risk of sexual exploitation and poor mental health. It has been suggested that too little is known about the pathways and trajectories of this group, and that specialist resources and services are required to address their needs (Carr and Pinkerton, 2015). The LGBTQIA+ youth in care network has a website dedicated to providing bespoke resources, support and advocacy for this group of care leavers.

Disabled care leavers

The Equality Act 2010, and the Disability Discrimination Act 1995, define a person as having a disability if they have 'a physical or mental impairment' that 'has a substantial and long-term adverse effect on the person's ability to carry out normal day-to-day activities'. (It therefore includes mental health conditions as well as other types of disability including intellectual disability, autism, physical and sensory impairments.)

Children and young people with disabilities are overrepresented in the care system, and face particular challenges when leaving care. These include difficulties getting formal recognition of their disability, which can be essential for access to some services (Kelly et al., 2016, 2022). Access to support can be patchy, in part because legislation is compartmentalised meaning an absence of one legal framework that outlines all roles, responsibilities and duties but rather a patchwork of legal provision. Access to services and support is further hindered because, unlike other groups of children leaving care who are referred to a children's leaving care service, children with disabilities when they reach age 18 are referred to adult services teams. This makes coordination with the pathway adviser more challenging. The recent English Government commissioned review of children's social care (MacAlister, 2022) noted that some local authorities have established bespoke children's disability teams offering support to children and young people up to 25 years old. The recommendation was for more of these.

It should be obvious that young people leaving care who are disabled are likely to need more help and support than others. However, there is some evidence that they actually receive less (Kelly et al., 2022). Harris (2008) point to anomalies in the legal provision for disabled care leavers – particularly in relation to those in regular respite care, who are mainly excluded from the leaving care provisions even though in some cases they may spend more time in respite placements than at home. Extra work may be needed with these young people to ensure that they are fully involved in planning, that they have real choices and options in relation to their accommodation and that their educational needs are met (and they are not put on courses simply as a way to occupy them). Young people with additional needs may need opportunities to acquire skills and confidence gradually. This work should not all be left to carers: specialist input may be needed and formal assessment of skills and abilities should take place well before young people leave care. Long-term advance planning is crucial for success in independent living.

Pathways to success?

So what factors really help to make for successful transition to adulthood? Just as young people leaving care have many different needs, so there are many different pathways to success after leaving care. For some, it is to *return home*, at least in the short term. We know that most young people, even those who have become completely separated from their families while in care, do at some stage return home (Neil et al., 2020). This may happen immediately on leaving care or later, and it may be for a brief or an extended period; but in whatever way, the overwhelming majority re-establish some form of contact with their families. There are a number of things that social workers can do to help make this return home successful, of which almost certainly the most important is to put real effort into helping children and young people to maintain links with their immediate and extended families during their time in care.

For others, the key is a continuing relationship with *foster parents*. The 'Staying Put' scheme (referred to earlier) that operates in England (and is available under differing names in the rest of the UK) is a good example of a successful policy initiative designed to support on-going relationships between care leavers and foster carers (Dixon et al., 2020). The evaluation by Dixon et al. (2020) indicates that the more that foster parents can offer continuing support to young people in the same way that most ordinary families do, the better the chances of those young people succeeding in their lives after care.

Most of us when we leave our parental home know that if we're stuck we can go back. We also know that we can always turn up for a meal, a chat, perhaps even a loan. Simply knowing that this support is available can sometimes make the difference between feeling safe and confident and feeling isolated and bewildered. If foster parents are to take on a similar role, they need to know that this is recognised by the agency – and they may also need help and support in dealing with the implications for taxes and benefits (the 'Staying Put Good Practice Guide' published by Fostering Network and NCB, undated, for example provides guidance on these issues).

The same applies in a different way to continuing relationships with *residential care* homes. If a children's home is where a young person has spent their teenage years, that is often where they will naturally look for support and guidance as a young adult. They need a clear message that this is OK, and not a feeling that they are being pushed out. As noted earlier, a positive example of policies designed to support young people leaving residential care (and the practice of corporate parenting) is the 'Staying Close' scheme. This mirrors the 'Staying Put' scheme for young people leaving foster care. The 'Staying Close' scheme was introduced in England (Narey, 2016, para 59) and its aim is to support young people previously in residential care 'to live independently, in a location close to their children's home with ongoing support from that home. Dixon et al. (2020) in their evaluation highlighted some positive impacts for young care leavers regarding independent living skills, increased stability regarding accommodation, increased engagement in social activities which all increased overall levels of happiness.

As we have already seen, *education* can be a key element in a pathway to success. Research indicates that success in education is connected with a range of other factors including personality characteristics and background experiences, placement stability, carers who appreciate the value of education, access to individual tutoring, hobbies and school-based activities, teachers who have high aspirations for children in care, early identification of talents and strengths (Chase et al., 2006; Gorham, 2009; Brady and Gilligan, 2019). Gilligan and Brady (2022) explore the reengagement of care leavers in education after a period of disengagement and using the concept of 'linked lives' (which stems from the lifecourse perspective and the interdependence of events, experiences, memories in people's individual lives over time) note that there is the potential for the development of learner identities over time. Gilligan and Brady (2022, p. 12) highlight 'the importance of better understanding what prompts and sustains educational re-engagement in adult life. Without the critical turning point of re-engagement, the promise of education cannot be realised for adult care leavers whose educational progress has been delayed or disrupted'.

What helps in practice?

What happens before a young person leaves care is critically important. The law imposes duties on Local Authorities and Health and Social Care Trusts based on a model of the 'corporate parent'. With this in mind, it is not enough just to deal with immediate problems or needs – being a 'corporate parent' means taking a parent's responsibility for planning ahead and for giving a child the best start in life. Calling this phase 'pre-aftercare' may help to remind us that what happens after a child or young person leaves care is not simply an afterthought, but an essential part of the whole story.

What types of services are offered is also of critical importance. It was suggested earlier that we think in terms of three distinct areas of service provision: services that are provided for care leavers directly; services that are provided for all young people in the age group; and services that are provided for young people in care before they leave. The provision of universal services and services for young people before they leave care sometimes tend to be overlooked in concentrating on projects once young people have left care. Universal services are important because care leavers do not necessarily want services that are set apart from those provided for other young people, and because many of their needs are also the needs of other people in their age group. The provision of services before young people leave care is also very important – indeed, in some ways the key to good leaving care provision is in how young people are looked after in the care system. Despite developments, there remain concerns about some of the services offered to support care leavers' transition into adulthood (Gonzalez et al., 2012; Hiles et al., 2013; Häggman-Laitila et al., 2020; Refaeli, 2020).

With regard to *accommodation*, for example, although there is a variety of accommodation, including local authority and housing association tenancies, private sector accommodation, voluntary sector schemes, and supported lodgings, some has been described as inadequate and, as noted earlier, concerns have been such that new regulations have come into force. There also remain concerns that although social services authorities now have the primary responsibility for financial support of care leavers, young people may still need advice and support in claiming additional benefits to which they may be entitled. Many of them will also need help and advice with budgeting. A concern regarding young care leavers and homelessness has been noted (Foley et al., 2021) despite the duty placed on local authorities in Wales, Scotland and England to prevent this (Foley et al., 2021). In Northern Ireland, while there is no such duty, it remains a priority to ensure that care leavers have suitable accommodation (Foley et al., 2021).

With regard to *education and employment*, if care leavers have had a successful experience of education and want to continue learning and gaining qualifications, they will still need information about what might be available, and support and encouragement to take advantage of it. If their experience has been poor, then it is much more difficult for them to see what they might gain from further education. There are projects and services that can help with this, and it is important for staff working with care leavers to be aware of these (Brady and Gilligan, 2019; Häggman-Laitila et al., 2020). Equally important is to have someone who the young person can see is really taking an interest in their progress and achievements, preferably someone who can model a successful use of educational opportunities (Jackson et al., 2005; Harvey, 2017). Careers advice and support is equally important, as is help with the practicalities of getting and keeping work – help preparing for interviews, support with costs of transport, smart clothes and so on. Local authorities are able to provide help through employability and mentoring schemes. As corporate parents, they have a responsibility to assist young people in care in producing effective CVs and preparing for interviews, and to provide employment experiences for them (Furey and Harris-Evans, 2021).

Young care leavers access to education and employment is inextricably linked to their *physical, emotional, psychological health and wellbeing*. There is a wide range of research that indicates the significant issues faced by care leavers and the difficulties they face gaining access to services (Jarczok et al., 2021; Häggman-Laitila et al., 2020; Kelly et al., 2022). Indeed, research indicates that not only are care leavers more likely to have mental health issues compared with their non-care experienced peers, but these mental health issues are likely to worsen on leaving care (Havlicek et al., 2013; Stein and Dumaret, 2011). Sulimani-Aidan (2022) explore psychological distress experienced by care leavers and risk and protective factors. They conclude that, reflecting resilience theory, factors such as successful engagement in education, good quality care environments and positive relationships can mitigate against some of the negative impacts of pre-care, in-care and after-care experiences which have the potential to worsen mental health difficulties. Other studies highlight the link between care leavers' mental health difficulties and their engagement in high-risk behaviour such as drug taking and alcohol abuse (Petäjä et al., 2023) and the over-representation of care leavers in the young offenders and/or prison population, for example (Carr and McAlister, 2016; van Breda and Frimpong-Manso, 2020).

In noting the varying needs of care leavers and the varied supports, the *unique identities, experiences, views, needs, histories and characteristics of care leavers need to be centre stage*. Respecting the individual lives, events and experiences and personal narrative of each person leaving care is fundamental to their rights and helps avoid the generalisations, stereotypes, assumptions and biases that are associated with the term 'care leaver'. As noted earlier, the role of the specialist leaving care team and their provision of positive, stable and consistent relationships can make a difference, as can support groups and mentoring (Brady et al., 2019). These supports and services are underpinned by values in which young people leaving care are respected as autonomous. Effective ways of helping them therefore depend on letting them lead the process and develop and use their own personal resources (both as individuals and as a group of people with shared interests and concerns); and empowering them, as experts by experience, to be fully involved in new service designs, service delivery and evaluations of services through becoming peer researchers for example (Pound and Sims-Schouten, 2022).

Summary and conclusion

We began this chapter by thinking about what is meant by 'leaving care', and what are social workers' responsibilities to all children and young people moving on from the care system. We then looked at the particular needs of young people leaving care in their teenage years, and the implications for providing services to them that are helpful, sensitive and accessible. We considered what is to be learned from research in leaving care, including what it can tell us about young people's views. We looked at the thinking underlying recent legislation on leaving care, which has itself been heavily influenced by research. One of the messages of the chapter is that not all care leavers are the same, and we focused on the needs of particular groups of care leavers – those from ethnic minorities, those who are disabled, LGBTQIA+ care leavers, and refugees and asylum-seekers. Finally, we looked at key messages for practice in this area. In conclusion, the key to success in this area of practice seems to be a combination of good general services with targeted specialist services that are accessible to young people when they need them, and practitioners who have a real commitment to working in partnership with young people, listening to them and taking notice of what they have to say.

GUIDE TO FURTHER READING

The best sources for research on leaving care are Stein (2006), Stein and Munro (2008), Wade (2011), Stein (2012), Stein (2019), Department for Education (2021). Other general texts that draw together existing policy and practice include Wheal (2005), Driscoll (2019), Mendes and Snow (2016) and Mann-Feder and Goyette (2019). For recent developments in law, policy and practice across England, Wales, Northern Ireland and Scotland, the report by Foley et al. (2021) is extremely helpful. Regarding support services for care leavers, Brady et al. (2019) on mentoring is very informative.

References

Atkinson, C. and Hyde, R. (2019) 'Care leavers' views about transition: A literature review', *Journal of Children's Services*, *14*(1), 42–58.

Barn, R. (2001) *Black youth on the margins*. York: Joseph Rowntree Foundation.

Barn, R. and Sidhu, K. (2005) 'Understanding the interconnections between ethnicity, gender, social class and health: Experiences of minority ethnic women in Britain', *Social Work in Health Care*, *39*(1–2), 11–27.

Biehal, N., Clayden, J., Stein, M. and Wade, J. (1995) *Moving On: Young people and leaving care schemes*. London: HMSO.

Bolaji, W. (2022) *Tiger! Tiger! What is the experience of trauma and transition into adulthood of African refugee and asylum-seeking care leavers?* (Doctoral dissertation, University of Essex & Tavistock and Portman NHS Foundation Trust).

Brady, B., Dolan, P. and McGregor, C. (2019) *Mentoring for young people in care and leaving care: Theory, policy, and practice.* Abingdon: Routledge.

Brady, E. and Gilligan, R. (2019) 'Exploring diversity in the educational pathways of care-experienced adults: Findings from a life course study of education and care', *Children and Youth Services Review*, *104*, 104379.

Brady, E. and Gilligan, R. (2020) 'Supporting care-experienced adults' educational journeys: "Linked lives" over the life course', *Child and Family Social Work*, *25*(2), 221–229.

Bywaters, P., Scourfield, J., Jones, C., Sparks, T., Elliott, M., Hooper, J., McCartan, C., Shapira, M., Bunting, L. and Daniel, B. (2020) 'Child welfare inequalities in the four nations of the UK', *Journal of Social Work*, *20*(2), 193–215.

Carr, N. and McAlister, S. (2016) The double-bind: Looked after children, care leavers and criminal justice. In Mendes, P. and Snow, P. (eds.) *Young people transitioning from out-of-home care: International research, policy and practice* (pp. 3–21). London: Palgrave Macmillan.

Carr, N. and Pinkerton, J. (2015) The experiences of LGBTQ young people in the care system in Northern Ireland. In Fish, J. and Karban, K. (eds.) *Lesbian, gay, bisexual and trans health inequalities. International perspectives in social work* (pp. 99–112). Bristol: Policy Press.

Chase, E. (2013) 'Security and subjective wellbeing: The experiences of unaccompanied young people seeking asylum in the UK', *Sociology of Health and Illness*, *35*(6), 858–872.

Chase, E. and Allsopp, E. (2020) *Youth migration and the politics of wellbeing: Stories of life in transition.* Bristol: Bristol University Press.

Chase, E., Simon, A. and Jackson, S. (eds.) (2006) *In care and after: A positive perspective.* London: Psychology Press Publishers.

Coleman, J. (1974) *Relationships in adolescence.* London: Routledge.

Coleman, J. (1978) 'Current contradictions in adolescent theory', *Journal of Youth and Adolescence* 7, 1–11.

Coleman, J. and Roker, D. (1998) 'Adolescence: A review', *The Psychologist*, December, 593–595.

Connolly, P., Sebba, J., Winter, K., Roberts, J., Tah, P. and Millen, S. (2023) 'The effectiveness of book-gifting programmes to enhance the reading skills of children in care: A randomised controlled trial of 'Reading Together' in England', *Children and Youth Services Review*, *153*, 107097.

Department for Education. (2021) Post-16 education and labour market outcomes for looked after children (LEO) research report. Available here https://assets.publishing.service.gov.uk/ government/uploads/system/uploads/attachment_data/file/993971/Post-16_Education_and_ labour_market_outcomes_for_Looked_After_Children__LEO__Research_report.pdf [accessed 02.04.24].

Devenney, K. (2020) 'Social work with unaccompanied asylum-seeking young people: Reframing social care professionals as 'co-navigators'', *The British Journal of Social Work*, *50*(3), 926–943.

Dixon, J., Cresswell, C. and Ward, J. (2020) *The break staying close, staying connected project.* London: Department for Education.

Driscoll, J. (2019) 'Strangers and estrangement: Young people's renegotiations of birth and foster family relationships as they transition out of care and the implications for the state as parent', *Children's Geographies*, *17*(5), 539–551.

Duncalf, Z. (2010) *Listen up! Adult care leavers speak out: The views of 310 care leavers aged 17–78*. Strathclyde: Care Leavers' Association.

Foley, S., Badinlou, F., Brocki, K., Frick, M., Ronchi, L. and Hughes, C. (2021) 'Family function and child adjustment difficulties in the COVID-19 pandemic: An international study', *International Journal of Environmental Research and Public Health*, *18*(21), 11136. https://doi.org/10.3390/ijerph182111136

Furey, R. and Harris-Evans, J. (2021) 'Work and resilience: Care leavers' experiences of navigating towards employment and independence', *Child and Family Social Work*, *26*, 404–414.

Gilligan, R. (2019) 'The family foster care system in Ireland. Advances and challenges', *Children and Youth Services Review*, *100*, 221–228. https://doi.org/10.1016/j.childyouth.2019.02.008.

Gilligan, R. and Brady, E. (2022) 'What helps adult care leavers return to education? Exploring the relevance of learner identity and the life course perspective', *Journal of Youth Studies* *26*(10), 1373–1386.

Gonzalez, R., Cameron, C. and Klendo, L. (2012) 'The therapeutic family model of care: An attachment and trauma informed approach to transitional planning', *Developing Practice: The Child, Youth and Family Work Journal*, *32*, 13–23.

González Álvarez, R., Armando Parra, L., ten Brummelaar, M., Avraamidou, L. and López López, M. (2022) 'Resilience among LGBTQIA+ youth in out-of-home care: A scoping review, *Child Abuse & Neglect*, *129*, 105660.

Gorham, H.S. (2009) *Educational success amongst looked after children in one London borough: The voice of the child* (Doctoral dissertation, University of London: Institute of Education).

Graham, M. (2007) *Black issues in social work and social care*. Bristol: Policy Press.

Häggman-Laitila, A., Salokekkilä, P. and Karki, S. (2018) 'Transition to adult life of young people leaving foster care: A qualitative systematic review', *Children and Youth Services Review*, *95*, 134–143.

Häggman-Laitila, A., Salokekkilä, P. and Karki, S. (2020) 'Integrative review of the evaluation of additional support programs for care leavers making the transition to adulthood', *Journal of Pediatric Nursing*, *54*, 63–77.

Harris, H. (2008) 'Meeting the needs of disabled children and their families: Some messages from the literature', *Child Care in Practice*, *14*(4), 355–369.

Harrison, N., Dixon, J., Sanders-Ellis, D. Ward, J. and Asker, P. (2023) *Care leavers' transition into the labour market in England*. Oxford: Oxford University, Rees Centre.

Harvey, A. (2017) *'The shadow falls': Understanding the factors involved in decision-making in local authority children's services*. London: University of East London.

Havlicek, J., Garcia, A. and Smith, D.C. (2013) 'Mental health and substance use disorders among foster youth transitioning to adulthood: Past research and future directions', *Children and Youth Services Review*, *35*(1), 194–203.

Hiles, D., Moss, D., Wright, J. and Dallos, R. (2013) 'Young people's experience of social support during the process of leaving care: A review of the literature', *Children and Youth Services Review*, *35*(12), 2059–2071.

Ince, L. (1998) *Making it alone*. London: British Agencies for Adoption and Fostering.

Ince, L. (2004) Preparing young black people for leaving care. In Barn, R. (ed.) *Working with black children and adolescents in need*. London: British Association for Adoption and Fostering.

Jackson, S., Ajayi, S. and Quigley, M. (2005) *Going to university from care*. London: Institute of Education, University of London.

Jarczok, M., Knecht Krüger, B., Mitrovic, T., Gérard, G. and Jud, A. (2021) 'Care leaver needs and accessibility: Findings from the first large-scale project in Switzerland', *Child and Family Social Work*, *26*(1), 11–25.

Kaasbøll, J., Pedersen, S.A. and Paulsen, V. (2022) 'What is known about the LGBTQ perspective in child welfare services: A scoping review', *Child and Family Social Work*, *27*(2), 358–369.

Kelly, B., McShane, T., Davidson, G., Pinkerton, J., Gilligan, E. and Webb, P. (2016) *Transitions and outcomes for care leavers with mental health and/or intellectual disabilities: Final report*. Belfast: QUB.

Kelly, B., Webb, P., Davidson, G., Pinkerton, J. and McShane, T. (2022) 'Raising the profile of care leavers with mental health and/or intellectual disabilities: A contribution from Northern Ireland', *Children and Youth Services Review*, *136*, 106434.

Kohli, R.K. (2011) 'Working to ensure safety, belonging and success for unaccompanied Asylum-seeking children', *Child Abuse Review*, *20*(5), 311–323.

MacAlister, J. (2022) *The independent review of children's social care*. London: Department for Education.

Mann-Feder, V.R. and Goyette, M. (eds.) (2019) *Leaving care and the transition to adulthood: International contributions to theory, research, and practice*. Oxford: Oxford University Press.

McCormick, A. (2018) *LGBTQ youth in foster care: Empowering approaches for an inclusive system of care*. London: Routledge.

McNamara, P., Montserrat, C. and Wise, S. (eds.) (2019) *Education in out-of-home care: International perspectives on policy, practice, and research*. New York: Springer Nature.

Mendes, P. and Snow, P. (eds.) (2016) *Young people transitioning from out-of-home care: International research, policy, and practice*. New York: Springer.

Munro, E. R. (2019) 'Reflections on upholding the rights of youth leaving out-of-home care', in Varda R. Mann-Feder, and Martin Goyette (eds), *Leaving care and the transition to adulthood: International contributions to theory, research, and practice*, Emerging Adulthood Series (New York, 2019; online edn, Oxford Academic, 21 Mar. 2019), https://doi.org/10.1093/oso/9780190630485.003.0005, [accessed 2 Apr. 2024].

Munro, E.R., Kelly, B., Mannay, D. and McGhee, K. (2024) 'Comparing leaving-care policy and practice across the four nations of the United Kingdom: Exploring similarities, differences, and implementation gaps', *Journal of Comparative Policy Analysis: Research and Practice*,1-18.

Mupaku, W.M., van Breda, A.D. and Kelly, B. (2021) 'Transitioning to adulthood from residential childcare during COVID-19: Experiences of young people with intellectual disabilities and/or autism spectrum disorder in South Africa', British Journal of Learning Disabilities, 49(3), 341–351.

Narey, M. (2016) Residential care in England: Report of Sir Martin Narey's independent review of children's residential care. London: Department for Education.

Neil, E., Gitsels, L. and Thoburn, J. (2020) 'Returning children home from care: What can be learned from local authority data?', *Child and Family Social Work*, *25*(3), 548–556.

Organisation for Economic Cooperation and Development (OECD). (2022) *Assisting care leavers: Time for action*. Paris, France: OECD.

Petäjä, U.K., Terkamo-Moisio, A., Karki, S. and Häggman-Laitila, A. (2023) 'The prevalence of high-risk behavior among adolescents in aftercare services and transitioning from out-of-home care: A systematic review', *Adolescent Research Review*, *8*(3), 323–337.

Pound, M. and Sims-Schouten, W. (2022) 'A systematic review of the principles of co-production in relation to the mental health and wellbeing of care leavers', *International Journal of Emotional Education*, *14*(1), 3–19.

Ramsay, A. (2020) *Social work with unaccompanied asylum-seeking children in Scotland*. Glasgow: The Institute for Research and Innovation in Social Services (IRISS).

Refaeli, T. (2020) 'Needs and availability of support among care-leavers: A mixed-methods study', *Child and Family Social Work*, *25*(2), 412–420.

Schoenwald, E., O'Higgins, A., Collyer, H., Ahmed, F., Whelan, E., Curtis, B., Ghedia, N., Clancy, C. and Alam, A. (2022) *Outcomes for black children in care. A rapid evidence review synthesis*. London: What Works in Children's Social Care.

Stein, M. (1997) *What works in leaving care?* Ilford: Barnardos.

Stein, M. (2006) 'Research review: Young people leaving care', *Child and Family Social Work*, *11*(3), 273–279.

Stein, M. (2012) *Young people leaving care: Supporting pathways to adulthood*. London: Jessica Kingsley Publishers.

Stein, M. (2019) 'Supporting young people from care to adulthood: International practice', *Child and Family Social Work*, *24*(3), 400–405.

Stein, M. and Carey, K. (1986) *Leaving care*. Oxford: Basil Blackwell.

Stein, M. and Dumaret, A.-C. (2011) 'The mental health of young people aging out of care and entering adulthood: Exploring the evidence from England and France', *Children and Youth Services Review*, *33*(12), 2504–2511.

Stein, M. and Ellis, S. (1983) *Gizza say? Reviews and young people in care*. London: National Association of Young People in Care.

Stein, M. and Munro, E. (eds.) (2008) *Young people's transitions from care to adulthood: International research and practice*. London: Jessica Kingsley.

Stein, M. and Ward, H. (2021) 'Transitions from care to adulthood. Persistent issues across time and place', *Child and Family Social Work*, *26*(2), 215–221.

Sulimani-Aidan, Y. (2022) 'Periods of uncertainty: The experience of at-risk young adult Arabs during the transition to adulthood in the wake of COVID-19', *Child and Family Social Work*, *27*(4), 805–814.

Thoburn, J., Chand, A. and Procter, J. (2005) *Child welfare services for minority ethnic families: The research reviewed*. London: Jessica Kingsley Publishers.

United Nations. (2010) *Guidelines for the alternative care of children. A/RES/64/142 (Sixty-fourth session)*. Geneva: United Nations. Available here https://www.refworld.org/docid/4c3acd162.html (accessed 27.01.24).

van Breda, A.D.P. and Frimpong-Manso, K. (2020) 'Leaving care in Africa', *Emerging Adulthood*, *8*(1), 3–5.

Wade, J. (2011) 'Preparation and transition planning for unaccompanied asylum-seeking and refugee young people: A review of evidence in England', *Children and Youth Services Review*, *33*(12), 2424–2430.

Wheal, A. (2005) *The leaving care handbook: Helping and supporting care leavers.* Lyme Regis: Russell House Publishing.

Zeira, A., Refaeli, T., Achdut, N. and Benbenishty, R. (2023) 'Economic self-sufficiency and the employment outcomes of care leavers: A 10-year follow up', *Child and Family Social Work*, *28*(3), 635–645.

11

CONCLUSION

Contemporary issues

CONTENTS OF CHAPTER

- Introduction: social worker role with children and young people in care
- Effectiveness
- Outcomes
- Rights
- Relationships
- Digital technology
- Innovation and social transformation
- Recommendations for policy and practice
- Guide to further reading

Introduction: social worker role with children and young people in care

As outlined in preceding chapters, the social work role with children and young people in care is multi-faceted and takes place in economic, political, geographical and social contexts which change over time, vary according to place and reflect wider societal developments. At the outset, it is important to remind ourselves of the internationally accepted definition of social work, most recently ratified by the International Federation of Social Workers ([IFSW] 2014), which defines social work as

> a practice-based profession and an academic discipline that promotes social change and development, social cohesion, and the empowerment and liberation of people. Principles of social justice, human rights, collective

DOI: 10.4324/9781003503194-11

> responsibility, and respect for diversities are central to social work. Underpinned by theories of social work, social sciences, humanities and indigenous knowledges, social work engages people and structures to address life challenges and enhance wellbeing.

In this final chapter, we focus on the social worker role, the contemporary influences on work with children and young people in care and how they shape practice. We have identified the following key issues and will discuss their impact on the social worker role considering each in turn: effectiveness; outcomes; rights; relationship-based practice and the digital age.

Exercise 11.1 Annie revisited

Return to the example of Annie when we first met her in Exercise 6.1.

1 As if you were meeting Annie for the first time, ask yourself:
How would you ensure that Annie has:
continuity and quality of education?
continuity and quality of health care?
continuity of relationships?
stability of placement?
What work, skills and resources would be needed to achieve this?
What obstacles might there be? How would you overcome them?

2 With the benefit of hindsight after reading the subsequent examples, ask:
What could have been done differently to ensure better outcomes for Annie?

Effectiveness

What makes for effective social work practice includes learning from the experience of other practitioners, learning from what children and young people and their families have to say, and learning from research (which may itself tell us about the experience of other practitioners and about what children and young people and their families have to say). Recently there have been several inquiries which have raised fundamental concerns about the effectiveness and quality of social work practice and the quality of care offered to children and young people who do not live with their birth parents. Most recently, the Independent Review of Children's Social Care (in England) (MacAlister, 2022) serves to highlight the challenges and issues involved. One challenge relates to effectiveness.

In the Independent Review, the word 'effective' appears 42 times. Key questions considered include are the right families and children actually and appropriately identified; does intervention happen in the right way, at the right time; are the right services offered at the right time, in the right place and in the right way; and are services effective in meeting their aims and objectives. While the Review highlights areas of effectiveness, it also notes much evidence of ineffectiveness in the structures, systems, processes and practices associated with the current system of care (evidence which should be of concern to all social workers, whose profession is underpinned by principles of social justice, equality and rights). These are reflected in other reviews, including the Independent Review of Children's Social Care Services (Northern Ireland). To achieve change, it is suggested that both additional resources and restructuring of teams, services and supports will be needed, to align services more towards family support (early intervention and support to prevent entry into care) and towards delivery that emphasises specialist knowledge, interdisciplinarity, skills mix and room for social innovation (that is bespoke services, designed with users to meet particular needs).

Creating more effective social work structures, systems, processes and practices matters because our aim is to improve the lives of children who come into care. With regard to the relevance for the social worker role, the effectiveness of what we do is impacted by lack of clarity about the remit of the role, its associated tasks, and responsibilities, challenges balancing competing priorities and lack of resources. Often too, teams and organisations can be slow and/or resistant to change. As social workers, we should remain open minded to multiple perspectives that seek to improve effectiveness, whilst also being advocates for wider social justice considerations including the distribution of resources because personal effectiveness as a social worker does not occur in a vacuum but is facilitated by team and organisational effectiveness in a wider context where the role of social workers is fully supported and resourced.

Outcomes

An outcome is the difference that a service makes to a child's development and wellbeing. The most familiar outcomes around which the 'looked after child' is constructed are the developmental outcomes – physical and mental health, education, social and emotional wellbeing, relationships, self-care skills and identity. On each of these domains, there is a wealth of research evidence that identifies what the problems are for children in care and how effective and impactful the care system is in addressing children's needs in these areas. It is important to note, that although superficially appearing straightforward, there are significant challenges in both defining and measuring outcomes, as outlined in the work of Forrester (2017). That said, there is a significant body of outcomes-based research. It shows that the care pathways for children coming into, living in and leaving care are complex.

In attempting to understand what improves outcomes, the specific outcome needs to be clearly defined and a range of factors need to be considered, especially a child's socio-economic background, their class and their ethnicity. Other factors can be grouped together under child characteristics and circumstances (in addition to the above this could include gender, disability, language, type of placement, length of placement for example), the carer(s) characteristics and circumstances, and wider contextual factors (community, neighbourhood) and these are all of relevance in securing good outcomes.

For example, a recent study (Asif et al., 2023) used a longitudinal dataset relating to children in care in Australia, to explore the relationship between placement stability and developmental outcomes. It concluded that placement stability, while controlling for other factors, had a significant association with various developmental indicators. The study also showed that children who entered care at a later age were less likely to do well on developmental indicators compared with children who entered care at a younger age. Furthermore, analysis of placement type showed that placement with kinship carers had a positive association with socio emotional development. Carer distress was also noted to have a negative impact on the developmental outcomes of children in care, while carer satisfaction was associated positively with socio-emotional development. These findings are borne out in similar research using longitudinal datasets for children in care (McGrath-Lone et al., 2020; Neil et al., 2019).

What the above study highlights is that the definition and measurement of outcomes requires an ecological-based approach taking account of the personal, the immediate context and wider social structural factors and the varying interrelated impact of all these on outcomes. So, for example, it is important for social workers to bear in mind how comparisons are drawn. For example, most children are in care for a short period of time and then return home. We know that if children come into the care system at an older age and/or have recurrent 'in care' episodes, they are more likely to have significant challenges that are difficult to address, and that these are likely to be exacerbated by disrupted living, education and therapeutic arrangements and changes of social worker. That said, if we compare outcomes between children in care and children in need (known to social services but not in their care), research indicates that the outcomes for children in need can be worse than those for children with similar characteristics who were in care (Sebba et al., 2015).

In considering how knowledge regarding outcomes relates to the role of the social worker, key considerations are: 'what difference do I make, what difference do the decisions I make have on the lives of children and their families, what difference do services make to children and families and what difference can be made to wider social structural conditions that adversely impact on the lives of children and families?' This suggests that the role of the social worker has a 'political aspect' to it, in that we have an obligation to be aware of what aspects of our actions, decisions and interventions make a positive difference (and those that do not). We also have an obligation, as noted in professional standards, to advocate on behalf of those whose social conditions adversely impact on parenting capacity, child developmental outcomes, wellbeing, and overall quality of life.

Rights

Returning again to the professional standards that all social workers sign up to, a fundamental aspect of these in their various iterations across the UK is the obligation of the social worker to uphold the rights of individuals. Children's and parents' rights are set out in the Human Rights Act 1998, the United Nations Convention on the Rights of the Child, UN Alternative Guidelines and in the CRC General Comments. Despite this, most social workers do not know much about children's and parents' rights as outlined in the UNCRC and the supporting CRC General Comments, except perhaps for Article 12 which relates to children and young people having a right to express a view and have it taken into account in decisions that are made. Given the obligations imposed by professional standards and supporting legal frameworks, it makes sense that the UNCRC and the supporting General Comments continue to be more effectively and explicitly stated in systems, processes, services and practices in children's social work, in particular through adopting children's rights indicators against which to assess practice and its impacts. Regarding the social worker role, it is incumbent on all social workers working with children in care to uphold, promote and safeguard children's rights on a daily basis, and in so doing address structural inequalities that lead to social injustice in the long and short term (see for example the report by the Northern Ireland Human Rights Commission on alternative care and children's rights, and the resource produced by the Children's Commissioner for Wales on rights in social care practice in 2022).

Relationships

The obligation placed on social workers through their professional standards and through legislation is to conduct all relationships with all families and children with respect for the dignity, value, and inherent worth of each individual. While social workers cannot be all things to all people, there are certain values and principles that should underpin the social worker role in forming, maintaining, and sustaining relationships no matter how short they are, and no matter how contested the context in which they take place.

These principles focus on working in partnership (not 'doing to' children and families but rather 'doing with' children and families) being real, respectful, resourceful, reliable, accessible, flexible, truthful, genuinely interested, empathic, committed, responsive in thoughtful ways, and also on being able to regulate one's own emotional responses and react responsibly to the emotions of others (Thomas and O'Kane, 1998; Winter et al., 2017; Stabler et al., 2020; Mitchell, 2022).

It is evident therefore that relationships are core to the social worker role, and yet social workers know that it can be a struggle to have meaningful and positive relationships with parents, children, and young people. Some social workers may not like the people they encounter, and some families and children may not like the social workers they encounter. Social workers ask children to trust them and expect them to engage in meaningful relationships, and yet they may fundamentally disagree with the social work intervention or find it hard to trust because of constant changes of social worker, social worker unreliability, lack of time and changes to plans. And some social workers may think that they mean very little to children and young people and will not be remembered, because their involvement is only short-term. However, all encounters, no matter how short, can carry meaning for children and young people coming into care, living in, or leaving care.

The social worker role in building meaningful relationships can be compromised by workload issues, bureaucratic demands, organisational norms, conflict, resistance, fear, lack of trust and/or the threat of violence in work with children and families. The requirement for relationships can be a risky business for social workers, families and children alike. This raises questions about how the role of the social worker in establishing and maintaining positive relationships can be supported. It seems that a systemic approach is needed which focuses simultaneously on strengthening the skills of individual social workers, supporting social workers through adequate informal and formal supervision mechanisms at team and organisational level, valuing the social worker role at a social structural level and harnessing the attributes, skills, knowledge and values of social workers to be effective agents for change at social, political and economic levels.

Digital technology

With regard to the role of the social worker, there is also an emerging body of research that highlights how digital technology means we are conducting our relationships differently, and a growing interest in its impact on social work with children and young people in care. A report on this theme by the Children's Commissioner for England (2017) showed that children in care were more likely than their non-care experienced peers to lack access to technology, skills and support in using it, and also to lack access to digital safeguarding. Since then, use of the technology by children and young people has continued to grow – not least because of the COVID-19 pandemic. Through successive 'lockdowns' and other social distancing measures aimed at reducing face-to-face contact, practitioners adapted by using digital platforms to communicate. Copson et al. (2022) found that there are benefits for social workers, children and families in using digital technology, including accessibility, flexibility, spontaneity and informality. However, they also note the existence of digital poverty (poor families who lack access) and recommend that the technology should complement and not replace relationship building through home visits and face-to-face meetings. In building and sustaining relationships, physical and sensory elements can be vitally important.

For children and young people in care, digital technology offers a means of continuing relationships with immediate and extended families in unstructured and unsupervised ways, reducing the obstacles created by living away from home. It is evident therefore that there are benefits and challenges associated with the access of children in care to digital technology. It offers new opportunities for learning and networking, and at the same time can expose children and young people to harm such as 'cyber-bullying', 'trolling' and sexual exploitation, as well as manipulation, and can even hinder their life chances when embarrassing personal information from the past can still be made public.

Digital technology is here to stay. It is an integral part of our own daily relationships with friends, family and colleagues and is also therefore an integral part of our social work practice with children and young people in care. The skills used in the private lives of social workers need to be translated to professional practice. The role of the social worker in this regard is to be creative in communication with families and children, recognising the role played by digital technology and also recognising the 'digital divide' and those families that could be excluded due to lack of access to digital technology.

Using research in practice

With regard to using research in practice, some social workers might query how far and in what ways this should be achieved. Reflecting on the professional standards that social workers sign up to, in England, one of these standards, for example, involves maintaining one's own professional development which includes keeping practice up to date and *recording how research, theories and frameworks inform practice*. There is therefore an obligation placed on social workers to be aware of research, publications, current research knowledge and its application to practice. We need to make it our business to be fully informed about current research.

Given the range of research and the pressures of the job, how can busy social workers access and apply research findings to their jobs? Part of the answer, of course, is to be selective, and also to make full use of the digests and summaries produced by government, by childcare organisations and by research centres. However, it is also an important aspect of the social worker role to insist on making space in one's working time for reading, thinking and keeping up to date with new ideas and new knowledge. Teams and organisations also have a responsibility to create time and encourage staff to use some of their time to update and refresh thinking. Furthermore, the social worker role does involve a responsibility to contribute to research and the exchange of ideas – by undertaking their own research, perhaps in collaboration with academics, publishing results and engaging in wider local, regional and national governmental initiatives and fora set up to consider the delivery of social work practice. This aspect of the social worker role can lead to social transformation, as outlined below.

Innovation and social transformation

While it is important to note that the social work role cannot solve all the inequalities and challenges that lead to children and young people coming into the care system, it can and should, as argued earlier, involve advocating for improvements and change and it can redress some of the imbalances for those children who are in and leave the care system. This is most recently outlined in Fitzsimons and McCracken (2020) which summarises seven outcomes, seven features of practice and seven organisational enablers identified in the most effective projects funded by the government through the Children's Social Care Innovation Programme.

The Children's Social Care Innovation Programme funded the development, implementation and evaluation of new ideas and new ways of practising to improve outcomes for children and to 'help create new energy into a practice system that had become jaded over time, often found to be over focused on process rather than focused on practice' (FitzSimons and McCracken, 2020, p. 4). It noted that the seven most effective features of practice emerging from successful projects included:

- using a clear, strengths-based practice framework;
- using systemic approaches to social work practice;
- enabling staff to do skilled direct work;
- multi-disciplinary skill sets working together;
- undertaking group case discussion;
- high intensity and consistency of practitioner;
- and having a whole family focus (Department for Education, 2022, p. 10).

These factors above do not stand alone, but are most likely to produce the best outcomes (defined as greater stability, reduced risk, increased wellbeing and resilience, reduced days spent in care, increased staff wellbeing, reduced staff turnover and agency rates, and better value for money) when combined with organisational enablers including the following:

- A strategic approach
- Strong leadership and governance
- Engaging and supporting the workforce
- Engaging partners/stakeholders/children and families to co-produce processes, services, and interventions
- Building the supporting infrastructure/apparatus
- Fostering innovation
- Judicious use of resources

Of course, all these indicate the need for well-qualified social workers in well-resourced, well-led, well-managed and well-structured organisations. But, as noted earlier, organisations are located within broader social structural systems and in varied ways their processes, procedures and practices reflect a combination of individual, team based, organisational and social structural influences. Recent reviews of children's social care (MacAlister, 2022; Jones, 2023; Scottish Government, 2020) highlight good examples of successes at all levels but there are also serious and ongoing challenges that require changes in ways of thinking and doing.

All this aside, children and young people with care experience should remain front and centre. In the recent reviews, children and young people highlight that they want the basic, simple and straightforward things including:

- a positive and meaningful relationship with their social worker;
- continuity in this relationship;
- reliability, availability, confidentiality, advocacy to be inherent in this relationship;
- a relationship in which the social worker enjoys spending time with the child/young person and has a genuine interest in them.

The sad fact is that this does not differ significantly from early research into the views of children and young people (see Box 11.1).

Recommendations for policy and practice

This chapter has considered the social worker role and some of the contemporary influences on the nature of that role. It has indicated that the social worker role exists in a complex context and that there is still

Box 11.1 'My ideal social worker'

When Claire O'Kane and I talked to children and young people in care about decision making in their lives, we asked them to tell us about their ideal social worker. This is what they said they looked for:

- *Good communication skills* – someone who is easy to talk to and who understands, and explains well.
- *A good listener* – listens to what you have got to say, let you have more say, don't butt in.
- *Understanding* – understands what you feel and your view of things.
- *Personal style* – the way they talk, not strict or boring, generally happy, their personality, good sense of humour, friendly, doesn't lose their temper, doesn't stare, similar interests, polite, fashionable.
- *Giving you time* – giving you information and time to think about decisions.
- *Helpful* – they sort things out, get you good foster parents, set boundaries, arrange things, put things into action, can help give you ideas.
- *Caring* – has time for us, kind, calms us down, like a friend, generous, determination, dedication, good at general conversation.
- *An advocate* – willingness to say difficult things on your behalf.
- *Someone you can trust.*
- *Being fair* – they don't take sides, listen to all sides and negotiate, honesty not favouritism.
- *Taking you out & treats* – visiting and taking you out, giving you chocolate!

(Source: Thomas and O'Kane, 1998)

some way to go to create the optimal culture and conditions in which social work practice with children and young people in care can flourish, in which children and young people feel valued and respected, achieve their full potential, and in which children and families see how their own perspectives shape and inform services and outcomes. In England, Wales and Northern Ireland, the future of children's services and the role of the social worker is actively being considered. At the time of writing, there are consultations on the recent reviews (MacAlister, 2022; Jones, 2023). In England, proposal include revised Working Together guidelines and in Northern Ireland, proposals include the creation of a new arms-length body for children's services.

Recommendations impact on the role of the social worker in so far as there is a greater emphasis on skills mix (the use of multi-disciplinary teams and approaches), lead practitioners (who do not need to be social workers), specialist skills and roles for social workers involved in child protection, a renewed emphasis on effective relationships with children and their families and a renewed emphasis on communicating with, listening to and seeking the views of children and young people. Taking account of wider developments, our own recommendations regarding the social worker role are simple in the sense that relationships are at the heart of all social work with children and young people. Relationships between social workers, children and families matter, and relationships between children and young people in care and their families and friends matter (Lewis et al., 2022). It is useful therefore to think about what can be done to commit resources and time to building, sustaining and growing consistent and caring relationships with children and young people coming into care, while they are in care and when they leave care for the last time or on one of several occasions. Anything that can be done to sure up this foundational aspect of social work practice is to be welcomed as it is from this foundational basis that the social worker role and its component parts can be the most effective at the level of the child, their family, their immediate context and in terms of advocating for their rights and social justice at a structural level. It is useful therefore to think about what can be done to commit resources and time to building, sustaining and growing consistent and caring relationships with children and young people coming into care, while they are in care and when they leave care - whether for the last time or on one of several occasions.

GUIDE TO FURTHER READING

There are several useful websites that provide accessible research knowledge to social workers including: What Works for Children's Social Care; Research in Practice; NSPCC; the Community Care magazine websites. Other social work websites have guides as to how to navigate your way around the growing social work research knowledge that is available. BASW for example have published this guide. Social work journals have open access articles which can be searched through Google Scholar or the journal. There are many social work journals of interest – a list of the top journals is available on the Scimago Journal Rank website. There are also a growing number of podcasts – see here for a list. Campaigns such as Care Day and National Care Leavers Week draw into the public domain the experiences of care experienced people. Organisations such as Become, CoramBaaf, The Rees Foundation, Voice of Young People in Care, Voices from Care Cymru and Who Cares? Scotland also publish informative material. The websites of the Children's Commissioners in each of the evolved nations also provide a wealth of information.

References

Asif, N., Breen, C. and Wells, R. (2023) 'Influence of placement stability on developmental outcomes of children and young people in out-of-home care: Findings from the pathways of care longitudinal study', *Child Abuse and Neglect*, 106145. DOI: 10.1016/j.chiabu.2023.106145

Children's Commissioner for England. (2017) *Growing up digital. A report of the growing up digital workforce.* London: Children's Commissioner for England. Available here https://assets.childrenscommissioner.gov.uk/wpuploads/2017/06/Growing-Up-Digital-Taskforce-Report-January-2017_0.pdf (accessed 28.01.24).

Children's Commissioner for Wales. (2022) *The right way. A children's rights approach for social care in Wales.* Swansea: The Children's Commissioner for Wales.

Copson, R., Murphy, A.M., Cook, L., Neil, E. and Sorensen, P. (2022) 'Relationship-based practice and digital technology in child and family social work: Learning from practice during the COVID-19 pandemic', *Developmental Child Welfare*, 4(1), 3–19.

Department for Education. (2016) *Seven features of practice and seven outcomes. Based on findings drawn from the evaluation of round one of the children's social care innovation programme.* London: Department for Education

Department for Education (DfE). (2022) Seven features of practice and seven outcomes. Based on findings drawn from the evaluation of round one of the Children's social care innovation programme. London. Department for Education. HYPERLINK https://assets.publishing.service.gov.uk/media/6344463dd3bf7f58733e2c94/Seven_Features_of_Practice_and_Seven_Outcomes.pdf [last accessed 02.05.24]

FitzSimons, A. and McCracken, K. (2020) *Children's social care innovation programme. Round 2 final report.* London: Department for Education. Available here https://assets.publishing.service.gov.uk/media/5fb7b9ce8fa8f559e44d2d03/Childrens_Social_Care_Innovation_Programme_Round_Final_Report.pdf (accessed 28.01.24).

Forrester, Donald (2017) Outcomes in children's social care. *Journal of Children's Services 12* (2–3), 144–157.

Jones, R. (2023) *Report of the independent review of Northern Ireland's children's social care services.* Belfast: Department of Health.

Lewis, S., Selwyn, J. and the Bright Spots Team. (2022) *Staying connected. The views of looked after children and young people on their contact arrangements.* Oxford: Coram Voice and the Rees Centre, University of Oxford.

MacAlister, J. (2022) *The independent review of children's social care.* London: Department for Education.

McGrath-Lone, L., Harron, K., Dearden, L. and Gilbert, R. (2020) 'Exploring placement stability for children in out-of-home care in England: A sequence analysis of longitudinal administrative data', *Child Abuse and Neglect, 109*, 104689.

Mitchell, M. (2022) "Because I'm a kid…': The struggle for recognition of children and young people involved in child and family social work', *Child and Family Social Work*, *27*(3), 526–534.

Neil, E., Gitsels, L., and Thoburn, J. (2019) 'Children in care: Where do children entering care at different ages end up? An analysis of local authority administrative data', *Children and Youth Services Review, 106*, 104472. https://doi.org/10.1016/j.childyouth.2019.104472

Scottish Government. (2020) *Independent care review.* Available here https://www.carereview.scot.

Sebba, J., Berridge, D., Luke, N., Fletcher, J., Bell, K., Strand, S., Thomas, S., Sinclair, I. and O'Higgins, A. (2015) *The educational progress of looked after children in England: Linking care and educational data.* Oxford The Rees Centre, University of Oxford.

Stabler, L., Wilkins, D. and Carro, H. (2020) 'What do children think about their social worker? AQ-method study of children's services', *Child and Family Social Work*, *25*(1), 118–126.

Thomas, N. and O'Kane, C. (1998) 'When children's wishes and feelings clash with their best interests', *International Journal of Children's Rights*, *6*(2), 137–154.

Winter, K., Cree, V., Hallett, S., Hadfield, M., Ruch, G., Morrison, F. and Holland, S. (2017) 'Exploring communication between social workers, children and young people', *British Journal of Social Work*, *47*(5), 1427–1444.

INDEX

Note: **Bold** page numbers refer to tables and *italic* page numbers refer to figures.